GRIEF AND ITS TRANSCENDENCE

Grief and its Transcendence: Memory, Identity, Creativity is a landmark contribution that provides fresh insights into the experience and process of mourning. It includes fourteen original essays by preeminent psychoanalysts, historians, classicists, theologians, architects, art historians, and artists who take on the subject of normal, rather than pathological, mourning. In particular, it considers the diversity of the mourning process; the bereavement of ordinary versus extraordinary loss; the contribution of mourning to personal and creative growth; and individual, social, and cultural means of transcending grief.

The book is divided into three parts, each including two to four essays followed by one or two critical discussions. Coeditor **Adele Tutter**'s Prologue outlines the salient themes and tensions that emerge from the volume. Part I juxtaposes the consideration of grief in antiquity with an examination of the contemporary use of memorials to facilitate communal remembrance. Part II offers intimate first-person accounts of mourning from four renowned psychoanalysts who challenge long-held psychoanalytic formulations of mourning. Part III contains deeply personal essays that explore the use of sculpture, photography, and music to withstand, mourn, and transcend loss. Drawing on the humanistic wisdom that underlies psychoanalytic thought, coeditor **Léon Wurmser**'s Epilogue closes the volume.

Grief and its Transcendence is required reading for psychoanalysts, psychotherapists, psychiatrists, and scholars within other disciplines who are interested in the topics of grief, bereavement, and creativity.

Adele Tutter, M.D., Ph.D. is Assistant Clinical Professor of Psychiatry, Columbia University; and Faculty, the Columbia University Center for Psychoanalytic Training and Research and the New York Psychoanalytic Institute. She is the author of *Dream House: An Intimate Portrait of the Philip Johnson Glass House* and editor of *The Muse: Psychoanalytic Explorations of Creative Inspiration*. Dr. Tutter is in private practice in Manhattan.

Léon Wurmser, M.D., Ph.D. is Past Clinical Professor of Psychiatry, University of West Virginia, and Training and Supervising Analyst at the Contemporary Freudian Society. He has authored and coauthored many books on the theory and practice of psychoanalysis, including *The Mask of Shame, Jealousy and Envy – New Views on Two Powerful Emotions*, and *Nothing Good Is Allowed to Stand*. Dr. Wurmser lectures extensively in the USA and abroad.

PSYCHOANALYTIC INQUIRY BOOK SERIES
JOSEPH D. LICHTENBERG
SERIES EDITOR

Like its counterpart, *Psychoanalytic Inquiry: A Topical Journal for Mental Health Professionals*, the Psychoanalytic Inquiry Book Series presents a diversity of subjects within a diversity of approaches to those subjects. Under the editorship of Joseph Lichtenberg, in collaboration with Melvin Bornstein and the editorial board of *Psychoanalytic Inquiry*, the volumes in this series strike a balance between research, theory, and clinical application. We are honored to have published the works of various innovators in psychoanalysis, such as Frank Lachmann, James Fosshage, Robert Stolorow, Donna Orange, Louis Sander, Léon Wurmser, James Grotstein, Joseph Jones, Doris Brothers, Fredric Busch, and Joseph Lichtenberg, among others.

The series includes books and monographs on mainline psychoanalytic topics, such as sexuality, narcissism, trauma, homosexuality, jealousy, envy, and varied aspects of analytic process and technique. In our efforts to broaden the field of analytic interest, the series has incorporated and embraced innovative discoveries in infant research, self-psychology, intersubjectivity, motivational systems, affects as process, responses to cancer, borderline states, contextualism, postmodernism, attachment research and theory, medication, and mentalization. As further investigations in psychoanalysis come to fruition, we seek to present them in readable, easily comprehensible writing.

After 25 years, the core vision of this series remains the investigation, analysis, and discussion of developments on the cutting edge of the psychoanalytic field, inspired by a boundless spirit of inquiry.

GRIEF AND ITS TRANSCENDENCE

Memory, identity, creativity

Adele Tutter and Léon Wurmser

Routledge
Taylor & Francis Group

NEW YORK AND LONDON

First published 2016
by Routledge
27 Church Road, Hove, East Sussex, BN3 2FA

and by Routledge
711 Third Avenue, New York, NY 10017

Routledge is an imprint of the Taylor & Francis Group, an Informa business

British Library Cataloguing in Publication Data
A catalogue record for this book is available from the British Library

Library of Congress Cataloging-in-Publication Data
Grief and its transcendence : memory, identity, creativity / Adele Tutter and
    Léon Wurmser, editors.
        pages cm
    Includes bibliographical references.
    1. Grief.   2. Bereavement.   3. Memory.   4. Memorialization.
I. Tutter, Adele.   II. Wurmser, Leon.
    BF575.G7G725 2016
    155.9'37—dc23
    2015011446

ISBN: 978-1-138-81286-4 (hbk)
ISBN: 978-1-138-81287-1 (pbk)
ISBN: 978-1-315-74853-5 (ebk)

Typeset in Bembo
by Apex CoVantage, LLC

MIX
Paper from
responsible sources
FSC   FSC® C013604
www.fsc.org

Printed and bound by CPI Group (UK) Ltd, Croydon, CR0 4YY

In memoriam: Robert Phillips
(A. T.)

To my children, grandchildren, and friends
with love and admiration
(L. W.)

CONTENTS

ILLUSTRATIONS AND CREDITS

All URLs were accessed on April 2, 2014. Every effort has been made to contact the holders of the copyrights of images reproduced in this volume. If any have been inadvertently overlooked, please contact the publishers to make the necessary arrangements.

ACKNOWLEDGMENTS

First and foremost, the editors would like to thank Dr. Joe Lichtenberg, editor of the Psychoanalytic Inquiry Book Series, for his consistent endorsement of our work, and, in a broader sense, for his enlightened support of relevant interdisciplinary psychoanalytic scholarship. We also owe a debt of gratitude to Kate Hawes, Senior Publisher and Editor at Routledge, for her stewardship of this endeavor, Kirsten Buchanan and Susanna Frearson for their tireless assistance. We thank Christine Cottone, project manager, for her patience, and for her scrupulous attention to the manuscript. We thank those whose images grace this volume: Ladislav Bielik, Jean-François Bonhomme, Raymond Depardon, Yair Haklai, Brian Harris, Andreas Huyssen, Ken Howard, Mike Hvozda, Jiří Jurečka, Anselm Kiefer, Jaroslav Kysela, Ad Meskens, Anton Tutter, Susan Tutter, Yory Wurmser, Éditions Galilée, the Lucian Freud Archive, the Prints and Photographs Division of the Library of Congress, the Moravian Museum, The Sigmund Freud Museum, and the Office of the Governor of the State of New Jersey. And we thank our authors for their individual efforts, which we are privileged to gather in this monograph.

Adele Tutter wishes to thank her coeditor, Léon Wurmser, for his emotional and intellectual generosity during this venture; her husband, John Hudak, and her children, Kaspar and Ursula Hudak, for their loving patience and steady support; and her friends and colleagues for their invaluable interest and support.

Last, Léon Wurmser wishes to thank his children, grandchildren, and friends for their support in hard times of loss and their sharing in hours of joy and togetherness.

CONTRIBUTORS

Jan Assmann, Ph.D. is Professor Emeritus of Egyptology, Heidelberg University and Honorary Professor of Cultural and Religious Studies, University of Constance. He is the recipient of many honorary doctorates and awards, including the Prix Européen de l'Essay, the German Historians' Prize, the Thomas Mann Prize, and the Order of Merit of the Federal Republic of Germany. Professor Assmann has authored many books on Ancient Egypt (*The Mind of Egypt*, *Death and Salvation in Ancient Egypt*), cultural theory (*Cultural Memory and Ancient Civilizations*), the origins of monotheism (*Of God and Gods*), the reception of Egypt in the West (*Moses the Egyptian*), Thomas Mann (*Thomas Mann und Ägypten: Mythos und Monotheismus in den Josephsromanen*), and Mozart's *Magic Flute (Die Zauberflöte – Oper und Mysterium)*.

Daria Colombo, M.D. is Assistant Clinical Professor of Psychiatry, Weill Cornell Medical College and Faculty, the New York Psychoanalytic Institute. Her essays have been honored by the Sacerdoti Prize of the International Psychoanalytic Association, among other awards. She sits on the editorial board of several journals, including the *International Journal of Psychoanalysis* and *Psychoanalytic Quarterly,* and maintains a private psychoanalytic practice in Manhattan.

Jane McAdam Freud is a Fellow of the Royal British Sculpture Society. She has had over forty solo exhibitions worldwide, and her works are represented in major public collections including the British Museum, the National Gallery of Greece, and the Victoria and Albert Museum. The great-granddaughter of Sigmund Freud, she has been an Artist-in-Residence at the Freud Museum, London. She is the recipient of the Key to the City of London, and the 2014 Trebbia

Foundation Award for Artistic Achievement. She lectures at the University of the Arts, London.

John Gale is CEO, Community Housing and Therapy, a mental health charity that oversees therapeutic communities for the psychotherapy of the psychoses, and President, International Network of Democratic Therapeutic Communities. A psychotherapist and former Benedictine monk, he has worked in therapeutic communities in the voluntary sector for over twenty years, and currently lectures on philosophy and church history. He is the author of many scholarly articles at the interface of philosophy, psychoanalysis, and spirituality, and is coeditor of *Insanity and Divinity: Studies in Psychosis and Spirituality* and *Therapeutic Communities for Psychosis: Philosophy, History and Clinical Practice*.

Otto F. Kernberg, M.D., F.A.P.A. is Professor Emeritus of Psychiatry, Weill Medical College of Cornell University; Past President, International Psychoanalytic Association; and Director of the Personality Disorders Institute, The New York Presbyterian Hospital. A Training and Supervising Analyst at the Columbia University Center for Psychoanalytic Training and Research, his many honors include the Sigourney Award and the American Psychiatric Association Distinguished Service Award. Dr. Kernberg is the author of numerous books and articles in the field of object relations (*Object Relations Theory and Clinical Psychoanalysis*)*,* narcissism (*Borderline Conditions and Pathological Narcissism*), and the treatment of severe psychopathology (*Severe Personality Disorders: Psychotherapeutic Strategies*). His most recent book is *The Inseparable Nature of Love and Aggression*.

David Konstan, Ph.D. is Professor of Classics, New York University; Past President, American Philological Association, and a Fellow of the American Academy of Arts and Sciences. The recipient of numerous honors, he has been a Fulbright Lecturer, a Guggenheim Fellow, and a Fellow of the Rockefeller Center at Bellagio, and has held visiting faculty appointments around the world. Among his many books are *Greek Comedy and Ideology, Friendship in the Classical World, Pity Transformed, The Emotions of the Ancient Greeks,* and *Before Forgiveness: The Origins of a Moral Idea*.

Jeffrey Karl Ochsner, F.A.I.A. is Professor of Architecture and Associate Dean, College of Built Environments, University of Washington, Seattle. A registered architect and Fellow of the American Institute of Architects, he has written on the psychoanalytic aspects of memorials and the interactive design process. Among the books he has authored and edited are *Lionel H. Pries, Architect, Artist, Educator; Furniture Studio: Materials, Craft, and Architecture; Shaping Seattle Architecture: A Historical Guide to the Architects;* and *Distant Corner,* about the rebuilding of Seattle after the fire of 1889.

Diane O'Donoghue, Ph.D. is the Senior Fellow for the Humanities at Tisch College for Citizenship and Public Service at Tufts University, where she served as chair of the Department of Visual and Critical Studies; and Faculty, Boston

Psychoanalytic Institute. A recipient of the Felix and Helene Deutsch Prize and the American Psychoanalytic Association's CORST Prize, she has been an Erikson Scholar at the Austen Riggs Center, a Fulbright Visiting Professor at the Akademie der Bildenden Künste in Vienna, and a Fulbright/Sigmund Freud Visiting Scholar at the University of Vienna and the Freud Museum. She is the author of *Reflection and Reception: the Origins of the Mirror in Bronze Age China* and the forthcoming *On Dangerous Ground: Freud, Visualities, and the Construction of the Unconscious.*

.**Marion M. Oliner, Ph.D**. is a Member of the Faculty, Contemporary Freudian Society. She has published many articles on a wide range of subjects, including reality, violence, trauma, and has authored two monographs, *Cultivating Freud's Garden in France* and *Psychic Reality in Context Perspectives on Psychoanalysis, Personal History and Trauma.* An ethics curriculum developed by Dr. Oliner is in wide use as a required course for licensing. She maintains a private practice of psychoanalysis and psychoanalytic psychotherapy.

Anna Ornstein, M.D. is Professor Emerita of Child Psychiatry, University of Cincinnati; Lecturer in Psychiatry, Harvard Medical School; and Codirector, International Center for the Study of Psychoanalytic Self-Psychology. A Training and Supervising Analyst at the Cincinnati Psychoanalytic Institute, and Supervising Analyst at the Boston Psychoanalytic Institute and the Massachusetts Institute for Psychoanalysis, she is the recipient of the American Psychiatric Association Distinguished Psychiatrist Lecturer Award and the Rosenberry Award for dedication to the care of children. She is the author of a memoir, *My Mother's Eyes: Holocaust Memories of a Young Girl*, as well as many articles on the psychoanalysis, psychoanalytic psychotherapy, child psychopathology, and the treatment of trauma.

Paul Schwaber, Ph.D. is Professor of Letters Emeritus, Wesleyan University and is Past President and Chair, faculty of the Western New England Institute. He is a practicing psychoanalyst in New Haven, Connecticut, and was for many years the Director of the College of Letters, Wesleyan's undergraduate major in Western literature, philosophy, and history. The author of *The Cast of Characters: A Reading of Ulysses* and coeditor, *Of Poetry and Power: Poems Occasioned by the Presidency and by the Death of John F. Kennedy*, he has published extensively on the relationship between imaginative literature and psychoanalysis. Among his many honors are the Robert S. Liebert Award in Applied Analysis of the Association of Psychoanalytic Medicine and the American Psychoanalytic Association Edith Sabshin Teaching Award.

Masayuki Sono, M.Arch. founding partner of CLOUDS Architecture Office, New York and visiting Associate Professor at Pratt Institute. He has lectured at the Royal Danish Academy of Fine Arts, AIA Staten Island, and Kobe University, Japan. From residential projects and public art to national museums, his work has been exhibited at the Venice Biennale Future Pass, MoMA PS-1, and Shanghai MOCA and has been reviewed in *The Politics of Urban Beauty, Architectural Record,* and *The New York Times,* among other publications. In 2005 his winning design for the international competition for the Staten Island September 11 Memorial was awarded the American Institute of Architects (AIA) New York Chapter Public Project Award.

Adele Tutter, M.D., Ph.D. is Assistant Clinical Professor of Psychiatry, Weill Cornell Medical College; Adjunct Clinical Professor of Psychiatry, Columbia University; and Faculty, Columbia University Center for Psychoanalytic Training and Research and the New York Psychoanalytic Institute. Her interdisciplinary essays have been awarded the American Psychoanalytic Association CORST and Menninger Prizes, among other honors. She is the author of *Dream House: An Intimate Portrait of the Philip Johnson Glass House* and editor of *The Muse: A Psychoanalytic Exploration of Creative Inspiration.* A member of the editorial boards of the *International Journal of Psychoanalysis, Psychoanalytic Quarterly, and American Imago,* she has a private practice in psychoanalysis and psychopharmacology in Manhattan.

Jeanine M. Vivona, Ph.D. is Professor and Chair of Psychology, The College of New Jersey, and Adjunct Clinical Faculty, the Pennsylvania Hospital in Philadelphia. She is the two-time recipient of the *Journal of the American Psychoanalytic Association* Prize for her writing on language and psychoanalysis and is the author of the forthcoming book, *Bridging the Verbal/Nonverbal Divide in Psychoanalysis: Theoretical and Clinical Implications of Language Research.* She is in private practice near Philadelphia.

Léon Wurmser, M.D., Ph.D. is Past Clinical Professor of Psychiatry, University of West Virginia. A Training and Supervising Analyst at the New York Freudian Society, he is the recipient of the Egnér Prize and the *Journal of the American Psychoanalytic Association* Paper Prize. He is the author and coauthor of many books on the theory and practice of psychoanalysis, including *The Mask of Shame; The Power of the Inner Judge; Torment Me, But Do Not Abandon Me; Jealousy and Envy – New Views on Two Powerful Emotions;* and *Nothing Good Is Allowed to Stand.* He lectures extensively in the United States and abroad.

FOREWORD

Daria Colombo

Mourning is an immemorial topic for artists and is contained and organized within the rituals of religious faiths and community practices. It has or will face all of us, but this universal, inescapable experience has been less than fully addressed in its most intimate register by psychoanalytic writing and theorizing, a notable absence. Freud wrote during the devastating unfolding of the First World War, "Death will no longer be denied; we are forced to believe it."[1] We don't need to believe in death for death, so to speak, to believe in us, and to confront us all – unpredictably, implacably, and inevitably. Confronting loss – "the price of love," and the hardest task forced upon us by life – can be thought of in various registers: as a developmental challenge; as an interpersonal experience; and as a fundamental intrapsychic paradox, both block and spur to growth.

Furthering the diminishing of the dominion of man begun by the Copernican and Darwinian revolutions, Freud's critical discovery that "the ego is not master in his own house"[2] inaugurated a world in which the powerful unconscious forces and conflicts informing psychic life were acknowledged. Yet his theory of mourning – that it is necessary to decathect the lost object – constricted both the difficulties and the possibilities facing the self seeking to master loss: to survive, love, create in its wake.

Adele Tutter and Léon Wurmser, who coedit as well as contribute to this wide ranging collection of essays, open up an unprecedented forum in which its authors navigate what Tutter calls the "conflict between the need to remember and the wish to forget." Wurmser notes that many of the contributions, including his own, traverse this territory with "great and personal specificity." The intimate experiences included in these essays are at the core of this work's enterprise, and the seam – jagged as it is – between what is known through theory and what is learned through personal experience and communion with art is thoughtfully, if painfully opened. Analysts who confront the losses of their patients as well as their own offer a perspective valuable not only within the boundaries of the consulting room, but also within the larger community, encompassing, indeed, all of us, who will face the task of mourning. Contributions by artists further enlarge the sense of connection created by this volume, as the essays, more than standing alone, seem to reverberate with each other, making common cause as they search for a path through mourning. Varied in their scope, these works comfort and accompany us, as they remind us of the power that both art and psychoanalysis have to unravel, witness, and contain the ineffable, that which cannot be borne.

This volume collects writers able to begin "talking in a common language" (Wurmser) about the isolation, shame, and despair that can reside within loss. Primo Levi, in writing about loss of a different order, states, "those who have seen the face of the Gorgon, did not return, or returned wordless."[3] He identifies himself and other survivor/writers as those who, in their ability to not only survive physically, but also to bear witness through writing, occupy a liminal space between life and death, neither turned to stone, nor (yet?) fully alive. It is deeply moving to witness and meditate upon the experiences described in these essays as they enliven discussions of mourning, liberating the topic from both the theoretical stiffness and, for many, the personal isolation in which it had been bound.

Elie Wiesel, another who did not return wordless, observed in *Night* that "every question possessed a power that was lost in the answer."[4] This volume demonstrates the power of such questioning. The opening of the 9/11 Memorial at the World Trade Center has caused an outpouring of public discussion about the way we mourn and memorialize, about retraumatization versus healing, and about how to confront individual loss and collective tragedy. To be able to write intimately about mourning, to wrench and reanimate from the stone of tragedies, monuments and cemeteries an enlivened emotional experience, to be able to gain comfort and community from the cultural and artistic products of mourning is to transform a forced and shattering belief in death into a different sort of belief, one in the value of, as Freud would have it, ongoing work and ongoing love – ongoing life.

Notes

1 Freud S. (1915/1957). *Thoughts for the times on war and death.* Standard Edition, 14: 273–300. London: Hogarth Press, p. 291.
2 Freud S. (1917/1955). *A difficulty in the path of psycho-analysis.* Standard Edition, 17:135–144. London: Hogarth Press, p. 143.
3 P. Levi, quoted in Hobsbawm E.J. (1995). *The Age of Extremes: The Short Twentieth Century, 1914–1991,* London: Abacus, p. 2.
4 Weisel E. (1982/2006). *Night,* trans. M. Weisel. New York: Macmillan, p. 5.

PROLOGUE: *GIVE SORROW WORDS*[1]

Adele Tutter

> *Thus the absent are present, and the poor are rich, and the weak are strong, and – what seems stranger still the dead are alive, such is the honor, the enduring remembrance, the longing love, with which the dying are followed by the living; so that the death of the dying seems happy, the life of the living full of praise*
>
> —Cicero, *De amicitia*[2]

1.

In July 2010, Queen Elizabeth laid a wreath at Ground Zero in lower Manhattan (Fig. 0.1). Speaking to those assembled, the normally reserved monarch paraphrased C.S. Lewis (1961), and said:

> *grief is the cost of love.*

Psychoanalysts have paid much attention to love and have placed great importance on attachment, intimacy, and the effects of early loss, but they have in general spent less time thinking about what happens when, under more typical circumstances, the loved ones to whom we are so closely attached are torn from us. On the surface, this is somewhat paradoxical, for despite the many differences that divide us, we all experience loss: as the philosopher Judith Butler (2003) puts it, "loss has made a tenuous 'we' of us all" (p. 10).

   The relative disengagement of psychoanalysis from grief and mourning, as compared with, say, the emphasis placed on trauma, can be understood as an instinctive response to the reality of the terrible inevitability of loss – something that lays bare

FIGURE 0.1 Prince Philip and Queen Elizabeth lay a wreath at Ground Zero, 2010.

the exquisite vulnerability with which we are invested by intimacy, and, ultimately, by mortality. By virtue of their aesthetic, intellectual, and linguistic distance, poets, philosophers, and artists have an advantage when grappling with this topic, as compared to psychoanalysts, who must sit with, contain, and manage not only their own anguish, but also that of their patients.

A year into World War I, Freud (1915) was moved to acknowledge that "death will no longer be denied; we are forced to believe it" (p. 291). The imprint of the war and its devastation on his theorizing is evident in "Mourning and Melancholia" (1917), in which he theorizes that mourning involves a painful process of reality testing, during which ties to lost objects are slowly withdrawn while the mourner oscillates between remembering them when they were alive, and remembering that they are now dead. It is not difficult to understand why loss must be "remembered" at all: often, the *fact* of loss is for some time incomprehensible, let alone acceptable. Moreover, when we sustain a loss – whether that of our beloved, our home, or our youth – we lose a part of ourselves, at least temporarily, and in some instances, forever. Again, I rely on the philosophers, in this case, Paul Ricoeur (2009).

> The loss of the other is in a way the loss of self . . . The [loved] other, because other, comes to be perceived as a danger for one's own identity . . . are we not able to anticipate, on the horizon of this mourning of the other, the mourning that would crown the anticipated loss of our own life?
>
> [p. 359]

How do we survive the death of those we cherish – an experience that Ricœur aptly terms an "amputation of the self" (p. 359)? Goethe goes even further, comparing some losses to death. As one contributor to this book noted, the poet wrote that we die twice – when we die, and again when we lose the ones with whom we shared our world (Kernberg, 2010).

The motif of the "double death" is most famously elaborated in the myth of Orpheus, who could not bear to lose Eurydice, the bride who died on their wedding day. Orpheus tried to "endure" his grief, "but Love overcame" him (Ovid, 1994, Met.X:35–36). Insisting that *he could not live* without her, he persuaded the rulers of Hades to return her to the world of the living. They agreed and allowed him to retrieve his beloved, but with one proviso: he must not turn back to look at her until they left the underworld.

As sculpted by Auguste Rodin (Fig. 0.2, left), Eurydice emerges from marble, as if escaping the imprisoning petrifaction of death; her *non finito* figure and closed eyes signal the ambiguity of her corpse-like state. Following his mandate, Orpheus covers his eyes with his right hand as he leads Eurydice out of Hades, "blind" to the reality of her death – an allegory for the desperate need to repudiate grief via magical denial. But when viewed from the right side (Fig. 0.2, right), we realize that Orpheus does indeed lift his hand from his face, an action that Rodin virtually narrates as we move from left to right around the marble group. The artist thereby demonstrates Orpheus's terrible ambivalence, and at the same time anticipates his fate: as much as he tries, he will not, he *cannot* prevent himself from looking back – from making sure his dead wife is really there behind him. By "looking" at Eurydice – in other words, by confronting and remembering the horrifying reality of her death – Orpheus affects her second death, losing her forever. From the right side of Rodin's sculpture, the vantage point of the lifted hand, Eurydice's face does indeed disappear from view. As Rodin confirms, she dies two deaths: her physical death and her effacement – literally and figuratively – in her lover's eyes.

In order to travel beyond grief (the "first" death), we must first look it in the eye. Doubtless myriad and variable mechanisms are involved in the reality testing of loss (the "second" death), the surrendering to grief and its eventual transcendence. Like myth, more contemporary masterpieces of art and literature also yield some clues.

FIGURE 0.2 Auguste Rodin, *Orpheus and Eurydice,* 1893, The Metropolitan Museum of Art.

Reversing the myth of Orpheus and Eurydice, Leo Tolstoy (1869) describes the recovery from grief in *War and Peace*: Natasha loses her beloved Andréi twice – first, when her indiscretions cause him to break off their engagement: and second, when after their happy reunion, he perishes from his war wounds. Natasha then sustains another crushing blow: the war claims her adored little brother, Petya. Her sorrow heightened by the reduplication of her loss, nevertheless, by caring for her yet more shattered mother, Natasha comes back to life.

> A wound in the soul, coming from the rending of the spiritual body, strange as it seems, gradually closes like a physical wound . . . a wound in the soul, like a physical wound, can be healed only by the force of life pushing up from inside. This was the way Natasha's wound healed. She thought her life was over. But suddenly her love for her mother showed her that the essence of life – love – was still alive in her. Love awoke, and life awoke. (. . .)
>
> She did not know it, she would not have believed it, but under the seemingly impenetrable layer of silt that covered her soul, thin, tender young

needles of grass were already breaking through, which were to take root and so cover with their living shoots the grief that oppressed her, that it would soon not be seen or noticed. The wound was healing from the inside.

[pp. 1080–1082]

Love awoke, and life awoke. How does this happen – this "healing from the inside"?

Freud (1917) understood the pathological reaction to loss – namely, melancholia – as resulting from the introjective identification of the ambivalently loved lost object. Today, however, most agree that identification is a far more generalizable, more often normal response to grief. Tolstoy anticipates this foundational premise of psychoanalysis: describing the anguished Natasha's "wounded soul," he all but states her identification with her beloved's wounded body. Whereas love was the cause of Orpheus's unbearable grief, for Natasha, love – for another wounded soul – was its cure.

At about the same time when Freud wrote "Mourning and Melancholia," Marcel Proust mined similar territory in his epic work, *À la recherché du temps perdu (1913–1927)*. Like Tolstoy, Proust employs a botanical metaphor for the generative processes of life after loss:

It is often said that something may survive of a person after his death, if that person was an artist and put a little of himself into his work. It is perhaps in the same way that a sort of cutting taken from one person and grafted onto the heart of another continues to carry on its existence even when the person from whom it had been detached has perished.

[Proust, 1993, p. 706]

Again, like Tolstoy, Proust evinces an intuitive awareness of the animated, dynamic processes of internalization in mourning, and the central role of generativity in the transcendence of grief.

In "The Ego and the Id," Freud (1923) extended the conclusions of "Mourning and Melancholia," theorizing that the essence of identity – the individual characteristics of the ego and superego – is formed in the crucible of relinquished, internalized object relations. Melanie Klein revised and extended Freud's theories of mourning within the framework of object relations, as explicated in Hannah Segal's (1952) famous explication of Proust. For Klein (1940), Segal explains, mourning is

a re-living of the early depressive anxieties; not only is the present object in the external world felt to be lost, but also the early objects, the parents; and they are lost as internal objects as well as in the external world. In the process of mourning it is these earliest objects which are lost again, and then re-created . . .

[p. 199]

One detects an echo of Freud's theory of reality testing in Klein's formulation of the depressive position, in which loss can be acknowledged and grieved, and the paranoid-schizoid position, in which it is not, and in which fantasies of omnipotence, which negate libidinal needs and resulting vulnerability, predominate instead. Klein's theory also draws on Freud's (1895) concept of *Nachträglichkeit*, the shaping of present experience as a function of the past. Responding to the sudden death of his beloved friend, Arthur Henry Hallum, Lord Alfred Tennyson (1849) composed the epic poem, "In Memoriam A.H.H.," over the next seventeen years. In the following excerpt, written a century before Klein, he demonstrates an acute awareness that loss in adulthood reverberates with, and resurrects, the first loss, what Andreas-Salomé (1921/1962) considered the primal psychic injury: the realization that "the circle of the breast" is not "I," and that the beloved mother is in fact "other."

> The baby new to earth and sky,
> What time his tender palm is prest
> Against the circle of the breast,
> Has never thought that "this is I":
>
> But as he grows he gathers much,
> And learns the use of "I," and "me,"
> And finds "I am not what I see,
> And other than the things I touch."
>
> So rounds he to a separate mind
> From whence clear memory may begin,
> As thro' the frame that binds him in
> His isolation grows defined. [XLV.1–12; p. 230]

It was also Klein (1940) who first situated creativity within a psychoanalytic model of mourning, positing that this process often gives rise to a creative impulse, as Tennyson so beautifully illustrates. She theorized that the creative work of art functions as a means of repairing the lost object; again, in Hannah Segal's (1952) words,

> only the lost past and the lost or dead object . . . can be made into a work of art . . . It is when the world within us is destroyed, when it is dead and loveless, when our loved ones are in fragments, and we ourselves in helpless despair — it is then that we must re-create our world anew, re-assemble the pieces, infuse life into dead fragments, re-create life.
>
> [pp. 198–199]

If Klein saw mourning as the reliving of the loss of the earliest objects, Hans Loewald (1962) saw the formation of the superego from their internalization as a necessary preparation for mourning later in life. Loewald (1973) felt that adult loss is transcended by the internalization of not only the lost object, but of the entire object relationship.

Vividly, Tennyson visualizes this experience: contemplating a yew tree at Arthur Hallum's grave, he imagines its roots "wrapt about the bones" (1849; II. 4; p. 205) and prefigures in the first person the vegetal metaphors of Tolstoy and Proust: "I seem to fail from out my blood / And grow incorporate into thee" (II.15–16). The success of his mourning is evident in the progress of the poem, which ends with the marriage of his sister Emily, formerly his dead friend's fiancé. Tennyson realizes that love is simultaneously grief's source and solace, recognizing the need to grieve and love: "Let Love clasp Grief lest both be drown'd" [I.9].[3]

Nor, as Loewald theorized, does love for the dead end; all of the psychoanalysts contributing to this volume concur, disagreeing with Freud's original notion that mourning is dependent on the decathexis of the lost object, a process he felt was finite, and the completion of which prerequisite to the establishment of new libidinal attachments (see also Hagman, 1995; 1996; Pollock, 1978; among others). As for Tennyson, love will survive his own death: "I shall not lose thee tho' I die" (CXXX.16, p. 287).

Freud himself had already disavowed the notion of finite mourning, if privately. In a letter to his friend Ludwig Binswanger written after learning of the death of a friend's twenty-year-old son, Freud (1929a) anticipates Loewald's emphasis on the preservation of the relationship to the lost object, albeit at great cost.

> We know that the acute sorrow we feel after such a loss will run its course, but also that we will remain inconsolable, and will never find a substitute. No matter what may come to take its place, even should it fill that place completely, it yet remains something else. And that is how it should be. It is the only way of perpetuating a love that we do not want to abandon.
>
> [p. 196]

He knew from experience. Nine years after the death of his twenty-seven-year old daughter Sophie in the Spanish flu epidemic, and six years after the death of her five-year-old son (Heinz or Heinerle) to tuberculosis, he grieved still – indeed, was "inconsolable" (Fig. 0.3). As he made clear in a letter written one year earlier to Ernst Jones, he experienced especially intense grief after the death of Heinerle: "Sophie was a dear daughter, to be sure, but not a child. It was only three years later, in June 1923, when little Heinerle died, that I became tired of life permanently" (Freud, 1928, p. 521).

But can we really believe that Freud mourned Sophie less because she was not, like her son, a child when she died? Or did he love – and mourn – Heinerle all the more because he had already lost Heinerle's mother? In any case, surely their losses were not as separate and independent as Freud would have presented them: in the workings of his own concept of *nachträglichkeit,* in losing Heinerle, he lost Sophie all over again – another double death.

FIGURE 0.3 Anna Freud with Sophie Freud Halberstadt's two sons, Heinz (Heinerle), left, and W. Ernst, right.

And yet one year after writing his resigned letter to Binswanger, and one day after his mother passed away, Freud wrote to Ferenczi that this "great event" affected him

> in a peculiar way . . . No pain, no grief . . . at the same time a feeling of libera-
> tion, of release, which I think I also understand. I was not free to die as long
> as she was alive, and now I am. The *values of life [Lebenswerte]* will somehow
> have changed noticeably in the deeper layers.
>
> [Freud, 1930, p. 399, emphasis added]

As Loewald (1962) stresses, and as Freud admits, loss can implicate a degree of emancipation. Somehow, after the loss of his mother, Freud found a way to free himself from the bitter indifference incurred by Heinerle's death – achieved, like Tolstoy's Natasha, via the values of life. A hint as to what those values were – and, perhaps, his personal avenue to the transcendence of his grief – may be found in *Civilization and its Discontents*, published just a few months before the death of his mother: "people . . . seek power, success and wealth for themselves and admire them in others . . . they underestimate what is of *true value in life [Werte des Lebens]*" (Freud, 1929b, p. 64, emphasis added). If Natasha's *true values* included nurturance and love, for Freud they included religion, scholarship, and art.

The release that followed his mother's death had a meaningful precedent: following the death of his father in 1896, Freud had a dream in which a placard reads: "You are instructed to close the eyes" (Freud, 1896, p. 202). Among the many meanings this phrase suggests is the wish to "close his eyes" to the death of his father – and to the liberation that this death seems to have entailed for Freud. He embarked on a self-analysis, formulated the Oedipus complex, and completed his dream book within a few years of his father's passing – an exemplar of the stimulus of loss to creativity.

2.

Like its Prologue, this book is divided into three parts, each consisting of several original papers that are then considered in one or two discussions. Three chapters of this volume – from Otto Kernberg, Anna Ornstein, and coeditor Léon Wurmser – were first presented at a panel ("Mourning, Identity, Creativity") chaired by this writer during the meetings of the American Psychoanalytic Association in January 2013. Wurmser suggested, and all panelists agreed, that these presentations should form the nucleus of a monograph. Collected here in Part II, where they are joined by a like contribution from Marion Oliner, these essays are distinguished by candid descriptions of intensely personal experiences of grief and its transcendence; all of them respond to the failure of the psychoanalytic literature to describe and account for those experiences. As Oliner states, "my experience of great losses early in life make me something of an expert, but I rarely find *myself* in the literature on the subject." Ornstein agrees, noting that in the psychoanalytic literature, mourning tends to be "described in a highly abstract language and individual differences are not taken into consideration."

Organizing the 2013 panel was motivated by my own wish to better understand how we survive the terrible losses of life – my father, mother, and much loved aunt and uncle having all passed away within five years of September 11, 2001. On that day, my husband and children watched the burning towers crumble and fall from our home across the harbor in Brooklyn. Henceforth, I gained a growing appreciation of the role of creativity in mourning – both through my own studies of artists and writers, and from the impetus to this work that my own losses proved to be.

Tackling the subjective experience of anguish is no job for the faint of heart. And yet "authenticity in such an exploration is only possible," Wurmser observes, "when it is done with great and personal specificity." It is precisely this need to situate theoretical inquiry squarely within "great and personal specificity" – both personally and historically – that this book aims to address.

Part I –"Family, Community, Society" – opens with classics scholar David Konstan's explication of Cicero's *De amicitia*, "Cicero on Grief and Friendship." Echoing Freud's loss of his daughter Sophie, Konstan views the *De amicitia* in the context of Cicero's response to the loss of *his* daughter, his beloved Tullia. Freud's rationalization for (consciously) grieving more for Heinerle than for Sophie seems more thin, juxtaposed with Cicero's experience, for i.e., as Konstan notes, Cicero observes that "no loss is more difficult to endure than that of a child, especially if it is an adult child, as [Cicero's daughter] Tullia was at the time of her death." Sounding a most salient theme, writing about friends and the mourning of their passing – the endurance of which made possible by "the hope or confidence that the memory of their friendship will endure forever," was a creative means for Cicero to grieve for Tullia. The consolation implicit in *De amicitia* anticipates psychoanalytic theory by some two thousand years: "it is as though Laelius can keep his ego intact by incorporating or internalizing the other into himself through recollection." Konstan argues that if by linking *memory* and *love*, Cicero found that loving "friendship is the cure for grief, a bond that is able to transcend time and loss," then love for a lost child can also "be invoked as a cure for sorrow . . . love, which made grief almost unbearable, was at the same time its antidote" – as it was for Tennyson and for Tolstoy's Natasha. *Love awoke, and life awoke.*

We then proceed from friendship and family to community, remembrance, and ritual. Erna Furman (1981), who expanded the study of mourning to include its manifestations in childhood, stresses its important social aspects: the role of family and community, memorial and ritual; "mourning alone," she contends, "is an almost impossible task" (p. 114). Several of the essays in this book further the discussion on the fundamental role of community and ritual, beginning with "Rituals of Memory," in which Egyptologist Jan Assmann interrogates the historical roots of the collective experience of memory and remembrance. Within an intricate "interplay between symbolic and corporeal dimensions," he explains, ancient Egyptian death rituals and the Jewish tradition of memory and learning kept, and keeps, the past alive and connected to the present. Moving deftly from the denial of death evident in elaborate Egyptian tombs to postwar Germany's postponed confrontation with the "sins of the fathers" and debate over Holocaust memorials, Assmann argues that memory is crucial for "the deep human need to not allow the dead fall away from the world in which we live – but rather to take them with us, at least as names and memory, into unfolding reality."

Memorials and monuments serve as a "symbol of union" in the community, notes cultural historian Peter Homans (1989); functioning as "the material soul of the group" (p. 277), they facilitate vital connections between individuals based on a shared past. Homans observes:

> mourning renders with great intensity and force what is perhaps the most fundamental of human paradoxes: it is a heightened individualizing and interiorizing experience which is also accompanied by a profound – if only transient – sense of unity between oneself and all of mankind.
>
> [p. 278]

However, that "sense of unity" is less a reflection of mourning, as several of the essays in this volume stress, than a prerequisite. The "sense of unity" that memorials help to provide has its genesis in their promotion of shared remembrance.

In "The Staten Island September 11 Memorial: Creativity, Mourning, and the Experience of Loss," Jeffrey Karl Ochsner takes as his subject the stunning community memorial, *Postcards*. A licensed architect and architectural historian with a deeply psychoanalytic sensibility, Ochsner draws on Winnicott and Volkan to meticulously explore how the memorial constitutes before a holding environment and a "space of absence." He emphasizes how the unprecedented degree of community involvement in the memorial, from design to installation, inscribed in it the memory of each individual Staten Islander lost on 9/11. Commemorating loss and confronting the absence it now frames, the memorial promotes the recovery of a devastated society.

Following this essay is "Designing the Staten Island September 11 Memorial," a personal statement from the designer of *Postcards*, architect and artist Masayuki Sono, who in his prize-winning design expresses his wish "to connect all the victims of September 11 back to us." Sono relates the painfully intimate process of working hand in hand with community members on one of its singular aspects, the facial profiles of the lost ones. Candidly, he describes the loss *he* incurred after September 11 of his "belief in the values of humanity and beauty." Transforming the lost twin towers into two graceful wings, Sono's achingly beautiful elegy helped him, and doubtless many others similarly affected by September 11, "to move forward again."

Responding to the essays of Part I, in "The Relics of Absence," theological scholar John Gale weaves the themes struck by Konstan, Assmann, Ochsner, and Sono with reflections on mourning in ancient Christianity, pulling from them a common thread: that "absence is experienced enigmatically as a presence." Finally, in his discussion of Part I, "Arcs of Recovery," Paul Schwaber sounds the central theme in this volume, describing "the arc of recovery," the shifting balance of remembering and forgetting. Ultimately, "our recourse is memory – and resolution."

Marion Oliner's formulation of an alternative dynamics of traumatic object loss inaugurates Part II, "Theory, Specificity, Authenticity." Departing from the more traditional psychoanalytic literature on trauma, in "Further Reflections on Object Loss and Mourning" Oliner draws on her loss of family, language, culture, and country to focus on the mechanisms that preserve what is left of a devastated world. After such overwhelming trauma, Oliner asserts, remembrance must be delayed until a new life can be built, allowing the prospect of mourning itself to become less overwhelming. This is facilitated by the strengthening of the ego by identifications and external replenishment; the integrative process of dreaming; and important defenses, especially unconscious fantasies of omnipotence, which guard against premature confrontation with loss.

Following naturally from Oliner's emphasis on defenses, in her essay, "The Function of Memorial Spaces: Mourning Following Multiple Traumatic Losses" Anna Ornstein outlines the conditions that must be satisfied in order to access and work through the sequelae of catastrophic loss. Also speaking from experience, she, too, normalizes the delayed mourning of many Holocaust survivors, arguing that in such situations it may be necessary to postpone mourning until enough time has been spent cultivating a more cohesive self and the concomitant increased capacity to tolerate intensely painful affects. Ornstein explains how the survivors of exceptional, often "unspeakable" losses are often deprived of the sustaining benefit of ritual remembrance and thus may greatly benefit from memorial works of art and literature that create a "memorial space" – a psychic territory that can "facilitate grieving and offset the alienation of traumatic loss."

Otto Kernberg summarizes his own experience of the loss of his spouse and similar experiences of colleagues, friends, and patients in "The Long-Term Effects of the Mourning Process." Building on his previous work on mourning (Kernberg, 2010), he explores the permanence of mourning on the one hand, and, on the other, the generative productivity that ego and especially superego internalizations can instill. Echoing Ornstein, who relates that the internalization of her murdered brothers' medical ambitions was "crucial in my decision to embark on an academic career," Kernberg focuses, firsthand, on the special example of the mourner who constructively assumes the life project of the lost beloved.

Coeditor Léon Wurmser also writes about the loss of his wife in "Mourning, Double Reality, and the Culture of Remembering and Forgiving: A Very Personal Report," in which he concentrates on the dynamics of shame and guilt that commonly accompany the death of a loved one. Disagreeing with Freud's theory, Otto Fenichel (1945) posited that the guilt associated with bereavement is inevitable and adaptive, while Leon Grinberg (1964) argued that it resulted from the feelings of deprivation and impoverishment incurred by loss. Similarly, Martha Wolfenstein (1966) proposed the sense of having lost part of the self, which almost inevitably accompanies loss, is the source of profound shame. In Wurmser's very different formulation, the guilt that accompanies loss results from the inevitable failure to actualize the demands of omnipotent responsibility, fantasies intrinsic to intimate relationships. Wurmser also stresses the critically supportive aspects of traditional mourning rituals. Shared remembrance, he writes, serves to "strengthen bonds to the community: 'shared suffering *(das Mit-Leiden)* is half the suffering.'" For Wurmser, too, "love, which made grief almost unbearable, was at the same time its antidote."

Extending her discussion at the 2013 panel, Jeanine Vivona considers Part II in "Nothing Gold Can Stay?," a critical synthesis of the currents of contemporary psychoanalytic thought on grief and mourning that Oliner, Ornstein, Kernberg, and Wurmser develop. Vivona makes the important distinction between what is "normative" and what is "adaptive" – suggesting that what constitutes "normal" mourning is in reality highly variable and entirely dependent on both individual and external circumstances.

Part III –"History, Ancestry, Memory" – begins with "Lost Wax to Lost Fathers: Installations by British sculptor Jane McAdam Freud," in which the great-granddaughter of Sigmund Freud shares her thoughts on two significant bodies of work: the first generated while Artist-in Residence at the Sigmund Freud Museum in London, and the second conceived in a consciously considered process of grieving her father, the painter Lucian Freud, who died in 2011. In becoming intensely familiar with Sigmund Freud's "aesthetic and tactile appreciation," she writes, "I was able to recognize my own, able to trace its precedent"; by drawing and sculpting her late father, McAdam Freud discovered a potent means to "keep him alive." Further consolidating her ancestral connection, she recently purchased a house on the medieval town square of the Moravian town of Příbor, just steps from Sigmund Freud's birthplace. Now, the home of her father's grandfather is her home, too.

The eternal pull of home is further explored by this writer in "Sudek, Janáček, Hukvaldy, and Me: Notes on Art, Loss, and Nationalism Under Political Oppression." I, too, draw on personal experiences to explore how the Czech composer Leoš Janáček and the Czech photographer Josef Sudek transform national identity into art, a potent defense against loss and the dehumanization of cultural erasure. Spurred by his early loss of his father, Sudek's annual pilgrimages to Janáček's Moravian hometown of Hukvaldy recall the Aboriginal songlines to which Assmann refers. Echoing the losses of Cicero and Freud, Janáček's grief over his daughter Olga's death gave rise to the timeless opera of love, forgiveness, and redemption – *Jenůfa*.

In a fortuitous concordance, Janáček was born in Hukvaldy not two years before Freud was born in Příbor, a stone's throw away. In her discussion of Part III, "Image, Loss, Delay," Diane O'Donoghue gathers the strands of memory, history, and ancestry in Freud's Příbor, Janáček's Hukvaldy, and beyond. O'Donoghue understands works of art as mediators between past, present, and future: both "memento mori and reminder of what is alive, what still remains."

My coeditor closes this volume with his Epilogue, "'Tis Nameless Woe," a meditation on the foundational humanistic wisdom that underlies psychoanalytic thought. Wurmser underlines the ubiquity of conflict in mourning, and the need to recognize the primacy of the inborn seeking for the other. For it is by remembering the instinctual human striving for connectedness and solidarity, as well as the very human vulnerability to shame, that psychoanalysts can expose and ease the woe that goes by no name. Urging curiosity, humility, and, above all, respect for human dignity, Wurmser epitomizes these aims in the best tradition of the psychoanalyst, humanist, and scholar.

3.

Emerging from this cross-section of disciplines and approaches are three clear themes: the centrality of memory in the mourning process, whether immediately or many years hence; the management and metabolization of grief via communal rituals and loving relationships, old and new; and the singular impetus of loss to personal and creative growth, including works of art that partake in, promote, and sometimes even permit the process of mourning. The constant counterpoint running through these themes is the very *fact* of loss: the reality thereof.

Alongside their healing, social aspect, rituals also serve to symbolize and bind the vicissitudes of reality – the conflict between the need to acknowledge loss and embrace change, and the pull to disavow loss and remain the same. Ceremony, rite, and prayer are distinguished by repetition, soothing the bereaved while recursively evoking their essential quality: their enduring and stable repetition over time. By structuring mourning within rituals, customs, and traditions that have been and will continue to be repeated, lives shaken by death and displacement gain a stabilizing ballast of permanence, a sustaining matrix of continuity. Whether by the draping of the mirrors or by the periodic traveling of ancestral paths, their familiar sameness is a consolation, assuring secure links with past and future and thereby mitigating the devastation of our worlds and our selves. And so we manage to keep on living, even when our loved ones do not.

Much like rituals, works of art can also transform and palliate unspeakable realities, if by different means. In *Sulamit,* the German painter Anselm Kiefer rejects the original intention of a proposed Nazi war memorial; recasting this ceremonial hall as a blackened crematorium, he lays bare the true legacy of Hitler (Fig. 0.4). Deep inside, a lit menorah glows, retransforming the burning specter of death and claiming the "fascist architectural space, dedicated to the death cult of the Nazis" for their victims (Huyssen, 1989, p. 43). *Sulamit*, an enlivened memorial for those incinerated in the death camps: a cenotaph for those left without a marker of their death, or of their very existence.

Yet, as some of the contributions to this volume have commented, there is the risk that by: repeating the past, rather than remembering it, a melancholic process of denial or retraumatization will proceed, rather than a true process of transcendence. Kernberg, Ornstein, and Wurmser all agree that creativity can reflect a compulsive attempt to negate loss, rather than mourn it. Greenacre (1958) was among the first to identify the potential for art to function as defense against the reality of loss; more recently, Kristeva (1989) observed that "if loss, bereavement, and absence trigger the work of the imagination and nourish it . . . it is also noteworthy that the work of art as fetish emerges when the activating sorrow has been repudiated" (p. 9). Huyssen (1989) also worries that *Sulamit* and like works of art can enact the reassembly and repetition of the past, as opposed to its remembering and reworking, but concludes that by looking the past squarely in the eye, *Sulamit* "evokes the terror perpetrated by Germans on their victims, thus opening a space for mourning" (p. 43).

But maybe it is never really possible to *completely* embrace and accept the reality of death and the disappearance of the receding past. Indeed, the preeminent tension emerging from the pages of this book derives from the balance of the push to recognize and grieve loss against the pull to deny and repudiate it. That the conflict between the need to remember and the wish to forget pervades the various essays collected here signals its persistence in the mourner – well beyond, I offer, the initial, finite phase of reality testing postulated by Freud, and perhaps forever. The line between remembering the dead and forgetting their death, always blurred, breaks down, less a dichotomy than an uneasy equilibrium. Hence, the

FIGURE 0.4 *Upper, Sulamith (Shulamite),* Anselm Kiefer, 1983. *Lower,* Wilhelm Kreis, design for *Funeral Hall for the Great German Soldiers,* 1939 (unbuilt).

episodic, unexpected confrontations with grief, long after "mourning" is thought to be "over"; hence, the recurring fantasies of reunion; hence, the mystical instances that Cicero describes when *the absent are present*, and *the dead are alive*.

Such experiences are not limited to the bereaved. Viewing the Staten Island September 11 Memorial, how easily we imagine the messages on our "postcards" conveyed, on those great white envelope wings, to their recipients alive in the heavens.

> *How are you?*
> *Where are you?*
> *We miss you.*

Not too unlike the Ancient Egyptians, who assured the dead permanent residence in their world, so, too, do our questions, feelings, and memories animate the dead in ours.

If, as Goethe said, we "die twice," then, as Elie Wiesel said, those who remember "live twice" (Wurmser, this volume, p. 207). In the ancient myths of metamorphosis, the essence of a transformed human being persists inside a new, strange form, embodying the fluidity of our past and future selves and allegorizing the survival of the beloved departed in the memories and identifications that take up residence inside us. Indeed, all of the creative works of art discussed in this Prologue concerns *transformation*. Setting and symbolizing memory in transformative works of art and literature that will live on helps us to *go* on – to honor, to commemorate, and, sometimes, to forget, but more often to remember and grieve – even as we temporarily neglect our own end. Assmann notes that in legend, the initiated drank from the waters of Mnemosyne to remember their past lives, while others drank from the river Leth to forget. How fitting that in legend, Mnemosyne, goddess of Memory, is the mother of the Muses, the incarnations of creative inspiration (Tutter, in press)! Borne of Mnemosyne and whet by her daughters, word, image, music, and memorial afford solace in the face of the abyss, the awful specter of death. If we can "conceive culture as a great collective memory," as Assmann suggests, then via its gifts we are, as O'Donoghue notes, "momentarily ransomed from mortality."

Every year, on September 11, twin beams of light of stunning beauty rise from the site of Ground Zero in lower Manhattan (Fig. 0.5). Extending far up into the sky, they can be seen for miles. For a little while, the devastated twin towers forestall their inevitable disappearance; transformed, they come back to life. And then, like Eurydice, they are lost all over again. But unlike Eurydice, they can, and will, return. An attestation to the words that render immortal their "living record," this work of art has become a *ritual*.

> *When wasteful war shall statues overturn,*
> *And broils root out the work of masonry,*
> *Nor Mars his sword nor war's quick fire shall burn*
> *The living record of your memory.*
>
> [from *Sonnet 55,* Shakespeare, 2008, p. 491]

FIGURE 0.5 *Tribute in Light,* September 11, 2004.

We are constantly losing the self we once were; grief transforms us in ways we cannot predict. But while we cannot know the future, we can mourn the ones we loved and the time we shared with them. In healing rites and rituals, in memorials and imaginative works of art, and in all the generative, and, yes, loving forms of work that enrich our lives and the lives of others, we preserve *the living record of their memory* as we pick up the pieces and start again. Together, we *give sorrow words.*

Notes

1 *Give sorrow words; the grief that does not speak / Whispers the o'er-fraught heart and bids it break.* Macbeth 4.3, W. Shakespeare, 1994, p. 1330; I thank Léon Wurmser and Dr. Zvi Lothane for this quote.
2 Cicero (1884), p. 19.
3 See Hamilton (1986) and Hsiao (2009) for further discussion of Tennyson's "In Memoriam."

References

Andreas-Salomé, L. (1921/1962). The dual orientation of narcissism, trans. S. Leavey. *Psychoanalytic Quarterly*, 31: 1–30.
Butler, J. (2003). Violence, mourning, politics. *Stud. Gend. Sex.*, 4: 9–37.
Cicero. *De Amicitia*, ed. & trans. A.P. Peabody. (1884). Boston: Little and Brown.
Fenichel, O. (1945). *The Psychoanalytic Theory of Neurosis.* New York: Norton.
Freud, S. (1895). *Project for a scientific psychology.* Standard Edition, I. London: Hogarth Press (1950), pp. 281–391.
————. (1896). Letter from Freud to Fliess, November 2, 1896. In: *The Complete Letters of Sigmund Freud to Wilhelm Fliess, 1887–1904,* ed. & trans. J.M. Masson. Cambridge, MA: Harvard University Press (1985), pp. 202–203.
————. (1915). *Thoughts for the times on war and death.* Standard Edition, 14: 273–300. London: Hogarth Press, 1957.
————. (1917). *Mourning and melancholia.* Standard Edition, 14:237–258. London: Hogarth Press, 1957.
————. (1923). *The ego and the id.* Standard Edition, 19:1–66. London: Hogarth Press, 1961.
————. (1928). Letter from Freud to Ernest Jones, March 11, 1928. In: *The Complete Correspondence of Sigmund Freud and Ernest Jones 1908–1939,* ed. R.A. Pauskauskas. Cambridge: Harvard University Press, 1993, pp. 643–644.
————. (1929a). Letter from Freud to Ludwig Binswanger, April 11, 1929. In: *The Sigmund Freud-Ludwig Binswanger Correspondence 1908–1938,* ed. G. Fichtner, trans. A. Pomerans & T. Roberts. New York: Other Press, 2003, p. 196.
————. (1929b). *Civilization and its discontents.* Standard Edition, 21: 57–146. London: Hogarth Press, 1961.
————. (1930). Letter from Freud to Sándor Ferenczi, September 16, 1930. In: *The Correspondence of Sigmund Freud and Sándor Ferenczi Volume 3, 1920–1933,* eds. E. Falzeder & E. Brabant, trans. P. Hoffer. Cambridge: Harvard University Press, pp. 399–400.
Furman, E. (1981). *A Child's Parent Dies: Studies in Childhood Bereavement.* New Haven: Yale University Press.
Greenacre, P. (1958). The family romance of the artist. *Psychoanal. Study Child,* 13: 9–36.

Grinberg, L. (1964). Two kinds of guilt – their relations with normal and pathological aspects of mourning. *Internat. J. Psycho-Anal.,* 45: 366–371.

Hamilton, V. (1986). Grief and mourning in Tennyson's "In Memoriam." *Free Associations,* 1: 87–110.

Hagman, G. (1995). Mourning: A review and reconsideration. *Internat. J. Psycho-Anal.,* 76: 909–925.

———. (1996). The role of the other in mourning. *Psychoanal. Quart.,* 65: 327–352.

Hobsbawm, E.J. (1995). *The Age of Extremes: The Short Twentieth Century, 1914–1991.* London: Abacus.

Homans, P. (1989). *The Ability to Mourn: Disillusionment and the Social Origins of Psychoanalysis.* Chicago: University of Chicago Press.

Hsiao, I. (2009). Calculating loss in Tennyson's "In Memoriam." *Victorian Poetry,* 47: 173–196.

Huyssen, A. (1989). Anselm Kiefer: The terror of history, the temptation of myth. *October,* 48: 25–46.

Kernberg, O. (2010). Some observations on the process of mourning. *Internat. J. Psycho-Anal.,* 91: 601–619.

Klein, M. (1940). Mourning and its relation to manic-depressive states. *Internat. J. Psycho-Anal.,* 21: 25–153.

Kristeva, J. (1989). *Black Sun: Depression and Melancholia.* New York: Columbia University Press.

Lewis, C.S. (1961). *A Grief Observed.* New York: Bantam.

Loewald, H.W. (1962). Internalization, separation, mourning, and the superego. *Psychoanal Quart.,* 31: 483–504.

———. (1973). On internalization. *Int. J. Psycho-Anal.,* 54: 9–17.

Ovid. *The Metamorphoses,* trans. C. Martin. New York: Norton, 1994.

Pollock, G.H. (1978). Process and affect: mourning and grief. *Internat. J. Psycho-Anal.* 59: 255–276.

Proust, M. (1993). *In Search of Lost Time, Volume V: The Captive, The Fugitive (À la recherche du temps perdu #5–6),* ed. D.J. Enright, trans. C.K. Scott-Moncrieff & T. Kilmartin. New York: Random House.

Ricoeur, P. (2009). *Memory, History, Forgetting.* Chicago: University of Chicago Press.

Segal, H. (1952). A psychoanalytic approach to aesthetics. *Internat. J. Psycho-Anal.,* 33: 196–207.

Shakespeare, W. (1952) *Complete Works,* ed. G.B. Harrison. New York: Harcourt, Brace, and World.

———. (2008). *The Oxford Shakespeare The Complete Sonnets and Poems* (Oxford World's Classics), ed. C. Burrow. New York: Oxford University Press, USA, 2008.

Tennyson, Lord Alfred. (1849). In memoriam: A.H.H. In: *Tennyson: The Major Works.* Oxford: Oxford University Press, 2009, pp. 232–292.

Tolstoy, L. (1869). *War and Peace,* trans. R. Pevear, & L. Volokhonsky. New York: Knopf Vintage Classics, 2008.

Tutter, A., in press. The mother of the Muses is Mnemosyne. In: *The Muse: A Psychoanalytic Exploration of Creative Inspiration,* ed. A. Tutter. London: Routledge.

Weisel, E. (1982/2006). *Night,* trans. M. Weisel. New York: Macmillan.

Wolfenstein, M. (1966). How is mourning possible? *Psychoanal. Study Child,* 21: 93–123. New Haven, CT: Yale University Press.

PART I

Family, Community, Society

1

CICERO ON GRIEF AND FRIENDSHIP

David Konstan

It is remarkable, but too rarely remarked, that Cicero (106–43 BC) begins his famous essay on friendship, *De amicitia*, with a reflection not on the joy of a friend's company, or on the advantages that friends afford, but rather with a scene of loss and sorrow.[1] Although Cicero wrote about grief in other dialogues, above all in the *Tusculan Disputations*, composed less than a year previous to the essay on friendship, it is worth examining how he treats such bereavement when it is not the focus of his attention but plays only an incidental role in explaining the occasion for the dialogue that follows. For it is in such unguarded moments, when one's mind is elsewhere, as it were, that we can often detect processes in the psyche that may be rationalized or denied when they come under the subject's direct scrutiny.

Cicero begins the essay by remarking that he often heard the augur, Quintus Mucius Scaevola, speak about Gaius Laelius, who was born about eighty years or so before Cicero. Laelius, whom Scaevola never tired of calling "wise" (*sapiens*), will be the main speaker in the dialogue that follows; he disclaims any philosophical expertise on friendship, and his ability to expound it rests, it is clear, both on his own excellent character and on his relationship with Scipio Africanus, which Cicero treats as perhaps the finest example of friendship in all of history. Cicero's own knowledge of the conversation in which Laelius discoursed on friendship is due to Scaevola, who recited it to Cicero and a few other intimate friends when Cicero was still a young man. For, as he explains, as soon as he came of age, which is to say, around sixteen or seventeen, his father had committed him to Scaevola's care, with the intention that Cicero should stick to his side so as to absorb all he could of the great man's wisdom. Indeed, Cicero committed to memory all his words, and, in particular, his recollection of the discourse concerning friendship that he records in the *De amicitia*. Upon Scaevola's death, Cicero notes, he betook himself to another Scaevola, this one *pontifex* rather than *augur*, to continue his education; but that, as Cicero says, is another story.

FIGURE 1.1 Bust of Cicero, Capitoline Museum, Rome.

Another story it may be, but we may note two points. First, Cicero inaugurates his essay with a recollection of the formative experience of his own youth. Second, the theme of death is already announced, since his studies with the first Scaevola were interrupted by his demise and were continued under the supervision of his cousin. But there may be yet another suggestion of death in the text: whereas it was Cicero's father who placed him in the home of Scaevola the augur, Cicero says that he enlisted himself with Scaevola the *pontifex*. Had his father died in the meantime, or does Cicero merely mean that he no longer depended on his father to manage his education? The small aside in which Cicero mentions the second Scaevola, only to note this is a subject for elsewhere, seems to have been inserted mainly to enhance the atmosphere of nostalgia for the departed that governs the entire preface of the *De amicitia*.

What moved the first Scaevola to recall Laelius's conversation in the first place was an episode on everyone's lips at the time – namely, a quarrel between two intimate friends who had loved each other dearly, but which resulted in a mortal hatred between the two. Atticus, Cicero's dearest friend to whom he dedicates the *De amicitia*, will readily remember the episode, Cicero says, since he was on close terms with one of the two men involved. This extraordinary rupture, then, put Scaevola in mind of Laelius's lecture, which he delivered in the company of his two sons-in-law, Scaevola himself and Gaius Fannius, only a few days after the death of Scipio. The dialogue proper begins with Fannius's fulsome praise of his father-in-law Laelius, who, he insists, has greater title than anyone alive to being called "wise." Cato and Atilius were granted this title in the previous generation, Fannius says, but that was because the latter excelled in knowledge of the law, whereas Cato was an expert politician, whether in the Senate or the forum, and was consistent in the positions he adopted; indeed, in his old age, the word *sapiens* was practically thought of as his cognomen.

But Laelius is wise not only for his natural gifts and character, but also in his studies and learning, to such an extent that, in the judgment of the most erudite and not merely the masses, he has had no peers in all of Greece, save perhaps for Socrates, for whose wisdom the oracle of Apollo himself had vouched. Laelius's wisdom is such, Fannius continues, that Laelius regards all that is his own as located strictly within himself, that is, under his control, and he holds that the accidents that may befall human beings are always subordinate to virtue – the view associated with classical Stoicism. It is for just this reason that people have asked Fannius how he was bearing up after the death of Scipio, especially since Laelius had missed a meeting of the augurs, a function he religiously attended in the past. Scaevola, however, observes that Laelius has been enduring the pain caused by the death of his friend with moderation, even though he is too humane to be wholly unmoved. As to the fact that he had been absent from the augurs' session, Scaevola chalked that up to illness, rather than to sorrow.

Laelius confirms Scaevola's interpretation and adds that he would never have been remiss with such a duty because of some personal inconvenience; indeed, it is his belief that under no circumstances will a man of sound character fail in his obligations or services. As for Fannius's compliment, Laelius judges it to have been motivated by affection, and that if anyone ever deserved to be called wise – something Laelius himself doubts – then it was precisely Cato, if for nothing else then for the way he bore the death of his son. Paulus and Galus, he says, had also endured such a loss, but their sons were still boys, whereas Cato's was already an adult and illustrious at that. Laelius will not even allow that Socrates was wiser than Cato, whatever the god might have judged; for Socrates was famous for words, whereas Cato's reputation depended on deeds.

It is not hard to see the relevance of Laelius's remarks to his own recent bereavement: if he deserves in any manner to be called wise, it will be, we are given to understand, for the way he is dealing with the loss of Scipio. Yet he seems to regard his own deprivation as a lesser trial than that of Cato, who on the grounds of fortitude in regard to grief is uniquely characterized as wise. Why should Laelius make Cato's endurance the basis of his title to wisdom when it would seem to undercut his own claim to the highest degree of virtue for the way he is managing his own loss? There is, I think, an answer, but it takes us outside the text and into the territory of Cicero's own life.

Less than a year before Cicero penned the *De amicitia*, his beloved daughter Tullia passed away. Cicero's grief at the event was profound and elicited efforts on the part of his friends, including Atticus, to console or at the very least distract him. In a letter that has survived, Servius Sulpicius Rufus reminded Cicero that Tullia had been lucky enough to enjoy many blessings during her lifetime and was fortunate to have died relatively young rather than witness, as her father must do, the end of the Republic (*To His Friends* 4.5). Indeed, Cicero went so far as to write a consolation to himself (now lost) in his effort to overcome his distress. In the *De amicitia*, Cicero plainly affirms that no loss is more difficult to endure than that of a child, especially if it is an adult child, as Tullia was at the time of her death (she was probably a little less than forty years old and died a month or so after having given birth).

Is Cicero, then, comparing himself with Cato and staking a unique claim for being considered wise on the basis of having suffered such a loss philosophically? Given what we know of his severe emotional reaction, he may rather be exalting Cato as far superior to himself, a model or ideal figure, whom he and others of his time cannot equal. Although he has dedicated his essay on friendship to Atticus, he seems to be hinting to him that, when it comes to spiritual fortitude, the death of a friend is not so intense a cause of mourning as that of a beloved child at a mature age. I do not necessarily believe that Cicero consciously intended to impart this message to his most intimate friend; rather, I think that his anguish has left a symptomatic mark on the text, a kind of incoherence in the argument – this is, after all, a book about friendship – that points to Cicero's underlying distress about his own loss.

We do not know just how Cicero imagined Cato's reaction to his son's death, but Laelius makes it clear that he, at all events, cannot pretend to be unmoved by that of Scipio, whatever wise men may think about the matter. It would seem that Cicero is driving a wedge between the truly wise, of whom Cato is perhaps an instance, and those who do not pretend to such a station or even believe it is possible for human beings, as is the case with Laelius.[2] Fannius, then, may have exaggerated Laelius's virtue when he affirmed that, for him, all that is his is located within himself and therefore under his control and that such virtue is superior to any accident that may befall a person. The language here is thoroughly Stoic: the Stoics maintained that the only good is virtue and lack of virtue the only evil; what is more, they held that there are few if any who have ever achieved perfect virtue and that those who fell short of virtue by even the smallest degree were to be classed among the foolish or unwise. Our virtue is the one thing that is wholly within our power, the only thing we truly possess, and in this sense all that is properly ours is within us; everything else is indifferent, as the Stoics put it, neither good nor evil. We can of course be deprived of such externals, but this is not something bad in the strict sense of the term, and so should not be a cause of sorrow. Indeed, the Stoics argued that none of the usual emotions, such as anger, fear, pity, or shame pertained to the sage: these passions all rested on false judgments of what is worth caring about and what is not. Hence, the death of another, however dear, was to be borne dispassionately, as not constituting an evil at all.

What are we to make, then, of Laelius's concession that he was moved by Scipio's death? Is he simply confirming his failure to live up to the strictest standards of philosophical disinterest, as the Stoics (and also the Platonists and Epicureans) approved? The answer is: not exactly. For the Stoics allowed for certain types of reactions that were below the threshold, as it were, of emotions in the narrow sense; and this included, I believe, responses to the loss of loved ones. The best account of such "preliminary forerunners of feelings," as the Stoic Seneca was to label them, is to be found in Seneca's treatise, *On Anger* (these "forerunners" correspond to what some Stoics, writing in Greek, called "pre-emotions" or "proto-emotions"). Seneca offers a rather lengthy list of such reactions, including shivering with cold, squeamishness at certain kinds of touch, hair standing on end in response to bad news, blushing, dizziness caused by heights, and the sentiments we experience when we see plays, read books, hear music, or see horrible paintings, or again when we watch people being severely punished even if they deserve it. What all these reactions have in common is that they are involuntary and do not depend on judgment or assent. When you are watching a tragedy, you may shudder instinctively at what is happening on stage but you know that there is no real danger; hence, you are not experiencing actual fear, and so your shiver is not fundamentally different (on this way of looking at things) from trembling because of a chill. Now, earlier in this same treatise, Seneca states that

> wild animals, and all creatures apart from human beings, are without anger; for since anger is contrary to reason, it does not arise except where reason has a place. Animals have violence, rabidity, ferocity, aggression, but do not have anger any more than they have licentiousness . . . Dumb animals lack human emotions, but they do have certain impulses that are similar to emotions.
>
> [*On Anger* 1.3.4–8]

They can be violent, to be sure, "but they do not have fears and worries, sadness and anger, but rather things that are similar to these" (1.3.4–8); so too, in his *Consolation to Marcia* 5.1, Seneca affirms that animals do not experience sadness and fear any more than stones do). Although Seneca does not say so explicitly, there is good reason to suppose that he believes that the quasi-emotions that animals experience are identical to the pre-emotions that are part of the sentimental repertoire of human beings.

What about grief, then? In his *Consolation to Marcia*, Seneca challenges the idea that grief for the loss of loved ones is natural. Seneca certainly recognizes that we may miss friends, provided that our sense of loss is moderate – just the way Cicero indicates that Laelius bore the death of Scipio. Seneca affirms that even the strongest minds will feel a certain sting at the mere departure to distant places of those who are dear, never mind their death. The problem, however, is that opinion or belief, of which only human beings are capable, adds more than nature requires. Dumb animals, Seneca says, also experience loss, and indeed do so intensely, but for only a brief span of time. As he puts it: "no animal has a lengthy sorrow for its offspring except man, who adheres to his grief and is stirred not to the extent that he feels it but to the extent that he has decided to feel it." In the ninety-ninth epistle in the collection of philosophical letters addressed to his friend and disciple Lucilius, Seneca again insists animals have only a brief awareness of loss: when we first hear news of the death of a loved one, we weep out of a natural necessity – tears that fall irrespective of our will, and hence do not involve our assent.

Now, the case is different with the tears that we shed at the memory of those we have lost. Seneca affirms that to forget loved ones and bury memory of them along with their bodies is inhuman; this is what birds and wild animals do, which love their young with a fierce passion, but it is extinguished after they have died.[3] Seneca concludes that a sensible person, on the contrary, will persist in remembering – but he will cease to mourn. Seneca again equates the pre-emotional sting that even a sage experiences upon the loss of a dear one with that of animals. But the point is that, after the initial, involuntary response (Seneca does not specify just how long this might last), pain should give way to loving recollection. One may rightly recall the dead, but not mourn them. There is no question of repressing the pain felt upon the acute loss of a loved one, and tears are entirely natural; but this initial response should last only for a short while. It is only when our ability to remember the departed converts the initial sense of loss into prolonged mourning that it becomes a pathology and requires a cure. To put it in Freudian terms, it is when mourning is transformed into melancholy that therapy is required; and this conversion is due, according to the Stoics, to our assent to false judgments, for example, that death is a bad thing and should be lamented, something to which animals, which do not have the capacity to form beliefs, are not susceptible.

Returning, then, to Cicero's essay, we might suppose that when Laelius concedes that he was moved by the death of Scipio, he meant not that he experienced the emotion of grief, which depends on certain beliefs (we shall consider just what beliefs in a moment), but rather the proto-emotion of loss, something that does not depend on judgment and which ordinary human beings share both with other animals and, indeed, with the sage. His term for being moved (in Latin, *moveri*) does not necessarily imply a full-fledged emotion of the sort the Stoics condemned. If this is so, then Laelius's response to the death of Scipio may lie well within the Stoic parameters for wisdom, and we may even imagine that Cicero is hereby suggesting that his own reaction to his daughter's death was compatible with the Stoic ideal of virtue. Whatever the sangfroid with which Cato reacted to the loss of his son, Laelius's humanity, and Cicero's own, made room for the shock and tears that naturally accompany such a loss, and not even a Stoic sage could disapprove. Yet it is also possible that the distinction that Cicero draws between Cato's wisdom and Laelius's more modest claim provides him with a more attainable model, one that permits a degree of mourning to which Cato, perhaps, was immune, but which is natural even at the loss of a friend and hence all the more so of a child, which is the standard by which Cato himself is judged wise.

But there is more. In explanation of his reaction to Scipio's death – whether this was a true emotion or rather the kind of preliminary to emotion that Seneca describes – Laelius offers the fact that he has been deprived of such a friend as never has been before, and, he opines, will never exist in the future. This seems the kind of overestimation of the beloved that Laelius had just a moment before detected in Fannius's asseveration that he, Laelius, was far the wisest of all. Is Cicero aware that his own Laelius may be estimating the quality of his friend by the depth of his grief? Could he have intuited that, in the case of his daughter, his grief caused him to exalt her virtues? Or does this insight emerge from the text, with all its tensions, rather than from the author's intention? In any case, Laelius adds at once that he stands in no need of treatment or therapy: he is capable of consoling himself – a possible reference to Cicero's own unusual gesture (he claims it is unique) of composing a consolation to himself as part of his own cure – and, Laelius adds, his chief solace is to be free of the error that causes the greatest anguish at the death of a friend, namely the belief that something bad has befallen the deceased. If anyone has suffered, Laelius says, it is he himself; but then, to be greatly distressed by one's own ills is the sign of one who loves, not his friend, but himself.

This last counsel of fortitude is practical, no doubt, but surely pain at the loss of a loved one is not mere egoism or narcissism. The stress is on "greatly": Laelius is managing, after all, and here he is, engaging in civilized conversation only days after Scipio's death. He is in fact doing much better than Cicero did with his bereavement. Just here one might have wanted some further elaboration about why sensitivity to one's own loss should so facilely be characterized as selfish, but Cicero leaves this pithy remark hanging and has Laelius proceed to demonstrate that Scipio has had as fulfilled a life as is humanly possible and that he achieved all he could have wished for, unless he desired immortality, which is impious and something to which Scipio never gave a thought. Laelius enumerates Scipio's achievements in the sphere of politics (twice consul) and war (two powerful enemy cities laid low), then mentions his kind nature, respect for and generosity toward his mother and sisters, his beneficence toward his own, his justice toward all; there was, moreover, universal grief at his funeral. What, Laelius asks, could a few more years have added to what he had? As for old age in itself, though Cato had assured Laelius and Scipio in the year before his death that it was not onerous, it nevertheless deprives one of that freshness or bloom that Scipio still enjoyed when he died.

Laelius has entered, perhaps without realizing it (or Cicero's realizing it), upon the genre of the consolation, addressed to those who need special encouragement to assuage their grief because, it would seem, they are indeed inclined to see death as an evil. For what difference should it make if one has died young or at the acme of one's career if death is not an evil, as both the Stoics and the Epicureans clearly affirmed? Indeed, Laelius had just now magnified the sagacity or philosophical accomplishment of Cato precisely because he endured the loss of a grown son rather than a mere boy, as Paulus and Galus had done. On this reckoning, losing Scipio at the height of his powers ought to have been all the more grievous. Yes, a wise man such as Laelius might, like Cato, have "bucked up" despite it all, but the list of Scipio's accomplishments would hardly be the best way to lessen the pain. The argument that Scipio was spared the discomforts and debilities of old age, in despite of Cato's own testimony, again seems rather hollow, the more so in that it recalls Servius Sulpicius Rufus's unsuccessful, not to say fatuous, effort to soothe Cicero's grief by assuring him that his daughter had enjoyed a prosperous life and escaped not merely the tribulations of senescence but also the destruction of the Roman Republic. I cannot help but feel that via Laelius, Cicero is giving voice, unawares, to the very arguments that could not comfort his own loss, thereby evading or concealing the intuition that manifested itself in negative guise in respect to Cato's son, namely that such a death is unbearable, even if Cato – but only Cato – could abide it.

Laelius adds yet other reasons why Scipio lacked for nothing when he left this world. For death came upon him swiftly, so that he did not endure prolonged suffering nor a sense of dying; and what is more, his penultimate day on earth was so glorious – he was escorted to his home by a throng of admirers, from senators and ordinary people to foreign allies – that "from so high a degree of majesty he seemed to have attained to the gods above rather than those below" (*De amicitia* 4.13). Though Cicero merely hints at it here (Laelius rather cryptically says that the circumstances of Scipio's death are obscure), there was some suspicion that Scipio might have been assassinated by supporters of the popular party associated with the Gracchi; Scipio was not universally revered – that much is clear. But even if Cicero represses it, the hint of politics taints the larger argument concerning grief for loved ones. Is our sorrow really diminished by the splendor or successes of our friends, even on their dying day? Does this really give us confidence that they have moved on to a better place, rather than a worse? And what of our grief for less distinguished loved ones, who have lived and died humbly? Did Laelius love Scipio for his achievements, and is this why he regarded him as so special a friend? Again, what does this say about Cicero's uncontrollable grief over his daughter?

Laelius goes on to condemn the recent doctrine, according to which the soul is said to perish along with the body and everything is extinguished at death. He adduces traditional rites honoring the dead, which, he says, the ancestors would not have practiced had they believed that the dead were wholly insensible, and to this he adds the authority of Socrates, who argued that the souls – or rather minds (*animi*, not *animae*) – of human beings are divine; and when they have left the body, the way back to heaven lies open to them and most expeditiously to the best and fairest. The teaching that Laelius rejects is, of course, that of Epicurus, who was in fact prior to the Stoics. The Epicureans maintained that it was the fear of death, and punishment after death, that more than anything else spoiled the happiness of human beings and was responsible for the irrational behavior that leads to wars and every kind of injustice. By and large, Cicero, who disapproved strongly of Epicurus's views – even though Atticus was an adherent of the school – tended to pooh-pooh the notion that rational adults believed in the old myths about Hades or suffered anxiety over torments in the afterlife, at least when he was attacking Epicureanism (see, for example, *Tusculan Disputations* 1.6.10, 1.21.48). Nevertheless, when it came to his consolation to himself on the loss of his daughter Tullia, Cicero not only insisted that the soul survives the death of the body – a view he has Laelius endorse in *De amicitia* and which he approves guardedly elsewhere as well (as in the famous "Dream of Scipio," with which he concluded his *Republic* and to which Laelius alludes here) – but also, and exceptionally for him, that it might experience either eternal bliss or eternal punishment.[4] There is a hint of this same view in Laelius's ostensibly positive assertion that Scipio's final moments gave promise that he would ascend to the upper deities rather than descend to the netherworld. Are these really alternatives? And if so, should we fear for ourselves and for our friends? For no one can be certain of the gods' favor or of having led a blameless life (as the Stoic Seneca put it, "we have all sinned.").

Laelius reports a vision that Scipio had of his adopted grandfather, the elder Africanus, which convinced him that the spirits of the best would fly up to the gods, and if so, Laelius opines, whose more likely to do so than Scipio's own? To grieve at Scipio's death thus seems to Laelius to smack more of envy than of friendship. But even if, Laelius adds, it is true that death marks the termination of mind and body alike, as Epicurus maintained, then death is no worse than never having been born. This is the so-called symmetry argument exploited by the Epicureans to show that we have no more reason to lament nonexistence after death than we do prior to birth, but Laelius's sentiment also recalls Plato's *Apology of Socrates*, in which Socrates affirms that death is either the cessation of all sensation, which is no evil at all, or the transition to a felicitous afterlife of the soul. But Laelius is still focused on Scipio's condition and whether he is to be pitied or bemoaned for having died rather than on his own feelings of loss. Of course, we may suffer the departure of a loved one less if we are persuaded that she or he is faring well, but grief is not a sentiment that we feel on behalf of others but by virtue of our own desolation: by shifting the argument to Scipio's state, Laelius avails himself of a consolatory commonplace that might justify courage in the face of one's own death but offers limited solace for the absence of another. Laelius seems out to convince himself that Scipio ought not to be mourned, even as he concedes that he is not unmoved by his death.

But the view that death is not an evil has the further function of preventing us from projecting our own pain onto the other, thereby providing ourselves with an objective motive for our distress. Grief can be managed if we recognize that the source of it is located in ourselves, not in the fate of the loved one. This view of grief was shared by Stoics, Epicureans, and Academics or Platonists like Cicero himself: one naturally experienced the anguish of the loss, but the crucial thing was not to turn it into a full-fledged emotion, that is, a *pathos* or pathology, based on a judgment that the loved one has suffered a genuine harm. If we concentrate on the sorrow in ourselves, we can seek strategies for tempering it. Thus, by way of compensation, Laelius insists not only upon Scipio's survival after death, but also upon his own abiding unity with Scipio in memory, now that he is gone; and he concludes by observing that, although it would have been more fair that he, the elder of the two, have departed this world first, nevertheless the memory of his perfect friendship with Scipio lets him realize that his life has been blessed (he nowhere intimates that he might join Scipio in the next world). His ability to bear up under the loss of Scipio is due not to a reputation for wisdom, which he abjures, but the hope or confidence that the memory of their friendship will endure forever, alongside those few mythical pairs (he is thinking of Theseus and Pirithous or Orestes and Pylades) famous for such a bond. It is as though Laelius can keep his ego intact by incorporating or internalizing the other into himself through recollection, with the added fillip that this view of their friendship will be shared by posterity.

Today, we might interpret Laelius's devotion to Scipio as an overvaluation of the love object, a cathexis in which one projects onto the other the virtues associated with one's own ego ideal and is thus left with a diminished or evacuated sense of self. This is not how Cicero perceives it, nor the thinkers with whom he communed in his own time. One worked to rid oneself of a groundless sense that the other was suffering, reminding oneself of the other's good fortune and chiding oneself for being moved more by envy than by love. One cultivated the memory of the deceased, who was thereby kept alive in recollection; as Cicero has Laelius declare, among the values inherent in friendship is that the dead still live (*mortui vivunt, De amicitia* 23). He also has Fannius affirm that the friendship between Laelius and Scipio will indeed join the ranks of those mythological pairs whom Laelius had earlier mentioned. This, too, is a form of immortality, as the Romans conceived it, and the prediction that Cicero places in the mouth of Fannius is realized by Cicero in this very dialogue, which memorializes their bond: for this is one of the functions of literature, to outlast the deeds it records – like Horace's monument (his odes), more durable than bronze. So too Seneca avowed that, by appearing in his letters, his friend Lucilius would achieve fame among future generations (Epistle 21).

The connection between mourning and friendship, then, is that friendship is the cure for grief, a bond that is able to transcend time and loss. There remains, however, a hidden irony in Cicero's account. When Laelius comes round to defining friendship, he offers an oddly stringent thesis: "Friendship, then, is nothing other than the agreement on all matters human and divine, together with goodwill and affection." Perhaps Laelius did enjoy such a total accord with Scipio, but we know that Cicero and Atticus differed considerably in their views of human and divine affairs: Atticus was, as we have noted, a devotee of Epicureanism, the philosophy that least appealed to Cicero. Among other things, the Epicureans denied that the gods were in any way concerned about human beings but lived a life of supreme contentment, removed from all care; what is more, they held that the soul perishes with the body. Laelius does entertain the possibility that the Epicurean view might be correct, so perhaps such a difference in creed was not so crucial as to disrupt a friendship, but Laelius goes on at once to criticize those who place the highest good in pleasure, again a principle at the heart of Epicureanism. Laelius has yet another disagreement with the Epicureans, however, and this one closer to the theme of friendship: he rejects the notion that friendship has its origin in need and dependency and insists rather that its natural source is love – he affirms, indeed, that *amicitia* is formed from the root *amor*. By way of demonstration, he adduces the love that even animals feel for their offspring and affirms that this affection is still more evident in human beings: it cannot be disrupted save by the most heinous crimes. The latter is a significant proviso, since it makes love between parents and children depend on their virtue or character, at least in extreme cases. Laelius adds that we love even strangers and indeed enemies if they manifest virtue and probity, which renders virtue the chief inducement to affection; as he says, "nothing is more lovable than virtue." This latter condition for love will constitute the dominant line of the treatise, but we must not allow it to override entirely the instinctive fondness that exists between parents and children, which we share with other animals; and this fondness does not depend on virtue, though it can, in human beings, be undermined by extreme vice.

After Tullia died, Cicero lamented that he had lost the only thing that still tied him to life. But at the invitation of Atticus, he took refuge in his home; among the myriad books in Atticus's library, he read the Greek philosophers and, despite his enduring grief, produced the extraordinary series of literary works, the *De amicitia* latest, composed only months before his own death at the hands of Marc Antony. As the Republic reeled with violent conflict, Cicero sought to recover an ideal of friendship, as he imagined it, that respected virtue above all. But subtending friendship was love, as he believed, a love most manifest in the bond between parents and children; the loss of a child was, accordingly, the most difficult of all to bear. But that same love could be invoked as a cure for sorrow, a way of keeping the beloved alive in spite of it all. Among the motives for Cicero's essay on friendship, perhaps at an unconscious level, was a desire to find another form of solace for his bereavement, in which love, which made grief almost unbearable, was at the same time its antidote.

Notes

1 The translations of Cicero's treatise, *De amicitia* are my own. A good text and translation with brief commentary is Powell's (2006). For Cicero's grief at his daughter's death and his efforts to console himself, see Baltussen, 2013; also Späth, 2010.

2 For a similar tension between a presumably Stoic impassivity in respect to the death of a son (illustrated in this instance by Anaxagoras's response) and Cicero's own, more complex attitude in response to the loss of his daughter in the *Tusculan Disputations*, see the brilliant discussion by W.H.F. Altman (2009).

3 *Editor's note*: Contrary to Seneca's observations, attachment and loss is not limited to humans. A growing literature describes prolonged mourning-like behavior in various animals, including elephants, which return to visit the bones of long-deceased members of their own species. See B. McKing, *How Animals Grieve*, Univ. Chicago Press (2013).—*A.T.*

4 See Lactantius's *Institutio christiana* 3.19.1–6; also, Setaioli, 1999, esp. pp. 156–163, 2001a, 2001b.

References

Altman, W.H.F. (2009). Womanly humanism in Cicero's *Tusculan Disputations*. *Trans. Amer. Philol. Assn.*, 139: 407–441.

Baltussen, H. (2013). Cicero's grief in context: *The consolatio ad se*. In: *Greek and Roman Consolations: Eight Studies of a Tradition and its Afterlife*, ed. H. Baltussen, Swansea: Classical Press of Wales, pp. 67–91.

Powell, J.G.F., ed. (2006). *M. Tulli Ciceronis, De re publica, De legibus, Cato Maior De senectute, Laelius De amicitia*. Oxford: Oxford University Press.

Seneca. *On Anger*. In Moral Essays, Vol. 1. Loeb Classical Library No. 214. Cambridge, MA: Harvard University Press, 1928.

Setaioli, A. (1999). La vicenda dell'anima nella Consolatio di Cicerone. *Paideia*, 54: 145–174.

Setaioli, A. (2001a). El destino del alma en el pensamiento de Cicerón (con una apostilla sobre las huellas ciceronianas en Dante). *Anuario Filosófico*, 34:487–527.

Setaioli, A. (2001b). Il destino dell'anima nella letteratura consolatoria pagana. In: *Consolatio*, ed. A. del Real Concepción, Pamplona: Ediciones Universidad de Navarra, pp. 54–55.

Späth, T. (2010). Cicero, Tullia, and Marcus: Gender-specific concerns for family tradition. In: *Children, Memory, and Family Identity in Roman Culture*, eds. V. Dasen & T. Späth, Oxford: Oxford University Press, pp. 147–172.

2

RITUALS OF MEMORY

Jan Assmann

Rituals of memory: I would like to approach this theme with some very general questions, first of all regarding a distinction between two German words, both often translated into English as "memory": *Erinnerung* and *Gedächtnis*.[1] What is *Gedächtnis*? What is *Erinnerung*? *Gedächtnis*, which can also be translated as either "recollection" or "remembrance," along with "memory," signifies the capacity we have to remember. *Erinnerung* signifies the mnemonic act that sets this capacity in play. What function does *Gedächtnis*, remembrance, serve? For one thing, it allows us to orient ourselves in time, and for another, to know who we are. This is precisely what patients suffering from Alzheimer's disease cannot do, in this way showing us why we recollect things. These two capacities, orientation in time and knowing who we are, temporal consciousness and self-consciousness, are clearly closely connected. Our self has a temporal character; it is not a momentary register or ad hoc invention but constitutes itself from the past, present, and future, from plans and results, events and inventories. For this reason I would like to define memory as an organ that constructs this continuous synthesis of time and self. How the organ functions in detail is a question for neurologists, brain researchers, and psychologists who have enormously enriched our knowledge in this area over recent years. I am an Egyptologist, and as such, a specialist in culture and religion; my own research has little to contribute to such detailed facets of the phenomenon of remembrance.

Now memory and remembrance have not only an individual but also a social and cultural side. When we inquire into rituals of memory, we have to grapple with aspects of remembrance. Rituals are social institutions; they are engaged in largely by and for groups, only very rarely completely alone. Rituals often have a more or less distinctive and elaborate form, and in this respect they are also cultural institutions – they typify not only a certain group but also a certain culture. We live in a strongly deritualized society, to the extent that we have to pause and think when looking for examples of such culturally formed rituals. In Constance, where I have lived for some years, there is a very pronounced carnival culture – in contrast to Heidelberg, where I lived before (it is entirely absent from Lübeck, where I grew up). The impression one gains in Constance is of a ritual that follows the same script year after year and that plays a huge role in the city's life. The city here celebrates itself. For those living elsewhere, the city is tied above all to its famous fifteenth century ecumenical council and in turn with Bohemian reformer Jan Hus, burnt at the stake in Constance as a heretic on the basis of devious and dishonest proceedings. It takes some searching to find the Hus monument in Constance. People often lay wreaths there: traces of a ritual of memory. But few if any of the wreaths come from the city administration or the Catholic church; rather, most come from the Czech Republic. What party wishes to ascribe the tragic destiny of Jan Hus to its own past? Not the church, which is proud of having salvaged its own unity at the Council of Constance; and not the city, which is proud to have been the council's venue; but the Czechs, who make pilgrimages to Constance to lay wreaths or flowers at the Hussenstein. On this ritual level, we find, then, the same two central factors at work that we encountered on an individual level: time and the self. Generated for individuals through recollection, this synthesis of temporal consciousness and consciousness of the self is generated for the group through rituals. They make it clear to us who we are and where we stand.

The close parallel drawn here, between individual acts of recollection and shared rites, renders the differences between them all the more apparent. When the synthesis of time and self fails on an individual level, a grave pathology such as Alzheimer's is in play. But we do not yet possess adequate analytic and diagnostic criteria for identifying, let alone treating, such failures on the collective level. In this respect, the past half century or so has been highly instructive. In the West, the 1960s and 1970s stood under the sign of a radical deritualization. In West Germany's universities, caps and gowns were done away with, hence the formal framework of academic celebrations – indeed the celebrations themselves – often vanished. For their part, the churches frantically tried to modernize their liturgies. No one wanted to have anything to do with monuments, memorial days, and similar things anymore. At the most, the protest culture marking those years developed its own rites, including, in West Germany, Easter and peace marches and sit-ins, reminding us that "rituo-clastic" society also needs its rites.

This all started to change in the mid-1980s. Now memorializing rituals emerged, for example on November 9, 1988, marking the fiftieth anniversary of the November pogroms, at locations where synagogues once stood in various cities. Soon after, following the dismantling of the Berlin Wall, a plan was formed to erect a monument to Europe's murdered Jews at a prominent spot along the former death strip.[2] It would be a decade before this plan could be realized – at first, so to speak, from below as a citizen's movement, then from above through parliament; and in these years it was possible to experience the meaning of rituals of memory – how collective memories struggle to find suitable forms and visible articulation. In the German debate concerning monuments and memorialization that then unfolded, two directions above all were evident; the confrontation was all the more passionate in that both sides shared the same opening premises. On the one side, some people insisted that memories of the Holocaust were too horrific and guilt-laden to find any appropriate form of monumental expression: any aesthetization, they argued, amounted to downplaying the enormity of the event; gaps, empty places, a 'nonmonument,' so to speak, would be the only fitting form of memory. Other people insisted that it was precisely the unprecedented nature of the event, a horror that needed to be never forgotten, that made memorial expression imperative; this was in their view especially the case – and such a point is decisive when it comes to identity and remembrance – because others, above all in Israel and the USA, had taken the lead with monuments and museums, rendering the absence of a corresponding culture of memory in the land of the perpetrators all the more unbearable. Strongly feeling this need for expression and action, my wife, Aleida Assmann, and I sided with the memorial's proponents and collected signatures at Heidelberg's weekly Handschuhsheimer market.[3]

A society needs rituals. It needs a self-image and a past and cannot pronounce itself free of all that, for two reasons: first, because as human beings we are supplied with the capacity to empathize with others – a capacity that extends into the past, leading us to sometimes be moved, indeed haunted, by past suffering and injustice; and second, because a group, nation, society does not stand alone in the world but rather is tied to the other societies with which it shares its past, and which in turn impose on each society their own. Empathy in part means being able to see oneself through the eyes of others, and this is also the case on a collective plain. Every country occupies a space of intervision within which it shows its face, and needs to preserve that face: a countenance that, in the German case, became horrifically deformed in the Nazi period and can only be partly salvaged within such a space.

Groups do not have the powers of recollection of individual beings – they lack the neuronal network for the storage of memories. But groups can produce memory for themselves. This is the point where culture comes into the picture. From this perspective, we could conceive culture as a great collective memory, the term being understood in terms of the two dimensions of memory and recollection we have distinguished on an individual level. Memory would signify culture as the general stock of texts, images, rites, monuments, buildings, cities, landscapes, food, dances, songs, and so forth. Remembrance would signify forms of active participation, such as reading, contemplating, celebrating, and inhabiting, forms of living circulation of what has been mnemonically stored.

If we bring together everything stored as memory and everything that circulates or is celebrated as remembrance, then the connection between ritual and memory on a collective level becomes clear. Ritual is the most important form of collective remembering (or remembrance), that is, collective participation in cultural memory. But the concept of culture comprises both what is stored and the institutions of circulation, celebration, and participation. Culture is memory *and* remembrance. When we speak of cultural memory, we are referring to memory in the sense of inventory, storage, and an enabling of remembrance; when we speak of a culture of remembrance, we are referring to institutions, media, forms, and functions in which this inventory is active in particular societies and periods.

The primal scene, as it were, of cultures of memory and the origin of religion is the cult of the dead. The earliest rituals of memory are rites for the dead. Evidently death represents the greatest and most primal challenge for remembrance – in particular, for collective remembrance. Human beings are relational by nature; they are what they are only via their relations with other human beings, the development of language, consciousness, and recollection derives from. Every person lives within a complex network of groups and communal formations, extending from the small family unit, to the extended family and clan, and onward to national and religious communities. The threads constituting this network are in a state of weaker or stronger emotional tension – they are affectively charged, which endows them with the power to stamp remembrance and recollection. Death produces a painful gap in the network; rites for the dead are aimed at healing the wounds, overcoming the crisis, repairing the torn threads. For early human beings – and in many places this presently remains the case – the dead did not disappear and vanish from reality but rather moved to another sphere. Maintaining ties with them was crucial for two reasons: first, because of their attachment to the dead, and not wanting to lose them from the group unit, and second, because of their wish to prevent the dead from moving outside cultural forms, haunting and afflicting the living.

When it comes to death and its connections with time, the self, and remembrance, the ancient Egyptians likely represent the most impressive example, albeit perhaps also the most extreme one. Extraordinarily, they prepared their own tombs during their lifetimes, and this was all the more magnificently and monumentally in proportion to a person's wealth. Inside these tombs, they represented themselves not as they were but as they wanted to have been (*wie sie gewesen sein wollten*), and spent the rest of their lives in view of this self-representation, which they placed before their eyes like a normative mirror of their idealized self. In the form of their tomb, they constructed a place where they wished to remain in contact with those born afterward, addressing them through inscriptions, as well as through prayers noted down for visitors to recite to them, so that their life-giving connections would not be sundered. In this way, the tomb was not merely built for oneself, but above all, for one's descendants. An ancient Egyptian maxim reads as follows:

> You shall build your house for your son.
> For then a place has been created for you in which you will be.
> Richly furnish your house in the realm of the dead
> And prepare your place in the west in an effective way.
> Take heed: death is not much to us,
> Take heed: for us life is placed on high.
> For the house of death is aimed at life.

[Helck, 1984, p. 6]

In Egypt, this maxim was repeated over millennia: *a human being lived when his name was named*. The ancient Egyptians placed their own tombs in closest proximity to their ancestors; they visited their tombs, wrote letters to them, and brought them sacrifices. That the cult of the gods emerged in Egypt from the cult of the dead is unquestionable – the congruities between rituals for the dead and for the gods are very strong. The ties that descendants built and entertained with their dead across death's threshold functioned as the primal scene or foundational model for every relationship between this human world and the world of gods beyond, and the funerary priests, their role accorded to firstborn sons, served as the model for the high priest in the cult of the gods.

If we consider the history of religions, we see that in general veneration of ancestors operates as religion's earliest form. Consistently, there is a paramount concern with retaining ties with the ancestors and moving in their tracks. Precisely the metaphor of moving along tracks, which plays such a large role in, for instance, Thomas Mann's "Joseph" novels, is taken very literally in the case of the Australian Aborigines, whose ancient culture is broadly acknowledged as manifesting one of the most elementary forms of religion. Here remembrance of one's ancestors is not expressed in monumental funerary fashion as in Egypt, but through "songlines" or "dream-paths," specific migratory routes in which the Maori tribes enter the mythical time of their ancestral spirits, who have left their traces on these paths. Such highly ancient ways of entering into contact with the dead, ancestors, and the beyond, form the origin of cultural memory. What is at work here is first and foremost a matter of rites, celebration, and performance – even in Egypt, where this remembrance took on forms of permanence in stone and writing.

If we now take a step further to ancient Israel, we enter into an entirely new world, indeed perhaps into a consciously anti-Egyptian world. For here what forms the center of Egyptian ritual memory is strictly proscribed. Death – in Egypt the source of sacredness and transcendence, the gate to the beyond and to the gods – is now the source of impurity, incurring the most rigorous taboos.

In ancient Israel, we encounter a completely new culture of memory, one with no parallel in ancient Egypt. I have argued that *groups* do not possess memory in the way that individuals possess it, but that they can *produce memory for themselves*. We here have a classical example of a group that produces remembrance. The decisive source in this regard is the fifth book of the "Pentateuch," *Devarim*, or Deuteronomy ("Spoken Words"). From the beginning to the end of this book, the salient focus is on memory. After their flight from Egypt and forty years of wandering, the Israelites have reached the banks of the Jordan, which they will cross the next day. Moses, who will not accompany them to the Promised Land, impresses on them, in a long parting speech, what they must on no account forget when they settle there. On the one hand, this is the story of the exodus from Egypt, under God's "signs and wonders"; on the other hand, it is the law the Israelites received at Sinai, including the strict commands and prohibitions they must strictly follow to stay connected with God and be able to live in the land. Moses, however, not only instructs them in the "what" of memory but also in its "how," in the form of a highly elaborated collective mnemotechnics that outline and enforce a connection between textual and ritual representation. The following seven procedures are summoned to preserve the law from being forgotten:

1. Learning by heart: "Take to heart these instructions with which I charge you this day" (6, 6).[4] "Therefore impress these My words upon your very heart" (11,18).
2. Instruct and discuss: "Impress them upon your children. Recite them when you stay at home and when you are away, when you lie down and when you get up" (6, 7; cf. 11, 20). We should also here note God's warning to Joshua following the death of Moses: "Let not this book of the Teaching cease from your lips, but recite it day and night, so that you may observe faithfully all that is written in it" (Josh. 1, 8). The law is thus meant not only to be in one's "heart," but in one's "mouth."
3. Phylacteries and mezuzahs: the law is meant to be bound to one's forehead and attached to one's doorpost. Reading, learning, teaching are insufficient: the covenant requires visible signs, so as to not only be remembered, but also publicly acknowledged: "Bind them as a sign on your hand and let them serve as a symbol on your forehead" (6, 8; cf. 11,18); "Inscribe them on the doorposts of your house and on your gates" (6, 9; cf. 11, 21).
4. Accompanying visible signs in the domestic sphere are monuments and promulgations in public space; the law is meant to be written on plastered stone, thus being both eternalized and made generally accessible:

As soon as you have crossed the Jordan into the land that the Lord your God is giving you, you shall set up large stones. Coat them with plaster and inscribe upon them all the words of this Teaching . . . upon crossing the Jordan, you shall set up these stones, about which I charge you this day, on Mount Ebal, and coat them with plaster. . . . And on those stones you shall inscribe every word of this Teaching most distinctly.

[27, 2–8]

The next two procedures comprising Mosaic mnemotechnics represent real rituals:

5. Festivals of collective memory, the three great festivals of assembly and pilgrimage in which the entire people, great and small, are meant to gather before God. The first of these is Passover (Pesach, the festival of mazzoth), commemorating the exodus from Egypt: "so that you may remember the day of your departure from the land of Egypt as long as you live" (16, 3).[5] The second is Shavuot, the Festival of Weeks, on which people are meant to "bear in mind that you were slaves in Egypt" (16,12).[6] And the third is Sukkoth – the Festival of Tabernacles, in whose course the entire Torah is meant to be read every seven years.[7]
6. Oral transmission, which is to say poetry as a codification of the memory of history:

Therefore, write down this poem and teach it to the people of Israel; put it in their mouths, in order that this poem may be My witness against the people of Israel. When I bring them into the land flowing with milk and honey that I promised on oath to their fathers, and they eat their fill and grow fat and turn to other gods and serve them, spurning Me, and breaking My covenant, and the many evils and troubles befall them – then this poem shall confront them as a witness, since it will never be lost from the mouth of their offspring.

[31, 19–21]

The biblical book closes with a great poem, again warning of the fearful results of faithlessness and forgetfulness in encapsulated form. This poem is meant to remain alive through spoken transmission by the people, who in this way are steadily reminded of their ties and obligations.

Oral transmission signifies public presentation and ritual form. The seventh and last procedure constitutes a kind of seal. It amounts to a command to neither add nor remove anything – what is meant to be remembered is to be remembered literally, and to remain unaltered from generation to generation.

All seven procedures are institutions and media of a culture of memory. They paradigmatically show how a society produces remembrance. The main priority is education and the institutions needed for trans-transgenerational transmission. Nothing has changed in that respect: beginning in the family, the education process continues in schools and universities. Then come the visible signs of memory, extending from the corporeal and domestic to public monuments. Third, we have the liturgical and aesthetic forms of memory, the great festivals of Passover, Shavuot, and Sukkoth (or Easter, Pentecost, and Christmas in the Christian realm) and the song of Moses, which I would extend to illustrate the role of art in the culture of memory. And finally, there is the principle of the "canon," the sanctification of this complex – to be always remembered, never forgotten – of law, history, and creed.

Much of this can be generalized into a broadly applicable theory of collective memory-centered culture: but much is specific to ancient Israel and Early Judaism, with few parallels in other cultures. One of the specific phenomena is "law," and with it the idea of religion as a formal covenantal contract made with God, based on maintenance of a complex legal code. That was a revolutionary idea in the ancient world, producing a completely new type of religion grounded in a written canon, and forging a path that Judaism, Christianity, and Islam would follow. But the political element evident in the religious contract is special to the Deutoronomic culture of memory.

At the same time, in a more general sense, this element directly reflects the political culture that prevailed in the Ancient Near East. Contracts were not only sealed, sworn on, and deposited in a holy place, but were also recalled for the sake of the memory of the contractual parties. The Hethite king, Hattuschil, for example, left his descendants a type of political testament, stipulating that "these tablets are to be read to you [the heir] once a month; in that way my words and wisdom will be repeatedly impressed in you" (Laroche, 1990, p. 314). Deuteronomy is itself presented as the testament of Moses. One text from the Assyrian state archives in Nineveh, stemming from the seventh century BCE (and hence dated far more closely to Deuteronomy then Hattuschil's testament), likewise refers to a political ritual of memory. Here as well the focus is on "producing remembrance," in this case by the subjects and vassals of the Assyrian Empire, whom King Esarhaddon made swear an oath of fealty to his son, King Assurbanipal, heir to the throne. The ritual is in fact based on the same experience that is central for Moses: with a drastic change of location, the ties formed in the old place threaten to be forgotten in the new place. For Moses, the desert and Promised Land are at stake; for Esarhaddon, it is the capital and the provinces. His subjects and vassals have come to the capital to give their oath; here, where everything recalls the power of their overlord, they will certainly not forget it. But once they have returned to their own provincial cities, this obligation will likely recede into the background and vanish from memory, a process that needs to be prevented. To that end, a mnemonic ritual is devised, meant to be periodically repeated for the sake of refreshing memory:

> She [Ishtar of Arbela] gave them water to drink from the sarsaru-jug,
> She filled a one seah [ca. 6 liter] drinking vessel from the sarsaru-jug and gave it to them, thus ["saying"]:
> In your hearts you will speak as follows: Ishtar − a narrow one is she! [either, "she is someone close at hand!" or "she is a local deity of restricted influence!"]
> And you will go to your cities and districts and will eat bread,
> And you will forget this covenant [adê, sworn obligations].
> But when you drink from this water,
> You will again remember this adê that I have concluded in respect to Esarhaddon.
>
> [Otto, 1999, p. 82][8]

Rituals enact an interplay between symbolic and corporeal dimensions. Drinking water is a strong image for the reincorporation of a memory that has been or is in danger of becoming forgotten, and thus is stored beneath the mnemonic mark of symbolic enactment.

According to beliefs circulating in the framework of Orphic and Bacchic mysteries, the dead move into the House of Hades, where, on the right side, two springs are located. By one spring there is a luminous cypress − hence the sign of an inverted world, since cypresses are dark. Guards stand over the other spring. The ordinary dead try to reach the source by the cypresses; but the initiated are supposed to avoid it and seek the source where the guards are located. The source for which the ordinary dead are destined is Lethe, forgetting. The other source is fed by the lake of memory, Mnemosyne; the souls of the thirty initiated are meant to drink from it. Via the waters of Mnemosyne, memory of what they learned and experienced in the mysteries streams to the initiated souls, rendering them capable of finding their way to Elysium and escaping the world of death. All religions offer examples of ritual drinking; often such rites are tied to memory. The most prominent example of the production of remembrance through ritual nourishment is the Christian Eucharist, a rite involving the ingestion of bread and wine that Jesus initiates with the words *toûto poieíte eis tēn emēn anámnēsin*, "do this in remembrance of me."

In his *Genealogy of Morality*, Nietzsche (1887) foregrounds this corporeal aspect of the production of remembrance. "As one can imagine," he writes,

> the answers and means used to solve this age-old problem were not exactly delicate; there is perhaps nothing more terrible and more uncanny in all of man's prehistory than his *mnemotechnique*. "One burns something in so that it remains in one's memory: only what does not cease *to give pain* remains in one's memory" – that is a first principal from the most ancient (unfortunately longest) psychology on earth . . . it was never done without blood, torment, sacrifice; the most gruesome sacrifices and pledges (to which sacrifices of firstborn belong), the most repulsive mutilations (castrations, for example), the cruelest ritual forms of all religious cults (and all religions are in their deepest foundations systems of cruelties) – all of this has its origin in that instinct that intuited in pain the most powerful aid of mnemonics.
>
> [pp. 37–38]

Strong – *unforgettable* – words: evidently Nietzsche is here above all thinking of initiation rituals, indeed often linked to horrible tests of courage and the endurance of pain – tests that continue to be used in some tribal cultures (and in American fraternity-initiation rites). What is at stake here as well is the production of memory. The community into which the initiated person is introduced understands itself as a community of memory, presiding over a store of myths and norms it wishes to hand on to the neophyte – over precisely what Deuteronomy is concerned with: rules and knowledge of history.

However, Nietzsche's ideas of the cruelty of such social mnemotechnics in the *Genealogy* rest on a false anthropology, one that conceives of human beings as born egoists who by their natures forget everything not to their direct advantage and for whom remembrance of both fellow human beings and obligations to society can only be cultivated in a painful way. For Nietzsche, social civility is a straitjacket into which a person must be forced for the sake of coexistence. Freud shares this pessimistic view of human beings and culture; if we go further back historically, Hobbes might also come to mind, with his view of people as lonesome, violent, and socially oblivious. For Hobbes, only constant fear of being murdered by one's fellows led to agreed-on contracts and the transfer of all violence to individuals who could guarantee civil peace. But since these authors wrote their classic texts, anthropological research, brain research, and the stunning success of various social networks has strongly pointed to such a view of humanity as false: that in fact human beings are oriented by their nature toward empathy, sympathy, and forming interpersonal bonds, and, having evolved as a social animal, are unable to live outside a social matrix. Many of their mental and emotional faculties emerge, then, through social connections. In this sense, *homo naturalis* is inherently *homo civilis*; it takes as much labor to raise an aloof wolf as what Hobbes and Nietzsche imagine it takes to raise a responsible person – for Nietzsche, the final result of painful mnemotechnics. Human beings live in various states of attachment, strive to expand their circle of attachments, wish to belong to that circle, and take up the obligations and memories tied to this – perhaps not always without resistance, but external constraints at least encounter an impulse stemming from within. In any event, rituals are indispensable to physically stabilize memory. In this point Nietzsche was doubtless right: the propensity to forget is always there; it is not annulled through the human drive to form attachments. For this reason, memory needs stabilizing mechanisms.

What makes memory liable to forgetting is its "anachronistic" character. We are concerned here with memories from a distance, of things outside the immediate present, and this in both spatial and temporal senses. Our examples have mainly shed light on the spatial sense: recollection in the Promised Land of obligations imposed at Sinai and in the homeland, of obligations imposed in Nineveh. But the temporal sense is even more important, involving memory of a normative past through which a group defines itself. In the case of Judaism, this is the exodus from Egypt. In Deuteronomy's narrative, this appears to have occurred forty years previously. But at the time when the fifth book of Moses emerged, this normative past was dated to a past lying eight hundred years back; in the ritual of the two Seder nights with which the Passover festival begins, Jewry continues to recall the exodus from Egypt. The Jewish Seder is likely the most elaborate conceivable mnemonic ritual, involving a reenactment of the event. In the Seder liturgy, the Haggadah, it is put as follows:

> In every generation [*be kol dor va-dor*] we should consider ourselves as if we ourselves have left Egypt, as it is said, "And you shall explain to your son on that day, 'It is because of what the Lord did for me when I went free from Egypt.'" [Exodus 13, 8] He not only redeemed out fathers but us with them, for as it is said, "and us he freed from there, that He might take us and give us the land that He had promised on oath to our fathers.

[6, 23]

In every generation, what is at stake mnemonically returns to an event thousands of years in the past. A roasted lamb shank bone is placed on the ceremonial plate, just as, back then, the Israelites smeared lamb blood on their doorposts so the Angel of Death would spare their own firstborn; and matzah, unleavened bread, is eaten in the Seder and for all the eight days of the festival, reenacting the consumption of unleavened bread during the exodus due to lack of time for the leavening process. The participation at work here is not only intellectual, but emotional and physical as well.

We now need to consider a decisive characteristic of Jewish culture of memory, emphasized by Jewish historian Flavius Josephus with unmistakable pride:

> Could there be a more saintly government than that? Could God be more worthily honored than by such a scheme, under which religion is the end and aim of the training of the entire community, the priests are entrusted with the special charge of it, and the whole administration of the state resembles some sacred ceremony? Practices which, under the name of mysteries and rites of initiation, other nations are unable to observe for but a few days, we maintain with delight and unflinching determination all our lives.
>
> [Josephus, *The Life. Against Apion*, 1966, II.188–189, p. 369]

Here we are presented with a distinction between Jewish and foreign, which is to say pagan, and in particular Greek, culture of memory. The pagans, Josephus indicates, have to wait a long time until they come into contact with their sacred traditions – put more generally, their cultural memory – in the mysteries of festive celebrations where the myths are reenacted and recited. The Jews, in contrast, live in permanent contact with their sacred traditions; in their case, every day is a celebration of mystery. From morning to evening they read their holy books and are instructed in them by the priests. What Josephus is here describing (in the process certainly doing injustice, through his polemic, to the reality of Greek *paideia* – "education, formation") is the difference between ritual and writing, the temple and the house of learning (the *bet midrash*, an institution Johanan ben Zakai anticipated by developing his school at Yavne), sacrifice and sermon. Here, the script replaces cult, reading replaces ritual. This profound transformation is tied to Deuteronomy. Through this book, the Jews became the People of the Book, pointing the way to the other scriptural religions by taking it with them into Babylonian captivity. There it became a support and the basis for their memories, identity, culture, and religion – a "portable homeland," as Heinrich Heine put it so aptly. Both the Temple and state was destroyed, the priesthood scattered, but the script in which everything was described remained and could replace the rites. Deuteronomy prescribed remembering, in the Promised Land, the exodus from Egypt; it would now be the basis for remembering Jerusalem, in Babylon and elsewhere.

At the same time, this step from ritual into writing, born from necessity and then enormously successful, was not unopposed. Already Jeremiah, who lived at the time of Deuteronomy's emergence, was criticizing the book when he wrote the following:

> How can you say, "We are wise,
> And we possess the Instruction of the Lord"?
> Assuredly, for naught has the pen labored,
> For naught the scribes!
> The wise shall be put to shame,

Shall be dismayed and caught;
See they reject the word of the Lord,
So their wisdom amounts to nothing.

[Jer. 8, 8–9]

It was also a massive step to codify the will of God. Countermovements were thus not lacking, the most momentous of them being the Jesus movement, whose main thrust was formulated by Paul: the letter kills; the spirit gives life (2 Corinthians 3:6). Paul here encapsulates the danger posed by a scriptualized culture of memory. Two things have to come to the aid of the text so that freezing of meaning does not take place: on the one hand, what Paul calls "spirit," and on the other hand the text's reembodiment in living, acting individuals. Spirit is taken care of by the interpreter – the rabbi in the Jewish tradition, the pastor, priest, or theologian in the Christian tradition and corresponding teachers and hermeneuticists in other scripture-grounded traditions. The text's reembodiment is taken care of by ritual. John's reference to the word becoming flesh naturally refers to Jesus alone; but in a more general sense, the divine word wishes to become flesh for every believing Jew, Christian, and Moslem.

Judaism maintained this principle most intensely; for this reason Paul criticized it as *sarkikos*, "carnal." The so-called Jewish ceremonial laws prescribe ritual behavior rendering visible memory of the covenantal obligations. But Greek Orthodox and Catholic Christianity are also rich in rituals – although the Second Vatican Council Catholicism cut back on its sensory presence, to the point that Alfred Lorenzer (1981) spoke of a "council of bookkeepers" and of a "disturbance of sensuality." In any event, Protestantism went farthest in the direction of deritualization. Nevertheless, religion, and with it memory, cannot fully transfer into text; nor can it desensualize and interiorize itself into a purely spiritual thing. It also needs celebration, to be seen – it has an aesthetic, performative side that needs to be asserted.

In Germany of the 1980s, such considerations were evident in the context of the memory of both the Holocaust and, with some delay, World War II, the bombing of German cities, and the flight and expulsion of civilians from the east. In this respect I would like to return to two points that I have already touched on. The first of these again concerns Deuteronomy and the motif of the forty-year wandering in the desert, finding an end with Moses's departing speech and the entry into the Promised Land. Why, in fact, did the Israelites wander around the desert for forty years instead of covering the route in three or four weeks? The answer to this question is clear: because God condemned them to wander. When the scouts that Moses sent out to spy on Canaan returned (Num. 13, 1–14, 45), their report on the huge size and strength of the inhabitants sparks panicky anxiety. "The whole community broke into loud cries, and the people wept that night" (Num. 14, 1). The next day, the people wanted to stone Moses and Aaron to death, but God intervened. God now wished to destroy the people but Moses dissuaded him, the death sentence thus being changed to a "life sentence." In other words, his generation will now wander about for forty years until it dies, with only the new generation being able to see and enter the Promised Land:

> Of all of you who were recorded in your various lists from the age of twenty years up, you who have muttered against Me, not one shall enter the land in which I swore to settle you . . . Your children who, you said, would be carried off – these will I allow to enter . . . But your carcasses shall drop in this wilderness.
>
> [Num. 14, 29–32]

"[N]one of the men," pronounces God, "who have seen My presence and the signs that I have performed in Egypt and the wilderness, and who have tried Me these many times and have disobeyed Me, shall see the land that I promised on oath to their fathers" (Num. 14, 22). This generation of witnesses is thus excluded from the Promised Land. At this point in the biblical narrative, a set of interconnected themes are clearly of central importance: generations, forty years, the "blessing of being born late" that spares everyone under twenty, the "sins of the fathers" grounding God's decision.[9] Evidently, the generation from whose perspective the story is being told has pronounced itself free of the fathers.

If we read the story from the present perspective, certain parallels in the German context come to mind: following World War II, it took forty years before the memory of Nazi crimes returned in Germany, with all the force present in the return of the repressed. The Bitburg scandal in 1984; President Richard von Weizsäcker's talk of May 8, 1985, in which he referred to Nazi Germany's capitulation forty years earlier as a liberation; and the internationally framed Historians' Controversy over how to properly approach the mass crimes all signified an entirely new public confrontation with the Holocaust that found its expression in countless rituals of memory. Aleida Assmann has described and analyzed the history of this memory in her books, *The Long Shadow of the Past* (2006) and *Remembered History* (2007). Forty years mark the threshold upon which both the perpetrators' and the victims' memories of traumatic events returns in their old age. Precisely that threshold marked the founding of the Spielberg Archive with its fifty-thousand video testimonies of Holocaust survivors and the similarly equipped, but methodologically different Fortunoff Archive, in which a rich literature of memory began to emerge for which there was previously neither language nor interest. The obvious conclusion to be drawn from this parallel is that only successive generations are able to remember and mourn "the sins of the fathers."

The other motif that I would like to take up in conclusion is that of haunting. In 1993, playing with the word "ontology," Derrida coined the term "hauntology," in reference to the ghost of Marxism that, following the collapse of Communism, haunted Europe more strongly than before; meanwhile, the term has been extended to take in the crimes of the Nazi period, above all the murder of Eastern

European Jewry, and has also gained a psychoanalytic dimension in connection with Nicholas Abraham and Mária Török's concept, "crypts of memory" (1976). I would like to understand the formula of being haunted by the past in this extended sense. Since the late 1990s in Germany, the past involved in this haunting has increasingly included the suffering of the Germans: the aforementioned bombing, flight, and expulsion, and the rape of women by Russian soldiers. These themes, once strikingly absent from literature and public debates, have since come to fill books, literary supplements, and exhibitions. At the center of the Holocaust-memorial debate of the 1990s was the consistent critique of memory "ordered from above" and of empty official rituals. The history of the past two decades shows how mistaken the critics were. The new culture of memory was largely a grassroots movement; it involved forms through which long-repressed memory on the part of a society haunted by its past could gain social expression. "Each person is alone with his conscience," declared the author Martin Walser (1998) in his controversial Peace-Prize speech at Frankfurt's Paulskirche on October 11, 1998; in it, he warned against a "cruel commemoration service" that equated remembering with blaming and would deteriorate into threat-filled routine. Everyone, Walser insisted, needed to be left alone with his or her memory and not constantly patronized by the media and politicians. These remarks of his were important because they provoked intensive discussion; indeed, a bitter dispute with Ignatz Bubis (head of Germany's central Jewish communal organization) and many others. In its course, the extent to which memory is a social phenomenon relying on rites and monuments became increasingly clear. Walser experienced every reminder of the Holocaust as an accusation and defended himself against that. But accusing the perpetrators is not the only reason for remembering the victims. The victims deserve our memory for their own sake, as well as for the sake of empathy, mourning, and the deep human need to not allow the dead to fall away from the world in which we live – but rather to take them with us, at least as names and memory, into unfolding reality.

Notes

1 This essay was translated from German by Joel Golb.
2 The "death strip" refers to the zone in between the two separate walls that comprised the Berlin Wall. Attempts to traverse this strip of land often resulted in death.
3 The debate continues. See A. Assmann, 2006; 2013.
4 This and following citations from Deuteronomy (indicated by chapter and verse) and other books of the Hebrew Bible are from *Tanakh: A New Translation of The Holy Scriptures According to the Traditional Hebrew Text*.
5 On Passover as *zikkaron*, feast of commemoration, see Ex 12, 14; Lev 23, 24. See the literature in Cancik & Mohr, 1990, notes 73–77.
6 In the post-biblical period Shavuot takes on the sense of a festival to recall the revelation at Sinai and the giving of the Torah. See Dienemann, 1937 and Hardmeier, 1992.
7 "Moses wrote down this Teaching" and ordered its regular reading every seventh year before the people (31.9,13). In Hethite contracts this corresponds to the standard stipulation that

the contract's text is to be read at regular intervals. See Korošec, 1931, p. 101. On every day of Sukkoth, Ezra reads the Torah to the people (Neh. 8, 1 and 18).

8 Cited from E. Otto, 1999, translated by S. Maul, both of whom I would like to thank for a great deal of scholarly support.

9 For the "sin of the fathers" and the importance of this motif in the Torah, see Bernhard Lang, 2011.

References

Abraham, N. & Török, M. (1976). *Cryptonomie: Le verbier de l'homme aux loups*. Paris: Aubier Flammarion, 1986. English translation, N. Rand, *The Wolfman's Magic Word: A Cryptonomie*, Minneapolis, MN: University of Minnesota Press.

Assmann, A. (2006). *Der lange Schatten der Vergangenheit: Erinnerungskultur und Geschichtspolitik (The Long Shadow of the Past: Cultures of Memory and the Politics of History)*. München: C.H. Beck.

Assmann, A. (2007). *Geschichte im Gedächtnis. Von der individuellen Erfahrung zur öffentlichen Inszenierung (Remembered History)*. München: C.H. Beck.

Assmann, A. (2013), *Das neue Unbehagen an der Erinnerungskultur*. München: C.H. Beck.

Dienemann, M. (1937). Schawuot. In: *Jüdisches Fest und jüdischer Brauch*, ed. F. Thieberger, Königstein: Jüdischer Verlag, 1979, pp. 280–287.

Cancik, H., & Mohr, H., eds. (1990), Erinnerung/Gedächtnis. In: *Handbuch religionswissenschaftlicher Grundbegriffe 2*, eds. H. Cancik, H., B. Gladigow, & M. Laubscher. Stuttgart: Kohlhammer.

Cancik, H., Gladigow B., & Laubscher, M., eds. (1990). *Handbuch religionswissenschaftlicher Grundbegriffe 2*. Stuttgart: Kohlhammer.

Hardmeier, C. (1992). Die Erinnerung an die Knechtschaft in Ägypten. In: *Was ist der Mensch ... ? Beiträge zur Anthropologie des Alten Testaments*, eds. F. Crüsemann, C. Hardmeier, & R. Kessler. Munich: Chr. Kaiser, 1992.

Helck, W., ed. (1984). *Die Lehre des Djedefhor und die Lehre eines Vaters an seinen Sohn*. Wiesbaden: O. Harrassowitz.

Josephus, *The Life. Against Apion*, trans. H. St. J. Thackeray, Loeb Classical Library, Cambridge, MA & London: Harvard University Press, 1966.

Korošec, V. (1931). *Hethitische Staatsverträge. Ein Beitrag zu ihrer juristischen Wertung (Leipziger rechtswissenschaftliche Studien 60)*. Leipzig: T. Weicher.

Lang, B. (2011). Die Zahl Zehn und der Frevel der Väter. In: *Buch der Kriege – Buch des Himmels. Kleine Schriften zur Exegese und Theologie*. B. Lang. Leuven; Walpole, MA: Peeters.

Laroche, E. (1990). *Catalogue des textes hittites, no. 6*. In: (1990), *Handbuch religionswissenschaftlicher, Grundbegriff 2m*, eds. H. Cancik & H. Mohr. Stuttgart: Kohlhammer 1990, p. 314.

Lorenzer, A. (1981). *Das Konzil der Buchhalter, die Zerstörung der Sinnlichkeit, Eine Religionskritik (The Council of the Bookkeepers, the Disturbance of Sensuality, a Critique of Religion)*. Frankfurt am Main: Europäische Verlagsanstalt.

Nietzsche, F. (1887). *On the Genealogy of Morality*, trans. M. Clark & A. Swenson, Indianapolis: Hackett, 1998.

Otto, E. (1999). *Das Deuteronomium*. Berlin: de Gruyter.

Tanakh: A New Translation of The Holy Scriptures According to the Traditional Hebrew Text. Philadelphia, New York, & Jerusalem: Jewish Publication Society, 1985.

Walser, M. (1998). Experiences while composing a Sunday speech. In: *The Burden of the Past-Martin Walser on Modern German Identity: Texts, Contexts, Commentary*, eds. T. A. Kovach & M. Walser. Rochester, NY: Camden House, 2008, pp. 88–94.

3

THE STATEN ISLAND SEPTEMBER 11 MEMORIAL

Creativity, Mourning, and the Experience of Loss

Jeffrey Karl Ochsner

The distance from lower Manhattan to Staten Island is only five miles, but it can seem much farther. In contrast to the high-pressure urban agglomeration of Manhattan, many neighborhoods on Staten Island retain small town characteristics as distinct communities.

It's a twenty-five minute ride on the Staten Island Ferry from the St. George Terminal at the northeast corner of Staten Island to the Whitehall Terminal, next to Battery Park, at the southern tip of Manhattan. For most of the day, ferries run about every thirty minutes; during rush hour, service is even more frequent. For commuters who take most of the 65,000 average daily trips, the ride is a familiar routine—in the morning, one prepares oneself for the a hectic day ahead; in the evening, the trip is a chance to "decompress," to remember the day, but also to get away from the demands of the financial district or wherever one works in the city. But on September 11, 2001, more than 250 commuters who rode the ferry to work never came home again, as Staten Island was one of the boroughs hardest hit by the 9/11 attacks.[1]

Today, approaching Staten Island by ferry, off to the right, more than a mile away, we can see the white "V" of the Staten Island September 11 Memorial (Fig. 3.1). As we approach the terminal, the structure seems less an abstract "V" and more like outstretched wings about to take flight. From the terminal, it is a short walk along the North Shore Waterfront Esplanade to the memorial. Although we approach on foot from the side, we are drawn into the gap between the two wings—the two parts of the memorial. The south end of the gap is narrow, only about seven feet wide at the base, but the wings splay so that at the north end they are just over fourteen feet apart.[2] The result is a kind of forced perspective that appears to draw Manhattan closer. The configuration also feels protective as we look to the north.

From the esplanade, which existed long before the memorial, there has always been a splendid view of the lower Manhattan skyline. Indeed, Staten Islanders gathered here to watch helplessly on the morning of September 11. Now the memorial

FIGURE 3.1 The Staten Island September 11 Memorial, Masayuki Sono, architect, view toward Manhattan and Ground Zero.

focuses our view, as its centerline points directly at the site of the missing twin towers. We know what should be there, but is not.

Looking toward Manhattan, we are not alone. If we turn to either side, we see, on the memorial walls, individual silhouettes – each one different and each looking to the north with us. They are the Staten Islanders who died as a result of the 9/11 attacks. Unexpectedly we are drawn in. We have a feeling of the presence of the dead, and we experience an extraordinary sense of loss.

Remembering 9/11

The process of dealing with grief and mourning following a death has traditionally included the making of a permanent record of the person who is gone. We know that memories will fail with time, and those who lived through an event, or who know those who died, will themselves eventually reach the end of their own lives. With the passage from one generation to the next, what guarantee is there that any of us will be remembered? One way of assuring that our loved ones are remembered is the creation of permanent markers. For most, the permanent record is the grave marker: – the inscription of the name (and often the dates of birth and death as well as a brief statement) on the surface of the stone placed at the burial site creates a permanent symbolic record.

In the aftermath of 9/11, the impulse to memorialize, to create markers of remembrance was extraordinarily powerful. As Oliner (2006), Ornstein (2010), and others have noted, in the aftermath of traumatic group loss, the creation of a shared marker – a memorial – can become an especially important part of the mourning process. After 9/11, many of the earliest memorials were found online, but these soon gave way to physical sites of remembrance. Mourners created temporary memorials at the attack sites and at American embassies and consulates across the globe. There was no question that permanent memorials would be constructed at Ground Zero, the Pentagon, and Shanksville, Pennsylvania, but many other communities from California and Texas to Florida and Massachusetts also built their own memorials. The memorials at the attack sites focus, for the most part, on the events and the deaths at each location. Those at distant locations tend to focus primarily on the events of 9/11 but seldom address individual deaths.

In the New York area, there is another group of memorials that particular to the different communities that suffered losses of loved ones on 9/11. Some were erected in firehouses or police stations, others in different boroughs and nearby towns. These memorials are similar in that they all concern the same traumatic event: located at a distance from Ground Zero, each of these memorials is nonetheless connected to it, for in each place there were loved ones who never returned home. Yet they are all unique, addressing groups of individuals from various communities who were lost. As a collection, these memorials suggest a variety of aesthetic and social responses to the losses of 9/11, and the variety of ways in which different groups have chosen to remember and to mourn.

In the more than fourteen years since 9/11, the major memorials have been extensively covered in the press. A number of scholarly books and articles also focus on the major memorials, addressing questions of design, commemoration, representation, visitor experience, and the like (Nobel, 2005; Simpson, 2006; Sturken, 2007; Doss, 2010).[3] Far fewer works look in detail at the less well-known memorials, particularly those in the smaller communities directly impacted by 9/11 (Lerner 2004).

This article focuses on just one of these memorials, the Staten Island September 11 Memorial. In this article, I first relate the story of its design and construction, and then discuss some ways in which this memorial may be understood. I argue that the process by which it was created, particularly in the development of the silhouettes, was an important part of the mourning process for those Staten Islanders who lost loved ones. I also maintain that this memorial is particularly effective as a site of mourning, that it owes its success to its essential incompleteness, and that it can only be understood by considering how it evokes human response. Furthermore, I argue that through its design, the Staten Island September 11 Memorial creates a kind of place apart. It can be read as a "holding environment" in the way it encloses, seemingly protects, but also allows us to look outward (Winnicott, 1967). It is a symbolic object that establishes a permanent link with the dead and can, I posit, be understood as a "kind of shared transitional object" (Homans, 1989, p. 278), a "revived transitional object" (Tutter, 2013), or a "linking object" (Volkan, 1972; 1981; 2009; Volkan & Zintl, 1993). Finally, it may be experienced as a special kind of linking object, a "space of absence," where the message is the absence of the dead, yet where we simultaneously feel their presence (Etlin, 1994, p. 172).

Conceiving a monument for Staten Island

On the morning of September 11, 2001, many Staten Islanders gathered at the North Shore Waterfront Esplanade to watch the unfolding catastrophe at the World Trade Center. Some family members of those who worked in the twin towers were among the group that witnessed the collapse. That day, Borough President James Molinaro vowed that there would be a memorial at the site.

In December 2002, Molinaro announced that he had arranged for two million dollars to be set aside for the Staten Island September 11 Memorial, and had appointed an Advisory Committee to oversee its creation. Working quickly, the Committee issued a Request for Proposals (RFP) on January 13, 2003, asking for conceptual design submissions for a memorial that was "solemn but uplifting." As a minimum, each design was to honor those whose lives had been lost by including their individual names and places of work; the RFP noted that some members of the community had suggested "the use of likenesses" of the victims. The RFP estimated that two hundred sixty-seven victims would be honored.[4]

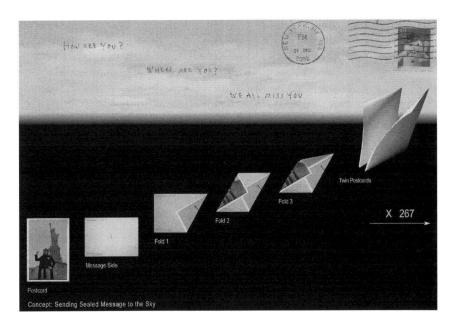

FIGURE 3.2 The Staten Island September 11 Memorial, final competition design, first of five boards submitted by Masayuki Sono on May 16, 2003. Penciled messages read, *How are you? Where are you? We all miss you.*

By the March 7 due date, the Committee received one hundred seventy-nine entries from nineteen countries (Fig. 3.2). After a month, the Committee announced six finalists and asked them to refine their projects and to provide more developed drawings and models. These were received on May 16 and were exhibited thereafter. On June 12, the six finalists discussed their projects in a public forum at the Center for the Arts at the College of Staten Island, followed the next day by final presentations to the Committee. On June 17, 2003, the Advisory Committee announced the selection of a proposal entitled "Postcards," designed by New York architect Masayuki Sono (*Wired New York*, 2004).

As Sono explained at the public forum, he routinely has postcards in his apartment. Although some are used for sending notes to friends and family, he also plays with these as a designer, using one or more postcards as material for small hand-made concept models. As he tried different ideas for the 9/11 Memorial competition, he realized that the postcards could be more than just model-making material; even with all the digital technology available, many people still continue to send handwritten postcards – perhaps these have a more personal feeling than electronic communications. Sono saw the idea of the postcard itself as a way to embody messages of love and remembrance.

FIGURE 3.3 The Staten Island September 11 Memorial in context; looking southeast, the Staten Island Ferry in the background.

Of course, in his final design, the concept of "postcards" is not entirely literal – the idea is a more metaphorical one. Still, the outsides of the two walls of the Staten Island Memorial show a slight pattern of layers each suggesting a postcard folded over onto itself, in fact more like an envelope, to keep a message personal or private (Fig. 3.3).[5] Sono positioned the pair of "postcards" to create an empty space, the axis of which directly points to the former site of the missing twin towers. The walls are closest to each other at the south and spread slightly to open toward the harbor and the sky. This configuration, along with the curved upper edges, transformed the parallelograms into softer shapes, which viewers often perceive as wings (*Wired New York*, 2004).

Inside the walls, Sono's design provided space for 267 "commemorative stamps" – another metaphor – in the form of individual granite silhouettes of the faces of the lost looking toward the harbor, each with an individual's name, workplace, and date of birth. The wall behind the silhouettes is perforated to allow the penetration of light so that each profile is highlighted by direct sunlight, diffused daylight, or, at night, backlit by artificial illumination. The changes in light and shadow were envisaged by Sono as both enlivening the memorial and as marking the passage of time.

Building a monument for Staten Island

From the time when Sono's design was selected, there were fewer than fifteen months to September 11, 2004, the date that had been chosen for the memorial dedication. Sono immediately arranged for a leave of absence from his employer.[6] He also invited his former university classmate Lapshan Fong, then working in Los Angeles, to join him in New York to work on the project.[7] The participation of Fong, who arrived by October, proved crucial to the success of the project as the schedule was so tight.[8]

Sono had originally intended the Memorial to be constructed of post-tensioned white concrete, but by November, he, Fong, and their engineers were researching alternatives. A carbon-reinforced composite structure had been used for the bell tower in the renovation of the New York City Hall, and Sono and Fong turned to its fabricator, New England Boatworks (NEB), a high-end boat builder in Portsmouth, Rhode Island. During this phase they sent digital sketches and 3D models to NEB to determine the appropriateness of their technology. In December, when the carbon fiber estimate came in at about half the price of concrete, they chose to go with this material. This choice had the fortuitous effect of enhancing the feeling of lightness, and even flight, that many experience at the memorial; even the smoothest concrete would likely have conveyed a feeling of heaviness.

Although Sono and Fong had already settled the structural concept and overall dimensions, the choice of the composite material required further refinement of the configuration of the plaques, the shelves, and the light shafts that were the key to how the silhouettes would appear. They built and tested multiple physical models, both outside and at a lighting lab, both in daylight and with artificial illumination.

NEB started constructing formwork about mid-February, and the actual casting of the wall shells began on May 23. Because each of the walls would weigh about fifteen tons, substantial foundations were required; demolition at the waterfront site began in mid-April. By late June, the cast-in-place concrete work was largely complete. NEB completed their work on August 14. The walls were shipped on separate barges, made a twenty-four hour journey to Staten Island, and were hoisted into place two days later.

Memorializing the dead

The Staten Island September 11 Memorial includes the names of two hundred and sixty-three Staten Islanders who died as a result of the 9/11 attacks. It continues the tradition of other memorials that list the names of the dead, most notably the Thiepval Memorial to the Missing of the Somme in France (1932) and the Vietnam Veterans Memorial in Washington, DC (1982).[9] However, the Staten Island September 11 Memorial provides more than just words. In response to the RFP suggestion of "likenesses," each of the dead is also represented in silhouette.

Sono began working on these silhouettes, or profiles, soon after he won the competition. Fong also worked on the individual profiles, and eventually a third member was added to the team, artist Toshihiko Oka.[10] As architectural tasks took priority during regular working hours when the consultants and contractor were available, most of the work on the profiles was done in the evening or on weekends.

To produce the profiles, Sono and Fong initially tried collecting photos from the families, sending sketches back and forth to secure approvals: they would send draft silhouettes to family members, who either approve them, or send back "redlined" sketches. Although some profiles were developed this way, Sono and Fong soon found that the best way to work was to meet with the families and sketch together once the initial drafts were ready. Sono explains, "we went to the arts and community center in Staten Island numerous times to meet the families and sketched together until they were satisfied with the silhouettes."[11] Through this process, the families developed a deeper understanding of the ideas that shaped the memorial, in addition to being directly involved in personalizing it. Sono describes the process as painful and exhausting:

> The families came with their albums and we talked and sketched over our drafts together. Most of them started crying when they opened their albums and saw their loved ones photos ... my belief is that this painful process was the very essence of remembering and memorializing the victims – and also of accepting their loss and considering a better future.
>
> [e-mail, M. Sono to J.K. Ochsner, January 9, 2010]

There is no doubt that through this process the families became deeply invested in the memorial.

The profiles were fabricated at Granite Importers in Vermont. To achieve the uniform white color they sought, Sono and Fong selected a special granite that lacked colored flecks. Although the installation of the profiles was the responsibility

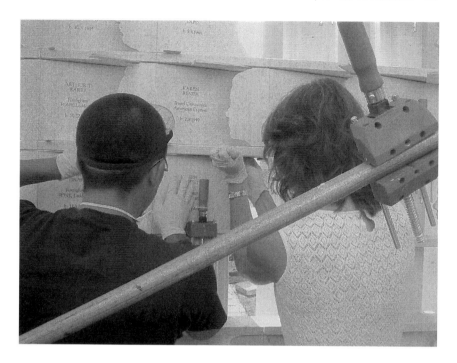

FIGURE 3.4 Family member (right) participating in the installation of a granite silhouette, August 2003.

of Brisk Waterproofing, a subcontractor, Sono and Fong assisted with the installation due to the delicacy of this phase of the construction. Some of the victims' families came to the site to witness, and even participate in, the placement of their loved ones' plaques (Fig. 3.4).[12]

One crucial aspect of the Staten Island Memorial is that its profiles are not organized or grouped in any apparent way. The names are not in alphabetical order, the birth dates are not ordered, and individuals who worked for the same organization are not found together.[13] Rather, the placement of individual profiles seems entirely random. The lack of order is deliberate: Sono and Fong used a computer program to randomize the placement of the profiles so that no patterns would accidentally emerge. This randomness creates a clear sense of equivalence – in death we are all equal. Were the names organized by alphabet or date of birth, their individuality would be minimized – reduced to points in an abstract system of letters or numbers. Randomizing the profiles allows each to be seen and experienced as an individual, and as part of a group without intervening distinctions. Differentiating individuals by grouping them by employer, or separating out the uniformed responders from those who were employed by companies in the twin towers, would similarly have disinclined the viewer to experience each individual loss as a unique and equal part of the cumulative loss shared by all Staten

FIGURE 3.5 Dedication ceremony, the Staten Island September 11 Memorial, September 11, 2004.

Islanders. While the individuality of each profile and their random arrangement lets us see each one as a real person, their common form as silhouettes makes them part of the group, allowing us to simultaneously understand that these people were all Staten Islanders, thereby circumventing the potential danger that the destruction of 9/11 might overwhelm the individuality of the dead – a point noted by Bernstein (2000) with regard to Holocaust memorials. The memorial thus supports both individual mourning, and the mourning of the Staten Island community as a collective whole.

The memorial was dedicated on September 11, 2004; the dedication ceremony was attended by an estimated three thousand people (Fig. 3.5). There have been memorial ceremonies at the site on September 11 of each year since 2004.

Symbolization and mourning

Memorial services are often part of burial rituals, traditional rites that often include the recounting of events of the deceased's life. Critical theorist Slavoj Žižek (1992) notes, "the funeral rite exemplifies symbolization at its purest: through it, the dead are inscribed in the text of tradition, they are assured that, in spite of their death, they will 'continue to live' in the memory of the community." The stories that are told as part of funeral rites allow those present to share how each knew the deceased, and to hear how others knew them. This sharing of stories from different perspectives confirms and expands the reality of the person who is no longer alive: what was once each individual's subjective perception becomes part of an understanding shared by the community. More than factual communication takes place at such rites. Because our inner emotional lives have been shaped by the loved ones now gone, the stories also recall for us, consciously and unconsciously, the feelings associated with the deceased; thus such rites can mark a first step toward the work of mourning as we begin to sense how our inner emotional world is inevitably linked to the deceased.

When Sono and Fong met with the families, their focus was on developing the silhouettes. Yet these meetings no doubt played a role similar to certain aspects of funeral rites. Each family shared pictures, told stories, and recalled their lost loved ones. As they did this, Sono and Fong developed sketches – beginning the transformation of ephemeral memories into stone. However, the creation of these permanent likenesses differed from the creation of a typical grave marker – in the United States, a grave marker most often bears a name, dates of birth and death, and perhaps an epitaph, but not a figurative representation of the person.

Creating permanent objects of remembrance draws on inner experience. The creation of permanent objects of any kind may be a link to one of the earliest experiences of human life, the recognition of object constancy, a step toward the distinction between inner and outer reality: things do not disappear when we cannot see them. But in death, the other *does* disappear and can unconsciously evoke the primal experience of loss described by Winnicott (1971), that we, as infants, first felt when we realized that our caregiver (usually our mother) was not there.

Rituals associated with caring for and burying the physical remains of the dead are a crucial element of most normal grieving and mourning traditions. But the destruction of the twin towers was so complete that many families were left with no remains. The inability to bury a loved one added an additional layer of complexity to the process of mourning that was already complicated by the trauma resulting from the suddenness and unexpectedness of these deaths, as well as the massiveness of the destruction and overwhelming scale of the losses (as also discussed by Ornstein, 2010, with respect to the Holocaust). As Pelento (2009) notes, if one is not able to carry out the rituals associated with the interment of remains, it can become "impossible to fulfill the necessary conditions to trigger and maintain the work of mourning." Although families without remains still held memorial services, they often experienced a sense of a ritual left incomplete, the permanence of death left unevidenced.

Symbolization can be used to make things permanent; we render ideas in symbols in order to communicate; we share feelings through symbols. Of course, the symbol is not the thing; as Žižek (1992) reminds us, symbolization always involves loss. But in death, symbolization is all that is available – the loss is real, and symbolization is one way of experiencing the loss as real and keeping the person alive in memory. The symbolic site offers a place where a person may be remembered and mourned and his or her memory preserved in perpetuity.

Of course, a silhouette is also an abstraction, yet it is an abstraction from a figurative representation, more viscerally representational than name alone. In constructing the profiles, families were forced to "see" their lost loved one again – not merely to glance or vaguely recollect, but really to think about what the loved one looked like, and in turn, who he or she was. Although the making of the memorial cannot be said to have been equivalent to the normal rituals associated with interment, participation in the creation and installation of the silhouettes – making a permanent marker and sharing stories and remembrances – may well have aided those whose grief and mourning were made even more complex by the absence of remains. In addition, while abstracted, the granite profiles are at the same time concretized and as such provide a physical embodiment of the departed. The transformation of memories into silhouettes in stone gave families a chance to recall and share memories of the person they lost, and a chance to share in the creative process of making a likeness that will survive, even as memories fade (Ornstein, 2010). And for those who participated in their installation, there was also a kind of finality – the permanent marker was now in its place, looking toward Manhattan with all the others who lost their lives. The experience of the families recalls Hannah Segal's (1952) discussion of Proust: "all his lost, destroyed, and loved objects are being brought back to life ... By virtue of his art he can give his objects an eternal life in his work" (p. 198). The families may not have been artists, but there can be no doubt that in their participation in the fabrication of the silhouettes, they took part in essentially the same process (a somewhat similar observation in another context has been made by Tutter, 2013).

Today, of course, visitors to the Staten Island Memorial include more than family members. For most visitors, the silhouettes do not evoke personal memories of the individuals portrayed, yet they are nonetheless evocative of real people; we can all imagine our own loved ones, or even ourselves, in silhouette form.

A linking object

One way to understand the power of the Staten Island September 11 Memorial silhouettes is to consider them as "linking objects," an idea conceived by psychoanalyst Vamik Volkan (1972). He initially formulated this concept in addressing pathological mourning, arguing that "the mourner sees [linking objects] as containing elements of himself and the one he has lost" (Volkan, 1981, p. 20); he considers them as a constituting "meeting ground" (p. 119), where the mourner may "resolve the ambivalence" about the deceased (p. 20). Volkan (2009) also argues that linking objects can serve to perpetuate the static, pathological mourning of "perennial mourners" (p. 100), and that while such objects can serve as an element in the work of grief, under certain circumstances, they may prolong the grief work (also see Volkan & Zintl 1993).[14] Of course, our memories of lost loved ones never fully disappear, so, in one sense, we may all have some experience of "perennial mourning"; indeed, today, normal mourning is seen by many as a lifelong process, as other contributions to this volume attest.

For family members, creation of the silhouettes was not a conscious attempt to create a "linking object"; rather, I suggest that the success of the silhouettes as sites for (unconscious) projection depends upon their not being consciously understood by family members that they might serve in this role. The psyche resists being choreographed, and unconscious processes follow their own paths. Yet when they participated in making the silhouettes, the family members were clearly aware of contributing to the shaping of stone, and the markers they created evoked, and will continue to evoke, personal memories and recollections.

Beyond the individual, the Staten Island September 11 Memorial is a site for group mourning. As explained by Volkan and others, group mourning processes follow traumatic events in which group members suffer significant losses (Volkan, 2009; Ornstein, 2010; Homans, 1989). In developing his thinking about the roles that monuments and memorials play in group mourning, Volkan came to see them as "shared linking objects" (Volkan & Zintl, 1993; Volkan, 2009). He argues that a memorial site may assist in the completion of a group's mourning by helping "members accept the reality of their losses," but he also argues that a memorial may also continually activate the hope of "recovering what was lost," or generate a desire for revenge.

The Staten Island Memorial, like most of the 9/11 memorials, is not heroic and presents no call for retribution – it is the sense of loss that is palpable. It clearly plays a role in helping the community that built it mourn by helping community members accept the reality of their loss, the deaths of former community members. Visitors see the silhouettes with the names and dates. We may not know anyone personally, yet we can identify with them, as we recognize their silhouettes for what they are: representations of people like ourselves, who once lived and now are gone. We can run our fingers along the surface of one or more silhouettes, feeling the individual form of each face – the effect is enhanced because the silhouettes are nearly life size.[15] We may run our fingers across our own faces for comparison – the identification we feel is not just through sight, but also through touch. We may each have different feelings or memories, but in a sense, those who died continue to live in the feelings they evoke in us.

The Staten Islanders shown on the memorial have become part of a permanent public site of memory. We see them individually, and we see them as a group – the number seems so large, and we know that Staten Island is, in some ways, still a small community. We experience the losses individually, and we experience the loss of the group. And as we turn toward Manhattan, we remember what should be there, but is no longer, and we sense the enormity of the shared loss (Fig. 3.6).

FIGURE 3.6 Family members and other visitors often leave flowers and other mementos at the Staten Island September 11 Memorial.

Experiencing the memorial

When we visit the Staten Island September 11 Memorial, we cannot help but be drawn into the space between the walls. We find the profiles all facing Manhattan, and we look there too. If one visits when few others are present, and the light conditions are just right, as at dusk, one may have a feeling that those represented in the silhouettes are somehow there with us – we look together across the water. We sense that the dead are gone, yet somehow still present, if only for a moment. Cultural historian Richard Etlin (1994) calls a space that evokes this response a "space of absence," which he describes as "a void whose overwhelming message is the absence of the dead person, no longer with us in life, and yet somehow present within the aura of the monument" (p. 172). He notes that the "space" need not be an actual space – an object can also evoke this response – but at the Staten Island 9/11 Memorial, it is when we are within the literally empty space (between the two walls) that we sense the presence of the dead.

The idea of a space of absence seems peculiar. We know that the memorial is made of inanimate material, yet somehow it seems to us to imbue the dead with some characteristics of being alive. Indeed, Etlin offers no explanation for the experience of a space of absence, noting only, "[i]t is about the encounter of two or more spirits or souls in a way that defies reason" (Etlin, 1994, p. 172). Since the enclosure is not alive, what makes it seem alive must come from us – it is our feelings that we unconsciously project into this space that makes it possible for us to feel the presence of the dead. As the dead remain alive in our own internal lives, it is the external object that provides a site onto which we can project and thus access our memories and our own internal living representation of the dead, so that we experience the dead as somehow present. We feel this within the space between the walls – walls that are inanimate.

A key aspect of the Memorial that helps foster this experience is its sense of containment. Although the Memorial is not completely encircling, its two walls are only seven feet apart at the base at the south. It is easy to walk inside, yet there is a subtle sense of the Memorial cradling us. We can understand it as a kind of "holding environment," a concept advanced by Winnicott (1967). Winnicott located the origin of the holding environment in the experience of the infant being held by and focusing on his or her caregiver (in Winnicott, typically one's mother). In the arms of the caregiver, the child feels safe and comfortable enough to look outward, knowing that he or she is safely held. The splay of the walls of the Staten Island 9/11 Memorial provides a subtle sense of protection, of being held so one can look outward. We relax, we see the silhouettes, and we look north, sharing the view with those who have died.

Although Etlin described and cataloged "spaces of absence," they may be considered sites that evoke projection. Since it is our projection that completes the space, a key aspect of a space of absence is that it must be in some way incomplete. If a space is too complete, then it cannot evoke projection. There must be "space" – a sense of incompleteness – into which the projection may occur. The challenge to the designer is to provide enough to evoke projection, yet leave enough incomplete so that we are the ones to complete it. If the "choreography" is obvious, if we feel manipulated, the psyche will resist. The space of absence is, therefore, elusive and unexpected – the first time we visit, we are surprised by what we feel.

The Staten Island September 11 Memorial is incomplete in multiple ways. The most obvious is the incorporation of the absent World Trade Center. The idea of a memorial incorporating other structures by orienting to them is not a new one. The two walls of the Vietnam Veterans Memorial point at the Lincoln Memorial and the Washington Monument, placing the Vietnam War deaths in the context of the American ideals represented by those two structures (Griswold, 1986; Ochsner, 1997). The axis of the Staten Island September 11 Memorial points to the site of the deaths, Ground Zero. This orientation places these deaths in context; but because the end of the axis lacks a physical focal point, it calls upon our imagination to remember what is not there.[16]

The Staten Island Memorial may also be considered incomplete in its openness to the sky. The importance of this aspect may not be readily apparent, but imagining the Memorial closed at the top, creating a closed space, indicates how important the sense of openness actually is. The experience of some visitors, of a sense of the dead floating up, is only possible because the V-shaped position of the walls creates a dynamic sense of lightness and movement.[17] The whiteness and the smoothness of the walls also add to this effect.

The most important way in which the Staten Island Memorial is incomplete is in the use of silhouettes. Again, if we imagine that an actual representative sculpture replaced each silhouette, we can see that the incompleteness would be lost. Indeed, Sono explained the design this way: "By keeping it simple, it allows us the space to feel and project our own imagination and memory onto the silhouettes" (*Wired New York*, 2004). The felt experience of presence and absence engages us to the extent that we may find ourselves running our fingers over the edge of the silhouettes. Even those who did not personally know any of the victims often find themselves touching the profiles. Because the silhouettes are incomplete, in that they do not provide the visual information of a portrait or sculpture, we use touch to confirm or expand the information provided by sight.[18]

The spaces behind the silhouettes – the gaps that allow light to come through – also contribute to the Memorial's incompletion, by their emptiness, and by adding to the changing experience of the Memorial with the passage of time, the movement of the sun and the changing of the seasons; each silhouette remains the same, yet our perception of them varies with each visit. Each silhouette is thus always seen as an incomplete representation, allowing us to experience this Memorial as a space of absence – the victims are "no longer with us in life, and yet somehow present" (Fig. 3.6).

We look outward with the dead. We experience their presence in a primary state of knowing – not through conscious intention, but through a preconscious, perhaps presymbolic way of understanding. For a moment we are together and we share a connection to those who are gone.

As at other recent memorials, visitors, especially family members, often leave something behind. It is common to find flowers on the shelves just below the portraits. Occasionally notes or photos, or even postcards, are left as well.[19] We understand the wish to contribute something of ourselves, to leave behind something to connect to those who were lost, to mark their absence, and to keep their memory alive – to leave something of ourselves as we retain something of those we lost.

Notes

1 Staten Island is the smallest of the five boroughs of New York City, with an estimated population in 2008 of 487,400. The next smallest borough, the Bronx, had an estimated population of nearly 1.4 million in 2008. Out of the five boroughs of New York, Staten Island lost the most citizens per capita on 9/11.

2 Other key dimensions are: height to highest point: 39'1" from ground; width at widest point: 44'5"; length at base: 38'6"; outside width at base: 11'0" expanding to 18'0"; inside space between the two walls: 7'1" expanding to 14'2".

3 The works cited here are only a small fraction of the many publications that deal with the memorials associated with the losses of 9/11.

4 The number 267 included in the RFP was an estimate because the exact number was not yet known. Today the actual number of silhouettes is 263. (Some recent newspaper accounts have suggested there are now 274 silhouettes, but this number is not correct.) The memorial includes all victims of the 9/11 attacks who lived in Staten Island at one point in their lives, not just those who lived there on 9/11/2001. Also included

is one passenger killed on United Airlines flight 93 in Pennsylvania, and one person killed in the 1993 World Trade Center bombing. They each have an additional line of text identifying the causes of their deaths. One woman who was several months pregnant and had decided on the child's name before the attack, has an additional line of text; at the family's request, the unborn son's name was included on her plaque. Some families who had moved from Staten Island were not included on the initial list, but after the 2004 dedication asked to be included. Ten were added in 2005 (one year after opening) and one more in 2006 (e-mails, M. Sono to J.K. Ochsner, January 8–9, 2010; January 6, 2014).

5 Some visitors might interpret the pattern of overlapping layers on the outside faces of the two walls as an envelope rather than a postcard. This effect is enhanced by the white color of the memorial – similar to an ordinary white envelope.

6 In 2004, Masayuki Sono was working at Voorsanger Architects in New York. He is now a partner in Clouds Architecture Office in New York.

7 Sono and Lapshan Fong met as graduate students at the University of Washington in 1995. When Sono completed the schematic design and realized he needed help, he invited Fong to join him. The project was a collaboration between Sono and Fong from design development through completion of construction. (In architecture, "design development" refers to the project phase after schematic design; in the design development phase, the details of the design are refined and technical issues are resolved. Once design development is complete, the architects are ready to produce the construction documents from which a project can actually be built.)

8 The full project team included, designer: Masayuki Sono; project collaborator: Lapshan Fong; profile art collaborator: Toshihiko Oka; structural and civil engineer: Weidlinger Associates, Inc.; geotechnical engineer: Han-Padron Associates; landscape design: Mathews Neilsen Landscape Architecture; lighting design: Fisher Marantz Stone; electrical engineer: PA Collins Consulting engineers; graphics and signage: That's Nice; Construction management: Bovis Lend Lease; Client: City of New York; New York City Economic Development Corporation.

9 The Thiepval Memorial to the Missing of the Somme, designed by Edwin Lutyens, completed in 1932, memorializes 72,090 missing servicemen from Great Britain and the Commonwealth countries who died in the Battle of the Somme and have no known graves. The Washington DC Vietnam Veterans Memorial, designed by Maya Lin, honors members of the United States armed forces who served in Vietnam and memorializes the over 58,000 dead and missing lost in the war. There is an extensive literature on both memorials.

10 Toshihiko Oka is a sculptor. When it became apparent that Sono and Fong could not complete all the profile sketches by themselves, they interviewed artists from New York and selected Oka to assist on part of the drafts. Sono and Fong met with the families and developed the profiles. Sono, who had previous experience in Japan with portrait painting, was responsible for final designs for all profiles.

11 E-mail, M. Sono to J.K. Ochsner, January 9, 2010.

12 In fact, some families had inscribed the names of their loved ones on the foundation concrete below the place their plaque would be later installed.

13 The identity of each person's employer is included on each panel with the person's name, which helps to answer the question why each person was in the World Trade Center on September 11. It also provides a way to identify the police and firefighters who lost their lives responding to the catastrophe. The profile is placed in front of the text panel with the identifying information so that, when illuminated from the rear, the profile is darker in contrast to the associated text panel, and the incised lettering is also dark.

14 Others have used somewhat different terms – "a kind of shared transitional object" (Homans, 1989, p. 278) or a "revived transitional object" (Tutter, 2013) – but describe essentially the same phenomenon.

15 Each individual module is 9" high and 13" wide overall. The visible portion of the text panel is 9" x 11" (from 9/11)—the actual outline of the face extends into this 9 x 11 area. The granite pieces are 3/4" thick. The type font is Goudy with letters 3/8" tall.

16 Since 2004, the view toward Manhattan has changed with the construction of One World Trade Center. However, it is not on axis, and does not substitute for the Twin Towers that we know are missing.

17 Sono's competition entry conveyed this idea with its visual suggestion of messages floating up. However, few visitors would know that this was intentional.

18 On 25 June 2008, Sono focused on the memorial's tactile character at a presentation about the Memorial at the St. George Library on Staten Island, sponsored by Art Education for the Blind and the New York Public Library.

19 Some families leave letters and small mementos, such as Christmas ornaments, the victims' photos laminated in plastic, and similar items. There have also been birthday balloons and ribbons. The city is in charge of periodic maintenance. The flowers are dried and crushed and used to fertilize the trees and flowers around the memorial. Other items are stored (e-mail, M. Sono to J.K. Ochsner, January 9, 2010).

References

Bernstein, J.W. (2000). Making a memorial place: The photography of Shimon Attie. *Psychoanal. Dial.*, 10:347–370.

Doss, E. (2010). *Memorial Mania: Public Feeling in America*. Chicago & London: University of Chicago Press.

Etlin, R. (1994). *Symbolic Space: French Enlightenment Architecture and Its Legacy*. Chicago & London: University of Chicago Press.

Griswold, C.L. (1986). The Vietnam Veterans Memorial and the Washington Mall: Philosophical thoughts on political iconography. *Crit. Inq.*, 12: 688–719.

Homans, P. (1989). *The Ability to Mourn: Disillusionment and the Social Origins of Psychoanalysis*. Chicago & London: University of Chicago Press.

Lerner, K. (2004). 9/11 memorials, not just in Manhattan. *Arch. Rec.*, 192:48.

Nobel, P. (2005). *Sixteen Acres: Architecture and the Outrageous Struggle for the Future of Ground Zero*. New York: Metropolitan Books.

Ochsner, J.K. (1997). A space of loss: The Vietnam Veterans Memorial. *J. Arch. Ed.*, 50:156–171.

Oliner, M.M. (2006). The externalizing function of memorials. *Psychoanal. Rev.*, 93: 883–902.

Ornstein, A. (2010). The missing tombstone: Reflections on mourning and creativity. *J. Amer. Psychoanal. Assn.* 58: 631–647.

Pelento, M.L. (2009). Mourning for 'missing' people. In: *On Freud's* Mourning and Melancholia, eds. L.G. Fiorini, T. Bokanowski, S. Lewkowicz, London: Karnac Books, pp. 56–70.

Segal, H. (1952). A psycho-analytic approach to aesthetics. *Internat. J. Psycho-Anal.* 33: 196–207.

Simpson, D. (2006). *9/11: The Culture of Commemoration*. Chicago & London: University of Chicago Press.

Sturken, M. (2007). *Tourists of History: Memory, Kitsch, and Consumerism from Oklahoma City to Ground Zero*. Durham, N.C., & London: Duke University Press.

Tutter, A. (2013). Angel with a missing wing: Loss, restitution, and the embodied self in the photography of Josef Sudek. *Amer. Imago*, 70:127–190.

Volkan, V.D. (1972). The linking objects of pathological mourners. *Arch. Gen. Psychiat.*, 47:215–221.

_____. (1981). *Linking Objects and Linking Phenomena: A Study of the Forms, Symptoms, Metapsychology, and Therapy of Complicated Mourning.* New York: International Universities Press.

_____. (2009). Not letting go: From individual perennial mourners to societies with entitlement ideologies. In: *On Freud's "Mourning and Melancholia,"* eds. L.G. Fiorini, T. Bokanowski, S. Lewkowicz, London: Karnac Books, pp. 90–109.

Volkan, V.D., & Zintl, E. (1993). *Life after Loss: The Lessons of Grief.* New York: Collier.

Winnicott, D.W. (1971). *Playing and Reality.* New York: Tavistock.

_____. (1967). The concept of a healthy individual. In: *Home is Where We Start From: Essays by a Psychoanalyst,* eds. C. Winnicott, R. Shepherd, M. Davis, New York: Penguin, 1986, pp. 22–54.

Wired New York. (2004). http://wirednewyork.com/forum/showthread.php?t=4726, April 3rd, 2004, accessed February 2, 2014.

Žižek, S. (1992). *Looking Awry: An Introduction to Jacques Lacan through Popular Culture.* Cambridge, MA & London: MIT Press.

4

DESIGNING THE STATEN ISLAND SEPTEMBER 11 MEMORIAL

Masayuki Sono

The heart of the design of the Staten Island September 11 Memorial came from a simple desire to connect all the victims of September 11 back to us. This was how the concept of sending letters and the use of individual profile silhouettes emerged. In materializing these ideas, the use of abstraction played a crucial role in creating an experience that allows multiple, personal readings of the piece on different levels.

Seen from certain angles, the overall form of this "folded twin postcards" was shaped in hope of potentially recalling a large V-sign, dove, or origami crane, among other things (which to me, together with the postcard of John Lennon making a "peace sign" used to illustrate the concept in the competition board, all symbolize peace). But personally, the most important aspect of the form is that its meaning(s) is entirely up to the viewer. The abstract form was carefully designed so that it looks very different from various angles, in order to stimulate people to see various things in it.

The profiles inside the walls were conceived of as instruments to enhance and extend connections between the victims and society through collective memory and imagination – from direct ties between families and friends, to links to the wider public and future generations (Fig. 4.1). Those who never had the chance to meet the victims in person are induced to think of the victims' lives as actual existences through the use of the silhouettes, abstract portraits that allow space for mystery and imagination.

The incorporation of these profiles led to an unprecedentedly deep involvement of the victims' families in the design of their loved ones' profiles. For me, the process of meeting the families and sketching together felt like mass mental rehabilitation – most of them could not hold back their tears once they opened their family albums. Their emotions and stories inevitably made my eyes wet as we sketched together.

Personally, what I lost on 9/11 was not a family member but a belief in the values of humanity and beauty – especially the latter, to which I had devoted much

FIGURE 4.1 Granite "negative" silhouette, Staten Island September 11 Memorial.

of my life as an architect and artist. After the twin towers, which I loved since my childhood, were destroyed, and I watched the subsequent breakout of war in the Middle East despite our efforts to protest against it, I became depressed and obsessed with feeling that what I believed in did not hold any meaning or power against violence and politics. Over time, this became part of my inner drive to submit a design to the memorial competition – to see if beauty and certain humane inspirations can still have meaning and existence in society, apart from being mere commercial instruments. In completing the memorial with families and seeing their children grow over the past decade, I now realize that the process was therapeutic not only for the family members, but also for myself, as I regained my ability to move forward again.

5

RESPONSE TO PART I

The Relics of Absence

John Gale

The past – whether encountered in rituals, texts, or architectural monuments – always speaks of an absence (de Certeau, 1967). This is powerfully illustrated by the way the authors of the preceding chapters elucidate the ambiguity of what Augustine called *memoria* – both what is remembered, and the act of remembering. For Augustine, *memoria* is more than a storehouse of concepts and fantasies: it has an intimate relationship with the will and the emotions. One of the key dynamic aspects of *memoria* is the ordering of interior experience in a way that approximates the psychoanalytic understanding of the unconscious. Indeed, Augustine considers the process of bringing together things "scattered and unarranged" (*quasi colligere atque animadvertendo*) central to the acquisition of self-awareness (Cary, 2000).

The absence invoked by the past is more than merely an interruption or a fissure, as Assmann suggests in this volume. It is, rather, the foundation of the symbolic (Lacan, 2006) and thus "the very place in which psychoanalysis dwells" (Ricœur, 1977, p. 369).[1] This foundation is mythologized in traces of memory that, as their historicity suggests, have been fabricated as well as reconstructed (Lacan, 2006). Our ability to record and transcribe the past is, of course, limited by the availability of materials and the conditions under which we preserve texts and artifacts. This fact alone immediately calls into question the objective historical status of these *objects*. But it is also called into question by the operation of repression. That is to say, the past as we enshrine it in memorials and in collections in archives, libraries, and museums is never uncontaminated. Rather, it is preconstituted: the result of a condensation and an ellipsis. As such, its relics are redacted and inscribed within a mythology that is dependent on a discordance (*Spaltung*[2]) between the past and the present that, in its turn, rests on a chronological model of temporality. This fragmentation or estrangement accelerates a process of petrification in which artifacts – rather than remaining meaningful in the present – become marginalized and defracted into the folkloric and seen, deceptively, as somehow "belonging" to the past (Lacan, 1994). Psychoanalysis turns this view of history on its head by recognizing that the relationship between the past and the present is not as one of succession, but one of imbrication and repetition (de Certeau, 1987). We are, as Assmann reminds us, haunted by the past.

But memory is not only constituted by absence: it also veils it (Ricœur, 2004). This veiling – or sheltering, to use Derrida's idiom – is a kind of forgetting characteristic of repression (Konstan, this volume). We find this masking of absence even where we least expect it – in Freud's concept of *Trauerarbeit* (literally, "mourning work"), which functions to eradicate the traces of loss (Ferber, 2006). It is a "work" that belongs not just to individual subjects, but to a particular mentality (Derrida, 1996). Indeed, even Cicero, the "*orator amplissimus*" (Augustine, *De Civitate*), experienced a grief (*dolor*) that was, as he records it in the *De amicitia*, inscribed within the lexicon of a specific culture (*paideia*), as Kostan notes. For precisely at the moment where utterance becomes dependent on a question, under the rubric of intersubjectivity, our history is experienced both as our own and yet at the same time, not our own. For it is the product of a specific place (Ahearne, 1995). In this it signifies a tradition (*paradosis*) in the sheltering of absence. This is one reason why some historical events occupy the forefront of a particular cultural awareness and other equally profound events are forgotten (Gadamer, 1975).

Archaeologies of grief and depression

Reading Konstan's study one cannot fail, from the very start, to notice the paradoxical nature of Cicero's text. On the one hand it is an exercise in recalling the past, and on the other, a written document, through which the author seeks to organize and master that past, and which continues to speak long after its author has died. These factors, and while interwoven, function according to different economies. As literature, the *De amicitia* is inserted into an archaeology of texts and usages. It thus reintroduces what it has sought to expel by a process of detachment (the "return of the repressed"). For this reason, de Certeau (1987) likens texts to tombs, erected by erudition, from which what is expelled 're-bites' (*remordent*). This is an archaeology that, in antiquity, amounts to a lexicography of grief, designated in manifold overlapping terms and genres, which discloses a dynamic process, founded on absence, that anticipates the views of Freud. Here, in intersecting private and public spheres, its essential link to death emerges (Liddell & Scott, 1863). This finds its expression in the deep sorrow and remorse (*penthos, katanuxis, lupē*), in the weeping and mourning that accompanies the loss of a loved one or a friend (Fraisse, 1984). This association with death indicates a further connection between grief and various forms of depression (*melancholia, akēdia*),[3] as well as with the penitential rituals associated with the "mortification of the flesh" as they change from the Middle Ages through to the seventeenth century (Foucault, 2004). But, as Assmann suggests, citing various key passages from sacred scripture, there may also be a Semitic provenance to the notion that positions grief in relation to a fictional castration (Egginton,

2007). Indeed, we know that Babylonian and Canaanite religious practices involved weeping and mourning rites, elements of which are found in the Old Testament (Huidberg, 1962). Pegon (1952) identifies one hundred and twenty uses of the verb *pentheō* (Greek, "mourning") in the Septuagint alone.

The Stoics, through a careful analysis of the emotions, noticed that expressions of grief change over time and may be voluntary or involuntary (Graver, 2007). As Konstan discusses, Seneca observes that only human beings grieve at any real length on the death of a loved one and that this grief, initially characterized by noisy weeping, involuntary sobs, and shaking, changes over time. While the first kind of grief is something natural (*naturalis necessitas*), the second indicates a person's humanity and will thus, to some extent, be controllable. Importantly, Seneca argued that these tears will be tinged with a certain joy at the memory of the loved one's kind deeds (Graver, 2007). Real happiness, he maintains in the *Epistulae Morales*, cannot be destroyed by loss, and thus the true friend, while he may shed some tears and feel a certain degree of pain, ought not to grieve when a friend dies; a person has responsibilities toward his family, and it will be of no service to them if that person is "laid low, or shattered, or dependent on the other, or reproachful towards god or humankind" (Graver, 2007, p. 178). Epictetus advises that we should love a child or a friend, remembering that death is a part of life (*Discourses* 3. 24–82ff). Cicero observes that guilt is often felt if happy emotions are experienced during mourning, but his concern is with those who are merely going through the motions of mourning for the sake of appearances (*Tusculan Disputations*, 3.63–4).

Tears, as an expression of a paradoxical satisfaction (*jouissance*) that the subject derives from grief, become commonplace in the early Eastern Christian tradition of asceticism (Müller, 2000). Here the focus is on compunction (Hausherr, 1944). To weep and mourn is now transposed into a spiritual exercise akin to those of the early Greek philosophers. The Stoics insisted that philosophy was not a question of learning a set of abstract principles, but a therapeutic exercise that causes us to *be* more fully and makes us better: a conversion that turns one's entire life upside down, changing the life of those who go through it (Hadot, 1987). For the early Christian ascetics, weeping and feeling remorse was a form of therapy, more than of penitence. Tears – which characterized the spirituality of many of the Byzantine monks – were at the same time painful and pleasurable (Hunt, 2004). Here we see a tight bond emerging between loss (grief) and the death drive (*Todestrieb*), which takes us back, as Assmann shows, to the Pauline exegesis of the Torah. In Lacan's (1999) words, "without a transgression there is no access to *jouissance*, and, to return to Saint Paul, that that is precisely the function of the Law" (p. 177). But while compunction was a central aim of the ascetic program, natural mourning was discouraged in monasteries; too much emotion toward deceased family members might draw the monk back to secular life. Even in the monk's prayer, he was discouraged from dwelling on the memory of his dead friends and relatives. Indeed, rather as the Stoic ideal, one of the hallmarks of the spiritual father was his ability to remain unmoved when his parents died. There was also some added discomfort in monastic circles at being overwhelmed by grief in the face of death, because it could indicate a lack of faith in the resurrection. Thus monks were encouraged to hold in mind simultaneously the day of their own death and the resurrection.

But monks also frequently suffered from what was known as *akēdia*, which indicates a particular form of depression.[4] It is a difficult term to translate; even Cicero (1999) (*Letters to Atticus*, 12.45.1) struggled to find a Latin equivalent, and many modern authors leave it in Greek. In German it is referred to without ambiguity as *Klosterkrankheit* (Geiger, 1882) or *Mönchskrankheit* (Flashar, 1966). It was transmitted to the West through the *Institutes* of John Cassian (Chadwick, 1950). Manifested in both somatic and psychological symptoms, such as fatigue, inertia, anxiety, despair, sadness, and boredom, symptoms of *akēdia* persisted well into the Middle Ages (Lampe, 1961). By the sixteenth century, it was more or less replaced by a revival of the ancient term melancholia – driven, to a large extent, by a preoccupation with the need to find a medical diagnosis of demoniac possession (Levack, 2013).

Freud began his collection of over two thousand statues, reliefs, busts, and fragments of papyrus in 1896, shortly after the death of his father (Burke, 2006). It was, he thought, a defense against the anguish he experienced at the loss (Mauries, 2002): a "game of substitution, in which the objects involved . . . were 'erotic equivalents,' items of conquest and desire offering relief, love tokens designed to soothe and heal" (Masson, 1985, p. 110). He had been quite overwhelmed by grief over the death of his father and recalled that it led him into a deep, prolonged period of mourning that was, nevertheless, highly productive (Masson, 1985). It was about this time that Freud first drafted what was the precursor of his deceptively short study, "Mourning and Melancholia" (1917). This essay represented a shift in Freud's thinking: here he argued persuasively that depression resembles mourning in a number of ways. In both there is a sense in which something had been lost, which leaves the person feeling uprooted.

The cult of the dead

Early Greek religious activity, Assmann notes, was centered on the tombs of heroes and altars erected there (Wright, 1982).[5] At least from the early seventh century BCE, myths were preserved in the form of iconographic relief, and legends already formed parts of ritualized repetition or liturgy (Coldstream, 1976). For the archaic period (800–500 BCE), we are reliant on Solon's legislation, which forbade ostentatious funerals, and on iconographic evidence (Boardman, 1955). The body of the deceased was to be laid out in the house so that friends and family could pay their last respects (the *prothesis*), with the burial taking place before sunrise the following day (Humphreys, 1980). The excessive expression of grief was proscribed; women under sixty were not admitted to the *prothesis* or the funeral, unless closely related to the deceased, and were not allowed to lacerate themselves or wail (*kōkeuein*). It was forbidden for anyone to lament for anyone other than the deceased (that is, those earlier interred in the same tomb). No ox was to be sacrificed at the graveside, no corpse buried with more than three garments (*himatia*), and nobody was permitted to visit the tombs of non kin, except at the funeral (Ahlberg, 1971). Men and women cut their hair and even the horses had their manes cut as a sign of mourning.

But by the third century BCE, the law of Gambreion suggests that speeches and sacrifices had become more common place both at cremations and at burials, and the friends and relatives of the deceased heaped earth up over the grave and burned offerings nearby (Humphreys, 1980). Now tombs were often grouped in small family enclosures normally holding two to ten graves, and it was common for family members to visit these tomb enclosures (Assmann, this volume). Commemoration was stratified by the Archaic period, and mounds and monuments indicated that those buried there belonged to the elite. The introduction of state funerals for those who had died in battle brought about a change; from then on, monuments and tombs commemorated the domestic virtues of the ordinary citizen. The funeral would end with a feast in the house of the heir and further commemorations were held on the ninth and thirtieth day after death, as well as monthly and annually.

Christians in antiquity largely continued these customs including the *dispositio* in a sepulchre (Adnès, 1980). Certainly there is evidence that from an early date in the post-New Testament period, the bodies of martyrs were venerated. Moreover, the dead were honored by a memorial service (Grégoire & Orgels, 1951), and from very early on in the Christian era, scenes showing Christ's miracles of healing appeared on sarcophagi as symbols of spiritual healing, a practice that continued in Europe into the early medieval period (Brown, 2000).

Subterranean burial is known to have been practiced in the early Church in North Africa and Asia Minor as well as in Rome where we find the most famous and largest of the catacombs. These were built outside the city and some forty survive to the northeast and to the south. Bodies were set in *loculi* or, for the more important members of the community, in *arcosolia* set into the walls of labyrinthine chambers. We know that the eucharistic liturgy was celebrated on these tombs on the anniversaries of the deaths of the martyrs, at least from the fourth century. Indeed, as Assmann notices, one of the earliest words used to describe the eucharist was *anamnēsis* ("remembrance," or "memorial"; Cabrol, 1924). Writing to Aurelius in Epistle 22, Augustine describes the deeply rooted African custom of holding banquets for the dead (Solignac, 1996). These *laetitiae*, as they were traditionally known, took place on the *natalitia* ("birthday") of the martyrdom (Quasten, 1940). Augustine defended the practice of honoring the relics of the martyrs while forbidding feasting at the tombs of the dead (Lancel, 1997); however, grave inscriptions and piles of wine amphorae scattered among graves indicate that these reforms went unnoticed elsewhere (Février, 1977). Early Christian cemeteries in Syria arose because the faithful had chosen to be buried close to the tombs of the early martyrs; they became places of deep veneration and were profoundly attractive to the devout. Other cemeteries were established in places where, according to popular opinion, the tombs of the great biblical characters were to be found (Vööbus, 1960). Believers were drawn to these places because they felt they came in contact with their departed relatives, as Assmann describes for the ancient Egyptians.

Christian monasticism, from the fourth to sixth centuries, flourished in an immediacy to absence. That is to say, in its hagiographical lexis, the motif of remembrance (*anamnēsis*) was closely interwoven with its development. This is illustrated in the myth of the desert (*erēmos*) – not so much a matter of geography but a trope for a certain kind of distancing and withdrawal from social relationships, particularly marriage (Goehring, 1993). As many of the sources show, absences or silences were embedded in a layered mythology about the past to which its apologists already looked back nostalgically.

We know little of the burial customs of the monks, as the literary and archaeological evidence is limited. But in Egypt, mummification was probably only abandoned gradually (Dunand, 2007). To preserve the body it was sometimes wrapped up in sheets with handfuls of coarse salt and juniper berries placed between the legs and over the trunk. In some of the graves, the bodies were covered with palm matting (Walters, 1974). Most of the inscriptions found at Kellia in Egypt commemorate deceased monks: the term used to describe them is *makarios* (blessed). These inscriptions give the names of the departed monks; their ecclesiastical rank and title, indicating their position within the hermitage; the name of the village or province from which they came; and the date of their death (Guillaumont & Daumas, 1969). The monks kept registers of deaths meticulously, and liturgical remembrances of the departed were common in monasteries (Brown, 1982). And in addition to liturgical and formalized memorials of the dead, individual monks also prayed privately in the tombs of departed members of their community. Thus, the monks continued customs far older than the advent of Christianity, surrounding themselves by the traces of absence. In so doing, the dead could, indeed, be said to haunt the living (de Certeau, 1987).

The topography of emptiness

As its Latin root indicates, architectural monuments honoring the dead are there to remind us of absence. They are, quite literally, a memorial (*monumentum*) to what has been erased. Architecture articulates this within a distinctive discourse of spatiality that characterizes the lost object. Walls, towers, and roofs wrap around an interior emptiness, creating containment (Ochsner, this volume). Boundaries establish an inside and make possible the bringing-in and preserving and the being in relation to what is, or is commemorated, within. But at the same time, like the sacred space that primitive man delineated with a circle of stones, the architectural space associated with the dead also intimates transcendence, a beyond (Eliade, 1959; also Konstan, this volume). This is what Le Corbusier (1948) famously described as "ineffable space" (p. 9) – or, as Sono (this volume) calls it, a "space for mystery," with its emphasis on silence. In other words, the dialectic between exterior and interior space, raises a question about alterity or transcendence (Hendrix, 2008).

Incubation, or pitching a tent on the graves of departed heroes, was known to have been common among Arab peoples, as well as among the Greeks where it was primarily associated with the cult of Asklepios (Dodds, 1951). This was done for therapeutic reasons, and it has been suggested that this may in some way have foreshadowed psychoanalysis (Meier, 1949; 1989). It was also not uncommon for relatives to have spent some considerable time living in the tomb of departed kin. Kavvadias (1891) argued that in the sanctuaries of Asklepios in the fifth to fourth century BCE, there was practically no medicine or therapy, properly speaking. The cures, he thought, were simply miraculous. However, Lefort (1906) positioned the practice of incubation, as it is found in its later stage, within the discourse of divination. While the link between healing and divination is well attested throughout antiquity, both from the literary and epigraphic evidence, the conflation of the roles of healer (*iatros*) and seer (*mantis*) into *iatromantis* does not appear before Aeschylus (Parker, 1983).

The practice of sleeping in tombs was continued by Christians, and there are examples in the Coptic passions of cures resulting from Christian incubation (Deubner, 1900). The fifth century historian, Theodoret of Cyrrhus, tells his readers of a Syrian monk named Peter, who spent his time in a tomb (Theod. *Rel. Hist.* IX:3). This tomb had an upper story and a balcony to which a ladder was attached to admit those who wanted to see him. He remained there for many years. Zeno, a former civil servant, settled in an inaccessible tomb on Mount Sipylus (Theod. *Rel. Hist* XII:2). From both Greek and Latin inscriptions, we know that one of the biggest monastic ruins in Northern Mesopotamia was originally a large second century tomb belonging to a local dignitary (Sachau, 1882). When Epiphanius was a young monk, he slept on one of the benches facing the grave of the five Syrian saints who had founded his monastery. In Armenia, too, we find examples of monks founding monasteries near cemeteries; this may have in part been to guard the resting places of their ascetic predecessors. At times the overlap between tomb and cell could be dramatic. Theodosius instructed each of his first disciples to prepare a *mnēeion*, which was to be used, initially, as living quarters. These single cells or alcoves could quickly be converted into tombs when their inhabitants died (Hirschfeld, 1992).

In Egypt, the spiritual biography of Antony provided an ideal pattern of monastic life in the early Church. It set out to be an inspiration for others, and here we see the saint, at a key moment in his ascetic journey, lying half dead on the floor of a tomb. There is clear evidence throughout Egypt that monks preferred to adapt and reuse pharaonic tombs and mortuaries at Deir el-Bahri rather than live in former temples (Brooks Hedstrom, 2007). It is unlikely that this was mere practicality as the monks were often adept architects and builders and erected well-designed, solid, and sophisticated residences (Halkin, 1932). That the tomb or cemetery seems to have been thought an ideal place for a monk to live has largely been overlooked, but it is worthy of attention for it illustrates the importance of the cult of the dead in early Christian monasticism.

There are interesting parallels to be made here with non-Christian forms of monastic life. For the tantric ascetics living on the famous cremation ground at Tarapith in West Bengal, the factor of place is of great importance for *sādhanā* (ritual practices). The sadhus who build their huts on the cremation ground are living above the remains of previous sadhus whose powers filter up to them through the earth (see also Assmann's discussion of the Aboriginal "songlines").

> But it would be too narrow to see this as the worship of relics. The sadhus who used to live there, the events that once happened there continue to inhabit the soil, the trees, the atmosphere, the very ambience of a particular spot and give to it its defining qualities. The repetition (*japa*) of a given mantra may be successful in one place, and unsuccessful in another. Only when its vibration coincides with the goddess in her auditory form does she appear to the adept in a vision of light, who becomes thereby a perfected being (*siddha puruśa*).[6]
>
> [Cantlie, 2013, p. 91]

Conclusion

The task of psychoanalysis has been described as reminding the patient that what is most essential has always already been forgotten (Lukacher, 1986). Freud had, of course, initially elaborated the concept of repression (*Verdrängung*) through an investigation of forgetfulness as he encountered it in patients suffering from amnesia (Breuer & Freud, 1893-1895). The conflict between forgetting – an action directed against the past (a loss) – and the mnemic trace, the return of the repressed, is staged in the arena of memory (de Certeau, 1987).

We see this clearly in Cicero's *De amicitia*, which – as Konstan shows in his detailed exegesis – is a treatise about friendship, permeated with absence. The literary context behind this text includes not just Xenophon's *Memorabilia*, on which Cicero overtly draws (*De amicitia* 62), but also, according to the testimony of Diogenes Laertius, a lost work by Theophrastus. While writing about expressions of grief (*maestitia*), mourning (*maestus*), funeral rites, and questions concerning the immortality of the soul, he mentions – in the first paragraph – the death of his father, and this is followed by frequent references to the deaths of Africanus, of Cato, and of Scipio, particularly in the first four sections of the work. He even mentions the death of Cato's son. Yet as Konstan demonstrates, Cicero's overwhelming grief over the untimely death of his only daughter just eighteen months earlier is apparently unconscious and unnameable. As he entered life before her, so had he expected to leave it before her (*De amicitia* 15), and somehow, despite his conscious wish to elaborate his thoughts on present friendship, his writing is constructed in relation to this loss. As she is absent from life, she exists in the text only by her elision, as an unsaid. Here we catch a glimpse of Cicero unconsciously working through his own grief, spelling out absence through its repetition, and thereby symbolizing it, even while it is disavowed. Thus the text articulates this lack via its enactment – much the same way the Staten Island Memorial commemorates the absence that it frames, and thus symbolizes.

In these studies we see the emergence of a symbolic network of interwoven sets of binary oppositions – past and present, forgetting and remembering, self and Other, pleasure and pain – which permeate the trope of absence (Vecchio, 1994). All of these resonate with the remembrance of death (Assmann, this volume). For the hidden basis of our individual yet shared history – our unconscious, in other words (Lacan, 2006) – is our finitude. In the context of religious responses to death, sickness, dying, and the care of the dead, absence is made present in the relationship between death rituals, and memorials, and the sacred spaces of the hospital, tomb, cemetery, mausoleum, and cenotaph, all of which function ambiguously both as a marker of alterity (*l'Autre*) and of a transcendence. As such, absence is experienced enigmatically as a presence (Lévinas, 1991).

Yet while disclosing death, structures of remembrance bear a double significa-tion, simultaneously camouflaging and veiling absence. That is to say, they rein-force a discourse in which death is an unthinkable and unnameable "elsewhere" (de Certeau, 1988). It is others who have died, their deaths existing in the past, and our own death becomes, right to the very end, something in the future, rather than a simultaneous aspect of present experience. Consequently, when not the object of historical research, the collective structures of remembrance – rituals (funerary and burial rites), monuments and archives (tombs, museums), and texts and inscriptions (necrologies, martyrologies) – often amount to no more than anachronistic dialects and antiquated quasireligious liturgies, empty of the faith that once inhabited them.

Excluded from and repressed by rites of remembrance, death is inscribed almost exclusively within the metaphors of psychoanalysis, where it takes refuge. The clinical encounter with the responses to loss (grief, weeping, depression, anger) reveals the extent to which our experience of life is articulated, precisely, "on the position of the subject with respect to death" (de Certeau, 1988, p. 192).

Notes

1 Lacan distinguishes between *remémoration* (recollection) and *mémoration* (remembering), which he considers symbolic processes, and *réminiscence* (reminiscence) which he considers imaginary.
2 Freud adopted the term *Spaltung* following Janet, but linked it to repression rather than seeing it simply as an incapacity for synthesis. On the background to the term discordance and its introduction into French psychiatry in 1912 by P. Chaslin, see the erudite study by Lantéri-Laura and Gros (1992), who demonstrate the origin of the term in Augustine's concept of *discordia*.
3 Stoic authors saw melancholia either as a form of insanity (mania) or as something that was often accompanied by insanity. For a discussion of the diagnosis of depression in antiquity, see Toohey (1990). Melancholia has an Arabic parallel in the word *ḥuzn*, which Avicenna suggests may be caused by the loss of a loved one.

4 Some modern commentators have been keen to emphasize the differences between *akēdia* and depression, but their arguments tend to be based on medieval Latin texts, which are heavily reliant on Cassian's translation of *akēdia* as *taedium*.
5 The excavations of prehistoric tombs at Prosymna show frequent Late Geometric deposits indicating hero or ancestor worship. In fact, there is evidence of continuous and intentional hero or ancestor worship from the end of the Mycenaean era through the Dark Age.
6 *Siddha* literally means boiled but is used metaphorically in the sense of perfected. A *siddhi* is a magical power.

References

Adnès, P. (1980). Mort (Liturgie de la) *Dictionnaire de Spiritualité*, 10: 1769–1777.
Ahearne, J. (1995). *Michel de Certeau. Interpretation and its Other.* Palo Alto, CA: Stanford University Press.
Ahlberg, G. (1971). *Prothesis and Ekphora in Greek Geometric Art.* Studies in Mediterranean Archaeology 32. Göteborg: Astrom Editions.
Augustine. (1967). *De Civitate.* In: *Augustine and the Latin Classics*, Vol II, ed. H. Hagendahl, Göteborg: Elanders Boktryckeri Aktiebolaq. p. 479.
Boardman, J. M. (1955). Painted funerary plaques and some remarks on prosthesis *The Annual of the British School of Athens* 50: 51–66.
Breuer, J. & Freud, S. (1893–1895). *Studies in Hysteria.* Standard Edition, 2:1-305. London: The Hogarth Press, 1955.
Brooks Hedstrom, D.L. (2007). Divine architects: designing the monastic dwelling place. In: *Egypt in the Byzantine World, 300–700*, ed. R.S. Bagnall. Cambridge, UK: Cambridge University Press, pp. 368–389.
Brown, P. (1982). *Society and the Holy in Late Antiquity.* Berkeley: University of California Press.
Brown, P. (2000). *Augustine of Hippo.* London: Faber & Faber.
Burke, J. (2006). *The Gods of Freud: Sigmund Freud's Art Collection.* Sydney: Knopf.
Cabrol, F. (1924). Anamnèse *Dictionnaire d'Archéologie Chrétienne et de Liturgie* II (2): 1880–1896, eds. F. Cabrol & H. Leclercq. Paris: Librairie Letouzey et Ané.
Cantlie, A. (2013). Divine madness: Tantric ascetics on the cremation ground in Tarapith, Birbhum District, West Bengal. In: *Insanity and Divinity: Studies in Psychosis and Spirituality*, eds. J. Gale, M. Robson & G. Rapsomatioti. London: Routledge, pp. 90–111.
Cary, P. (2000). *Augustine's Invention of the Inner Self.* Oxford: Oxford University Press.
Cicero. (1923). *De Amicitia.* In: *De Senectute, De Amicitia, De Divinatione*, trans. W.A. Falconeer. Loeb Classical Library. Cambridge: Harvard University Press.
_____. (1999). *Letters to Atticus, Vol I.*, trans. D.R. Shakleton. Loeb Classical Library. Cambridge: Harvard University Press.
_____. (1945). *Tusculan Disputations*, trans. J.E. King. Loeb Classical Library. Cambridge: Harvard University Press.
Chadwick, O. (1950). *John Cassian. A Study in Primitive Monasticism.* Cambridge, UK: Cambridge University Press.
Coldstream, N. (1976). Hero-cults in the Age of Homer. *Journal of Hellenic Studies*, 96: 8–17.
de Certeau, M. (1967). Les sciences humaines et la mort de l'homme. *Etudes*, 326: 344–360.
_____. (1987). *Histoire et psychanalyse entre science et fiction.* Paris: Gallimard.
_____. (1988). *The Practice of Everyday Life*, trans. S. Rendall. Berkley: University of California Press.

Derrida, J. (1996). *Archive Fever. A Freudian Impression*, trans. E. Prenowitz. Chicago & London: University of Chicago Press.

Deubner, L. (1900). *De Incubatione*. Lipsiae: B.G. Teubneri.

Dodds, E. R. (1951). *The Greeks and the Irrational*. Berkeley, CA: University of California Press.

Dunand, F. (2007). Between tradition and innovation: Egyptian funerary practices in late antiquity. In: *Egypt in the Byzantine World, 300–700*, ed. R.S. Bagnall. Cambridge, UK: Cambridge University Press, pp. 163–184.

Egginton, W. (2007). *The Philosopher's Desire: Psychoanalysis, Interpretation and Truth*. Palo Alto, CA: Stanford University Press.

Eliade, M. (1959). The *Sacred and the Profane: The Nature of Religion*, W. R. Trask, trans. New York: Harcourt Brace.

Epictetus. (1891). *The Discourses of Epictetus with the Enchiridion and Fragments. 2 Vols.*, trans. G. Long. London: George Bell and Sons.

Ferber, I. (2006). Melancholy philosophy: Freud and Benjamin. *Revue électronique d'études sur le monde Anglophone 4.1.* http://erea.revues.org/413

Février, P.A. (1977). A propos du culte funéraire: culte et sociabilité. *Cahiers archéologiques*, 26:29–45.

Flashar, H. (1966). *Melancholie und melancholike in den mediziniscen Theorien der Antike*. Berlin: Walter de Gruyer.

Foucault, M. (2004). *Abnormal. Lectures at the Collège de France*. New York: Picador.

Fraisse, J.-C. (1984). *Philia. La notion d'amitié dans la philosophie antique*. Paris: Vrin.

Freud, S. (1914). Remembering, repeating, and working-through (Further recommendations on the technique of psycho-analysis, II). Standard Edition, 12:145–156. London: Hogarth Press, 1958.

———. (1917). Mourning and melancholia. Standard Edition, 14:237–258. London: Hogarth Press, 1957.

Gadamer, H.-G. (1975). *Truth and Method*. London: Sheed & Ward.

Geiger, L. (1882). *Renaissance und Humanismus in Italien und Deutschland*. Berlin: Grote.

Goehring, J.E. (1993). The encroaching desert: Literary Production and ascetic space in Early Christian Egypt. *Journal of Early Christian Studies* 1: 281–296.

Graver, M. (2007). *Stoicism and Emotion*. Chicago & London: University of Chicago Press.

Grégoire, H. and Orgels, P. (1951). La véritable date du martyre de Polycarpe (23 Fevr. 177) et le *Corpus Polycarpianum. Analecta Bollandiana*, 69:1–38.

Guillaumont, A. and Daumas, F. (1969). *Kellia I, Kom 219, fouilles: exécutées en 1964 et 1965*. Cairo: Institut français d'archéologie orientale.

Hadot, P. (1987). *Exercices spirituels et philosophie antique*. Paris: Études Augustiniennes.

Halkin, F. (1932). Les Paralipomènes *Sancti Pachomii Vitae Graecae* 34–42. Subsidia Hagiographica 19. Brussels: Société Bollandistes.

Hausherr, I. (1944). *Penthos: La doctrine de compunction dans l'Orient Chrétien*. Orientalia Christiana Analecta 132. Rome: Pont. Institutum Orientalium Studiorum.

Hendrix, J.S. (2008). *Architecture and Psychoanalysis. Peter Eisenman and Jacques Lacan*. New York: Peter Lang Publishing.

Hirschfeld, Y. (1992). *The Judean Desert Monasteries in the Byzantine Period*. New Haven & London: Yale University Press.

Huidberg, F.F. (1962). *Weeping and laughter in the Old Testament. A study of Canaanite-Israelite religion*. Leiden: Brill.

Humphreys, S.C. (1980). Family tombs and tomb cult in ancient Athens: Tradition or traditionalism? *The Journal of Hellenic Studies*, 100:96–126.

Hunt, H. (2004). *Joy-Bearing Grief. Tears of Contrition in the Writings of the Early Syrian and Byzantine Fathers*. Leiden/Boston: Brill.

Kavvadias, P. (1891) *Fouilles d'Épidaure.* Athens.

Lacan, J. (1994). *Le Séminaire. Livre IV. La relation d'object 1956–57*, ed. J. – A. Miller. Paris: Seuil.

———. (1999). *The Ethics of Psychoanalysis 1959–1960. The Seminar of Jacques Lacan. Book VII*, trans. D. Porter. London: Routledge.

———. (2006). *Écrits. The First Complete Edition in English*, trans. B. Fink. New York/London: W.W. Norton and Company.

Lampe, G.W.H., ed. (1961). *A Patristic Greek Lexicon.* Oxford: The Clarendon Press.

Lancel, S. (1997). Modalité de l'inhumation privilégiée dans la nécropole de Sainte-Salsa à Tipasa. *Comptes-Rendus de l'Académie des Inscriptions et Belles-Lettres* (Algérie), 141:791–812.

Lantéri-Laura, G. & Gros, M. (1992). *Essai sur la discordance dans la psychiatrie contemporaine.* Paris: E.P.E.L.

Le Corbusier. (1948). New World of Space. New York: Reynal & Hitchcock.

Lefort, L.Th. (1906). Notes sur le culte d'Asclépios. Nature de l'incubation dans ce culte. *Le musée belge*, X:21–37, 101–126.

Levack, B. P. (2013). *The Devil Within. Possession and Exorcism in the Christian West.* New Haven & London: Yale University Press.

Lévinas, E. (1991). *Entre Nous: Essais sur le penser-à-l'autre.* Paris: Éditions Bernard Grasset et Fasquelle.

Liddell, H.G. and Scott, R. (1863). *A Greek-English Lexicon.* Oxford: Clarendon Press.

Lukacher, N. (1986). *Primal Scenes. Literature, Philosophy, Psychoanalysis.* Ithaca & London: Cornell University Press.

Masson, J.M. (1985). *The Complete Letters of Sigmund Freud to Wilhelm Fliess, 1887–1904.* Cambridge, Mass and London: Harvard University Press.

Mauries, P. (2002). *Cabinets of Curiosities.* London: Thames & Hudson.

Meier, C. A. (1949). *Antike Inkubation und Moderne Psychotherapie.* Zurich: Rascher Verlag.

———. (1989). *Healing Dream and Ritual.* Einsiedeln: Daimon Verlag.

Müller, B. (2000). *Der Weg des Weinens. Die Tradition des 'Penthos' in den Apophthegmata Patrum.* Göttingen: Vandenhoeck und Ruprecht.

Parker, R. (1983). *Miasma: Pollution and Purification in Early Greek Religion.* Oxford: Clarendon Press.

Pegon, J. (1952). Componction *Dictionnaire de la Spiritualité*, 2:1312–1321.

Quasten, J. (1940). Vetus superstitio et nova religio. *Harvard Theological Revue*, 33:253–266.

Ricœur, P. (1977). *Freud and Philosophy: An Essay in Interpretation*, trans. D. Savage. New Haven: Yale University Press.

Ricœur, P. (2004). *Memory, History, Forgetting.* Chicago and London: The University of Chicago Press.

Sachau, E. (1882). Edessenische Inschriften *Zeitschrift der Deutschen Morgenlandischen Gesellschaft*, 36:142–167.

Seneca. (1917). *Epistulae Morales 1–65*, trans. J.W. Basore. Loeb Classical Library. Cambridge: Harvard University Press.

Solignac, A. (1996). Notes complémentaires. In: *Oeuvres de Saint Augustin* ed. M. Skutella, trans. E. Tréhorel & G. Bouissou. Paris: Études Augustiniennes, 13, pp. 529–634.

Toohey, P. (1990). Some ancient histories of literary melancholia. *Illinois Classical Studies*, 15:143–161.

Vecchio, S. (1994). *Le Parole come Segni. Introduzione alla linguistica agostiniana.* Palermo: Edizioni Novecento.

Vööbus, A. (1960). *History of Asceticism in the Syrian Orient. A Contribution to the History of Culture in the Near East II. Early Monasticism in Mesopotamia and Syria.* Corpus Scriptorum Christianorum Orientalium 197. Leuven: Peeters.

Walters, C. C. (1974). *Monastic Archeology in Egypt.* Warminster: Aris and Phillips.

Wright, J. C. (1982). The old temple terrace at the Argive Heraeum and the early cult of Hera in the Argolid. *Journal of Hellenic Studies*, 102:186–201.

6

DISCUSSION OF PART I

Arcs of Recovery

Paul Schwaber

When someone beloved and close dies, we hurt. The wound can plunge deep and the anguish of loss seems total. We might feel strangely unprotected, even helpless – and then, slowly, begin to remember qualities and tonalities, looks, interactions, episodes with the person, while trying also, perhaps unconsciously, to deny, to put the painful loss out of mind. And so bolstered, albeit hesitantly and sadly, we go on. That is the paradigmatic arc of recovery. We live in time, though now a loved one has left it. The world may well seem diminished, possibly stopped – unless, by processes of remembering and integrating, painful though they be, we learn to accept living without that actual presence. Our recourse is memory – and resolution. We call on the past to aid with our grief, and we struggle to continue.

The essays published together here testify to just such painful losses, and their grouping implies a significant relatedness. David Konstan's commentary on Cicero's *De Amicitia* mentions lesser losses but focuses on the death of particularly close friends. Cicero invokes expectable philosophical forms of grieving that endured but also allowed gradually more inclusiveness of private feelings. The expectation, certainly for admired public figures, was for Stoic reserve in behavior and mind. As a boy, Cicero listened to his tutor Scaevola speak so commendingly of Gaius Laelius's discourse on friendship that he committed it to memory. Decades before Cicero's essay, Laelius, a much-admired man, praised for his wisdom, was responding to the death of his loved friend Scipio, who had died suddenly and at the height of his attainment. Cicero praises Laelius's Stoical control of his emotions, appropriate for so exemplary a man but allows hints too of more pained and private feelings. Laelius concedes being moved by Scipio's death. He disclaims being praised for wisdom, moreover, comparing himself unfavorably to Cato, who had suffered the death of his adult and accomplished son, the worst loss a man can suffer, but exemplified the Stoic standard of emotional calm and "virtue." In contrast, Laelius admits sorrow over Scipio's death. Thus the Stoic standard was undermined (or expanded), yet still upheld favorably in Cicero's commentary on friendship and loss. Professor Konstan proposes further, with considerable psychological cogency, that Cicero's focus on the friendship of Laelius and Scipio, including the celebration of Cato, displaced – whether consciously or not – his own anguish about the loss of his beloved adult daughter, Tullia, soon after giving birth; an agony he admitted to, less publicly, elsewhere.

The matter of personal suffering in great loss, as well as of communal expectations and the requisite of courage and virtue thus are introduced. A far wider perspective on loss, pain, and memory is provided in "Rituals of Memory," by Jan Assmann, who explores rituals as social and cultural symbols of group memory and identity, serviceable for transgenerational transmission of tradition, history, and values. Rituals, he explains, present culture as collective memory and performance, orienting us in time and helping us to define ourselves – as each Sabbath Jew read aloud from the written Torah and annually celebrate Passover, telling "in each generation" of the escape from Egypt and the bond with Moses and with God. He mentions Shavuoth and Succoth too – all three tied to leaving Egypt, receiving the Torah, and reading it aloud to the assembled. Education thus is crucial, as are rituals that embody collective memory. Josephus's pride in the Jews' daily performative connection to their sacred history and obligations, and their reliance on script as "a portable homeland," in Heinrich Heine's phrase, Assmann cites as central to Jewish cultural remembrance and hence survival as a group in the Babylonian exile – and, we might add, through centuries of diaspora experience and hostility in Europe and elsewhere. Assmann also cites the Germans' conundrum some forty years after the Second World War and fifty years after *Kristallnacht*: how to include adequately the Nazi's slaughtering of millions of Jews as part of that history. What kind of memorial could help to acknowledge such horror, perpetrated by their own kind as part of the nation's accepted culture of memory, to be included and pondered by generations present and future? And what of the Germans' own suffering in the war? What emerged for the Memorial to the Murdered Jews of Europe in Berlin was a nonrepresentational, symbolic physical structure suggestive of waves of graves on a broad swath but consisting of nearly three thousand rectangular gray stone slabs, each unique in shape and size. My experience being there was initial astonishment, followed by a feeling of being invited in to linger, sit, stand, or wander, to realize and to think, and to sense an infinitude of sadness.

Personal and communal grief find intriguing expression indeed in the Staten Island September 11 Memorial, both in its architectural accomplishment and in Jeffrey Karl Ochsner's commentary on it, which nicely illuminates his subtitle, "Creativity, Mourning, and the Experience of Loss." Masayuki Sono, the Memorial's architect, provides felt and confirming remarks. The bold, graceful structure, imaginatively conceived and dramatically placed, functions very much as a ritual in art form, a way of empathically recognizing and remembering the shock and grief of the families, friends, and neighbors of the more than two hundred fifty Staten Islanders who went to work in Manhattan by ferry that day and never returned. The Memorial is at once so arresting and effectively symbolic as to embody for current generations, and no doubt future ones, the horror and losses suffered that day—encompassingly through America, but in this Memorial, by the particular victims, their families, and fellow denizens of Staten Island.

Ochsner describes (as the illustrations show) the two white walls standing parallel and tall, yet as they rise higher, bending away from one another, opening to the sky while affording to someone standing between those walls a clear view of lower Manhattan, and of the place where the Twin Towers once stood. The structure itself thereby suggests flight and incompleteness—of lives, tasks, and futures undone, of challenges, disappointments, and fulfillments cut short. Within those walls too, arranged on shelves and looking toward Manhattan are silhouettes in white granite of likenesses of the faces of the victims, devised with the help of their families, almost life size, with plaques next to them giving names, birthdates, and places of work – but in no recognizable order, alphabetical or otherwise, testifying to the uniqueness of each person lost, none more important than any other and each part of the community of the mourned. The care with which the architectural team, sculptor, and families went about their work together, all dealing with the poignant fact of no remains to bury and vivid memories, is touching to read and gratifying to know about. Families opened to their grieving and memories while the architectural team provided empathic and containing listening. The process apparently translated creatively into those silhouettes at once recognizable to family and friends yet suggestive, not distinct as portraits or photographs would be – and thus proving easily imagined and identifiable with by visitors to the Memorial, some of whom evidently touch the granite silhouettes, run their fingertips gently on them.

Taken together, these essays offer moving recognition of private, shared, and communal griefs, and, in retrospect, open the consideration of loss and creativity, not alone in the magnificent Memorial but in the ways groups and individuals manage to mourn, survive – and live.

PART II

Theory, Specificity, Authenticity

7

FURTHER REFLECTIONS ON OBJECT LOSS AND MOURNING

Marion M. Oliner

Reflections on the history, the story, and the audience

Object loss, along with trauma, are concepts dear to us as psychoanalysts. My own work on these topics, and my experience of great losses early in life, make me something of an expert, but I rarely find *myself* in the literature on the subject. This reaction has given me cause for the reflections that are the subject of this essay.

A previous essay called "The Babel of Trauma," which examined the current literature on the subject, ended up in the proverbial drawer, forgotten, partly out of doubts that my criticism of well-established theories could be justified. Recently, however, I was encouraged to reexamine my response to the theories of trauma in general and object loss specifically. I had the unforgettable experience of recounting the losses I suffered during World War II in an address to a large audience at the 2007 International Psychoanalytic Congress in Berlin, where I was accorded the warmest reception imaginable.

My story told of hardships during World War II, as my family and I tried to evade deportation and death, followed by the gradual loss of everything and everyone I knew. I told of the massive struggle for me, born in Germany, to reconnect after years of analysis with love for the only identity I knew before coming to the United States. In my presentation, I tried to portray events in light of the knowledge available to the people I described when in that situation. My story pales in comparison to the stories told by survivors of concentration camps, yet it moved the audience to tears.

There were two striking aspects of this presentation that continue to preoccupy me and that I want to examine more closely: my unusual reaction to writing the presentation and the reactions of the listeners. By the time I had written it and guarded against all the foreseeable traumas, such as an empty room (I could not guard against harsh critics), I felt an uncharacteristic and unprecedented confidence in the finished product. I believe this stemmed from the conviction that I had told the truth as I see it, while accepting and stating all the possible distortions and uncertainties that accompany a personal history. It was clearly subjective, but true nevertheless. It is still hard to grasp the reaction of the listeners. The audience seemed to be grateful, personally touched, as if my story of wartime experiences and object losses had personal relevance for them, and my sharing it was a most precious gift.

In trying to understand this unexpected but most welcome reaction, I have thought, as I often do, that my trauma could not possibly compare to that of those who have truly suffered, and I suspected that this made it easier for me and the audience. This thinking, reminiscent of Primo Levi's (1988) attitude toward his experiences, is contrary to fact: I am among those who know about loss and the impact of persecution, because by age thirteen I had lost my birthplace, my nationality, my language, my possessions, my parents, and my basic trust. How is it that the audience was so moved? Some of the answer is clear. My presentation conveyed the experiences that I remember with clarity but also acknowledged uncertainty around specific emotional responses to the events when they occurred.

The facts of the immediacy, the vividness, the uncertainty, and the nature of my memories connect to my feeling that well-accepted theories do not reflect my experience. Especially fruitless is the notion that the essence of trauma consists in a breach in the stimulus barrier or excitement that overwhelms the defenses. The theory, based on a quantitative, economic approach that has otherwise been eclipsed, presumes that the victim was helpless and unprepared for the traumatogenic event. It describes a situation of utter passivity that has become one of the prototypes for understanding trauma and traumatic stress disorders (Freud, 1920, p. 29), and it accounts only for those traumas that lead to the flooding of posttraumatic stress disorder and flashbacks. We know now that this paradigm does not cover many responses to experiences generally accepted as traumatic, including mine. I will offer an alternative, in which the much-maligned defenses serve an important function by allowing loss to penetrate gradually, either when part of it becomes unavoidable or when one is ready to face a portion of it.

A more encompassing formulation of the dynamics of trauma suggests that the prototype of a traumatic event is structured entirely by the demands of external reality, eliminating the operation of the pleasure principle and unconscious fantasy, either temporarily or throughout most of life. This comes closer to most situations in which victims of traumatic loss still have defenses at their disposal that enable them to remain conscious of their surroundings, but at a very restricted level of functioning: these defenses are diminished in some respects, and heightened in others, such as perception. The recognition of this constriction informed my presentation and clearly moved the audience.

The puzzle regarding the popularity of a model of trauma that has such restricted application might be solved to some degree if we consider that the listener who hears a story of trauma or object loss, whether an analyst or not, is not prepared for it or guarded against it. In a sense, the listener confronts a traumatic history from a wider perspective than the person who is experiencing it. The defensive narrowing of consciousness and perception does not set in for the witness as it does for the person living through a calamity. We could speculate that the temporarily "defenseless" witness takes in the totality of the situation and can accept the explanatory theory of a breach in the stimulus barrier, whereas most victims experience trauma piecemeal. I do not want to be misunderstood as making light of cataclysmic events, such as that of September 11, 2001, which can and do befall people and for which their victims are unprepared. This classic theory may apply to such situations but cannot define all trauma.

My story was of losses that caused the hope and expectations of my family to diminish gradually, in which our unconscious omnipotence clung to the small victories that we won over an inevitable fate; the situation of total helplessness in which we found ourselves was mostly kept out of awareness. Even if one attempts to comprehend massive losses by identifying with a situation with all one's knowledge and faculties, one cannot know it the way most victims experience it. It is difficult or impossible to be empathic unless it is clear that the experience of the person caught in an extreme situation is *not* the same as the listener, nor, for that matter, for the one who tells the tale as it is remembered. I recounted experiences that were not known to me to their full extent until later.

The narrowed focus of the victim's knowledge is illustrated by a joke. Two policemen ring the doorbell and a woman opens the door. "Are you the widow Brown?" they ask. "No, I am Mrs. Brown" is her answer. Whereupon they respond with: "Want to bet?" An observer would grasp the poor woman's plight immediately, but not someone who has to postpone the knowledge of loss signified by the appearance of policemen at the door.

My presentation in Berlin focused on my memory of the time when the traumatic events occurred. I believe that by doing so, those events became more accessible and less strange. The presentation emphasized how victims, too, have defenses that work to prevent psychic catastrophe. The story I told included the description of such massive defenses that enabled me to survive without such symptoms as the overwhelming emotions that are so often cited in the literature as constituting trauma by causing a breach in the stimulus barrier. I believe that the audience could be moved, even to tears, because it was not overwhelmed, just as I was not shattered but seriously diminished. In emphasizing the defenses against the impact of loss, I did not minimize the lasting damage caused by the experience but made it more specific. The pathology caused by the losses and the defenses against the awareness of their magnitude led not to flashback memories but rather to emotional constriction, the prevention of further losses (Krystal, 1985, p. 152), and depression. The audience apparently understood that to undo some of the consequences, many years of analysis were needed.

Reflections on object loss without mourning

When I crossed the ocean after the war, I made the conscious resolve not to look back because I believed that I would drown if I turned around. A picture of the vast Atlantic Ocean as my grave accompanied this thought. In a similar vein, in

the Bible, the angels warned Lot and his family, the sole survivors of the destruction of Sodom and Gomorrah, "do not look back or you will turn into pillars of
salt" (Genesis 19:26). Thus the usefulness of memory for the process of mourning
was questioned: remembering came with the warning of the possibility of death,
inertia, and petrification. But the literature on mourning appeared to lean toward
considering this attitude a failure, and therefore I felt that I had failed to appreciate the virtue of remembering. Upon further reflection, I realized, as so often in
other quests for understanding, that in psychoanalytic thinking there are very few, if
any, absolutes. Most understanding comes from appreciating the context in which
behavior occurs, and in my case the context involved the total destruction of the
world I knew. Hence, the need to look ahead and outside took precedence over
remembering, because it promoted life.

The Jewish ritual of mourning starts with the washing of hands after the funeral
before the survivors enter the house where the Shiv'a takes place, because contact
with death is considered a contamination. Once inside the mourners are helped to
remember the dead: mirrors are covered and friends and neighbors bring food to
facilitate this process. But what is supposed to be done in the service of memory
actually involves replenishment for the mourners.

The induced passivity treats mourners as diminished, also symbolized by the
covered mirrors. In "Mourning and Melancholia," Freud (1917) suggested tenta-
tively that mourning involves the loss of the *object* whereas in melancholia, there is
loss of self-esteem. It may be more accurate to think that in mourning, the ego is
also diminished through loss and that internalization could be viewed as strengthening the ego, by its *being* the object: the prelude to mourning.

In Freud's formulation, the internalization of the object has a specific result:
the creation of the superego, which, when coupled with aggression, results in the
famous "shadow of the object" that falls on the subject. Thus the superego, which is
set apart from the ego, has more of the qualities of an object than the ego internalizations that involve *becoming* the object. Freud's account is almost too well known
to be repeated here, but I shall nevertheless include it in order to compare it with
some notions I have derived from Loewald's work that I find more helpful. According to Freud (1917),

> An object-choice, an attachment of the libido to a particular person, had at
> one time existed; then, owing to a real slight or disappointment coming from
> this loved person, the object-relationship was shattered. The result was not
> the normal one of a withdrawal of the libido from this object and a displace-
> ment of it on to a new one, but something different, for whose coming-about
> various conditions seem to be necessary. The object cathexis proved to have
> little power of resistance and was brought to an end. But the free libido was
> not displaced on to another object; it was withdrawn into the ego. There,
> however, it was not employed in any unspecified way, but served to establish
> an identification of the ego with the abandoned object. Thus the shadow of
> the object fell upon the ego, and the latter could henceforth be judged by a

special agency, as though it were an object, the forsaken object. In this way an object loss was transformed into an ego loss and the conflict between the ego and the loved person into a cleavage between the critical activity of the ego and the ego as altered by identification. [p. 249]

The lack of clarity in this well-known passage concerns the specificity of the "abandoned object," as if the process of internalization were restricted to "forsaken objects." It seems to me that rather than regarding the process described by Freud as applicable only in special cases, the process of *being* the object, which constitutes identification, might better be regarded as a universal reaction to loss. We are dealing with objects that do not survive and therefore are not dependable. This, I believe, applies to all 'lost' objects.

Loewald (1962) introduces a different way to view the conversion from outside to inside: the object ceases to be "objectified" and the ego is enlarged as a result. Thus the change from object love to narcissism causes a deadening of emotions. According to Loewald's notion, identification with the lost object leads to the enlargement of the ego prior to any freeing up of object libido for new objects. This complicates the picture of mourning. When *new* objects are invested again after the period necessary for mourning, they are genuinely *new* for reasons that Loewald explains: having undergone the transformations caused by the process of identification, the new objects are invested differently than the old loves. As he points out, were the libido withdrawn from incestuous objects reinvested in unmodified form in new objects, these new objects relations would essentially be infantile, incestuous, and therefore forbidden.

Sources of replenishment

The enlargement of the ego as a result of the internalization of the lost object enables the individual to use the senses to reconnect with the outside world. As I mentioned earlier, massive losses also include aspects of the inanimate world, so that the subsequent process of taking in the (new) external world through the senses complements, in an important way, the ritual preliminary meal. Turning away from losses and replenishing oneself by all means possible relies on the denial that is supported by unconscious omnipotence and manifested by *enabling fantasies* (Gottlieb, 1997). That this *use* of the external world is related to mania goes without saying, but it is distinguished from it by its temporary nature and by a sense of reality that tempers unconscious omnipotence. This "refueling" should not be confused with Winnicott's (1969) notion of *use* which entails the acceptance of and attachment to a dependable object that remains outside the individual's sphere of omnipotence. Instead, the first use that an individual whose objects did not survive destruction can make of the external world is more in the nature of an extension of a narcissistic enhancement. I am suggesting that *conscious* coping, being "realistic" or even opportunistic, and knowing how to limit one's expectations can act in the service of *unconscious* omnipotence, as I suggest in my book, *Psychic Reality in Context*:

> The defense on which survival [after massive losses] depends, in that it per-
> mits the adaptive attitude toward external conditions, is indeed *realistic* and
> basic to a productive life, while at the same time, reinforcing an irrational
> sense of omnipotence.
>
> [Oliner, 2012, p. 35]

I now think that this unconscious omnipotence, based on one's ability to adapt to
ever-changing realities (life lived as a sausage ready to be sliced), served to buttress
my previous belief in the efficacy of dissociation and denial as factors favorable to
the coping with loss. This notion has been supported by quotations from other
observers; thus reports by survivors, and those who have treated them, stress the
eclipsing of the sense of self, which I have questioned:

> Whether or not an individual can be cut off from emotions and inner pro-
> cesses, and, if so, to what degree and for how long, is a question that requires
> more thinking about. Do we assume that the person does not sleep and does
> not dream? It corresponds to the illusion created by the total attunement to
> the external world in order to survive, but still be untenable as a theory about
> the way the mind functions.
>
> [Oliner, 2012, pp. 7–8]

The duality of the inner and the external world has made it difficult to discuss the interaction between the two, and thus the role of the external world as
a source for replenishment and stimulation has been minimized in the literature.
Therefore I shall return once more to that aspect of experience before attempting
to suggest how they might be seen in relation to each other, while doing justice
to both.

The German analyst Ilse Grubrich-Simitis (2004) demonstrates how Freud's
conflict concerning the impact of external attributes as against internal factors
became manifest. In her meticulous analysis of Freud's interpretation of Michelangelo's statue of Moses (Freud, 1914a), she stresses his heightened sensitivity to
sensory stimuli. She is struck by his concentration on the *visual* details of the work
in order to understand its meaning and points to Freud's conscious conflict manifest in this exclusive focus on externality. According to Grubrich-Simitis, Freud
nevertheless persisted, thereby overlooking the issue of mortality that is essential to
the meaning of the statue. She suggests that experiences of childhood loss, leading
to discontinuities in his life, might have predisposed Freud to this intense response
to art and the concreteness of his reaction, which restored unity (Grubrich-Simitis,
2004, p. 49).

Marcel Proust also seems to have compensated for childhood trauma with a
keenness of observation. In a charming passage in his epic novel, *Remembrance of
Things Past*, he alludes to the importance of the perceptible world by describing
how *taste* functions to connect the individual to the past. The taste of a *madeleine*
dipped in tea brings back to life a world that was dead to the narrator. In this

context, Proust introduces a Celtic belief to describe this life-giving process, and its dependence on the qualities inherent in the material object:

> According to that belief, the souls of those we have lost are captive inside an inferior being. We liberate the souls from the spell if by chance we come close to one of these. Being liberated by us, they have triumphed over death and come to live with us.
>
> [Proust, 1913, p. 59]

This lovely, poetic invocation depicts the power of the material world over our innermost being: its capacity to bring the past to life. Thus the taste of the *madeleine* is the key to the resurrection of a lost world (Oliner, 2012, p. 68). Proust elaborates further:

> And so it is with our own past. It is a labour in vain to attempt to recapture it: all efforts of our intellect must prove futile. The past is hidden somewhere outside the realm, beyond the reach of the intellect, in some material object (in the sensations which this material object would give us) of which we have no inkling. And it depends on chance whether or not we come upon this object before we ourselves die. [1913, pp. 59–60]

> But when from a long-distant past nothing subsists, after the people are dead, after the things are broken and scattered, taste and smell alone, more fragile but more enduring, more immaterial, more persistent, more faithful, remain poised a long time, like souls, remembering, waiting, hoping amid the ruins of all the rest; and bear unflinchingly, in the tiny and almost impalpable drop of their essence, the vast structure of recollection. [pp. 63–64]

While I believe that the psychoanalytic literature tends to underestimate the importance of the external world, especially after object loss, Proust's exclusion of the inner world, as evocative and beautiful as it is, has to be taken as poetic license. It is based on the same illusion as that which promotes the feeling among survivors of object loss: that *new* experiences after massive losses are *replacements*, dissociated from the trauma. I am now convinced that this belief is based on the defenses needed to survive traumatic losses, supported by the psychoanalytic literature that emphasizes dissociation and loss of self. It is based on the image many survivors have of their new lives and supports unconscious omnipotence, which according to Winnicott (1960) accompanies every experience of trauma.

Silent nightly processes

I have stressed throughout the previous sections that the picture of the traumatized individual, unable to integrate emotionally the losses they have suffered, leaves out something that escapes notice; the picture of a fragmented or divided person is a partial picture, to which we need to add an important element. I have alluded to the unforeseen impact of my retelling in Berlin of the events associated with the destruction of the world I knew, namely, its unexpected healing consequences. Most surprising was the way it influenced what happens in my sleep. In my autobiographical sketch I mentioned that:

> I have had a recurrent dream, which causes me to wake up in a low mood. With minor variations, it starts with my being in a new apartment or house. The last dream took place in a house. We had just moved in, and I did not like the way the furniture was placed, but I did not know if my husband would agree to a change. He will say that it is too much work. The house was well constructed and had twenty acres of land around it. I said to myself that I should be happy with it, but I keep trying to understand why we sold the old one, the one about which my daughter said: you have to buy it, this is "your" house and then we bought it. The new one is sturdier, it has more ground, but when I look out the window I don't see the acreage, and what I see are some poorly growing shrubs without greenery. Why did we sell the house on the water with the beautiful view? Was there something financial? Perhaps, but surely the construction of the new one is better, and so the argument goes as I try to think of the new house as a potential improvement. I wake up sad, feeling that I lost something I loved, and only slowly, it comes to me that the loss was only in a dream and that I still have the old house.
>
> [Oliner, 2012, p. xxxii]

This was in fact the last occurrence of this dream. After the presentation in Berlin led to its disappearance, I was reminded of the power and the mystery of the unconscious and the role of sleeping and dreaming in the integration of the personality, even after massive trauma.

The process that literally takes place in the dark and brings an elusive source of strength to the individual consists of a constant effort to integrate that which in waking life is kept separate. From this perspective, those individuals who saw themselves as being able to live "next to their trauma" were most likely able to make a sharp division between their dreams and waking reality. We cannot know the part played by the traumatizing events during sleep. The isolation between the two states of consciousness keeps nightly attempts at integration between inside and outside, past and present out of awareness, preventing a premature return to a past that has not yet been mourned, and therefore only on the way to being appropriately integrated. The integration during *sleep* uses the residue of the previous day, makes it available to the senses (either visually or through sound or touch), and attempts to integrate it with the inner world of the sleeper. This presupposes that the ordinary function attributed to dreams will eventually gain the upper hand. It is this part of human endowment that consists of *repeating emotionally charged experiences by making them real* — in dreams (Freud, 1914b, p. 151) or in actions — that will manifest itself again and again and eventually bring and bestow a greater sense of *self* on the experience of external reality. Thus the posttraumatic, gratifying *sensory* experiences with the external world, previously described as replenishing the ego, can also function as the *day residues* that instigate a nightly integration between past and present. When defenses are successful, the narcissism of the individual, based on unconscious omnipotence, is sufficiently gratified to allow the dreaming part of the personality greater access to the integrative process, and paves the way for denial to yield gradually to genuine, conscious mourning. It is the incremental meeting of the inner and outer world, represented in tangible form (Oliner, 2010).

The external world, necessary for the ego depleted by loss and absence, can be considered the equivalent of food that the body needs for survival. But the intake of food is useless without an intact digestive system that works to extract its vital energy. The same is true of the sensory impressions that connect the individual to the here and now. They must undergo a process of assimilation and metabolization, which takes place just as automatically as the use of food for nourishment. Once more, this depends on the individual's capacity to disengage from the external world enough to sleep, and during sleep, to use the sensory impressions from the external world to form a dream. In successful cases, this allows the meeting between the inner and outer world and the beginning of their integration. According to Botella & Botella (2007, p. 31), dream work, which takes place in silence, is neither perceptible nor conscious, but has the same dynamic and economic value as those processes accessible to consciousness while awake. They stress that dreaming is a constraint necessary for the survival of psychic life. It is the place at which two modes of comprehension meet, creating a symmetry necessary for psychic equilibrium and permitting the dreamer to succeed where waking reality fails (paraphrased from Botella & Botella, 2007, p. 36, my translation).

In this way, conscious adaptation to present reality masks the awareness of the past, which in most cases is evident in mourners' implicit experience of the objects in their present life as *stand-ins* for the lost ones, a sign that loss continues to be registered in some part of the mind. And despite the impoverishment of fantasy life and the tendency toward a factual approach to experience, the ability of traumatized individuals to distinguish between day and night is essential to maintain the certainty of the substitute nature of the gratifications they can obtain and the derivative nature of love, thereby avoiding a manic solution to object loss. I believe that the problem of denial of loss is the reason for Hillel Klein's considering survivor guilt as a desirable phenomenon (Klein, Biermann, & Nedelmann, 2003). This caution was especially applicable to Israel, where Klein lived and functioned, as the country was built on a break with the past, that is, the break between Jews being abjectly murdered and Jews building and planting new life. As an analyst living within this cultural phenomenon, he learned firsthand to respect the interplay between the focus on the positive perceptual world and the psychic reality of devastating losses, without losing sight of either one.

Unfortunately, some survivors of massive losses have serious difficulties with sleep, some temporarily and some for rest of their lives. This was true of a woman who survived the murder of her parents in Auschwitz. She claimed that she was always a poor sleeper, but it is also possible that her difficulties with sleep were exacerbated by the remarkable manner in which she was told about the fate of her family. At the time, her Swiss foster parents took her to a special place where she was told that her parents perished, and then she was put to sleep for two weeks. It is the only time I have heard of this procedure based on the belief in the benefits of sleep. It is possible that this artificial intervention may have deprived her of a more normal way of processing this knowledge and interfered with her ability to sleep for the rest of her life.

Not every sufferer is able to sleep and forget his or her dreams. But those who can may well return to the past during sleep in a way that is tolerable to the sleeper. I may have been one of those fortunate ones, because I only remember one dream in the year after my parents were deported: we were together in India, riding on an elephant as if in a parade, and I had a problem keeping myself from slipping down the side of the elephant. Waking up was upsetting because I had to confront my loss. Forgetting nighttime activities that reworked the past allowed me to maintain an orientation to the present reality, as if the past had no relevance for the present and could be ignored. Keeping this conscious organization intact avoided the regressive search for perceptual identity – looking for the hallucinatory dream images upon waking – and with this, the prevention of unbearable pain over losses that had yet to be mourned.

In my own case, psychoanalytic treatment was essential. Unconscious omnipotence, the great *enabler* available to many survivors, also becomes the great accuser. When it is not manifested in survivor guilt, it is evident in an underdeveloped, unrealistic sense of self. The sense of loss that I thought I was not facing was evident in my never confusing the substitute character of the persons in my life who seemed to take the place of my parents, despite my faith in the solution I adopted in the many years before I consulted analysts. I felt inferior because I did have a family until I married an American. This choice was conscious and based on my wish for my children to have their own country and their own language, just like their father's. I did not make my own history taboo, but in order to "spare" them, I created distance.

In this way of thinking, a favorable outcome depends on the capacity to dream. It entails the ability to enter a state in which external reality is allowed to fade from consciousness. In a sense it is letting go of an anchor, possibly the only anchor after massive losses. When this is possible, it allows for daytime eclipsing of the loss and adaptation to the new, while refinding vestiges of what remains of the old during sleep, out of conscious awareness. Those objects that are lost are reminiscent of objects that do not survive destruction, as described in Winnicott's article, "The Use of the Object" (1969): the process of waking obliterates them, because objects that do not survive are useless. As I understand it, the destruction manifests itself in forgetting. Before they are properly mourned, these remembered lost objects are only burdensome until the integration of past and present is underway. This process, which can clearly only be inferred, is based on my own experience and the evidence I have observed.

Conclusion

My reflections on object loss are meant to include not only the loss of persons, but also of the very important assets constituted by language, home, and nationality. I have referred to the defenses against the experience of loss and their long-term consequences. The need to forget loss can harden the personality to the point at which the practice (of forgetting) has been made perfect, according to the motto "out of sight, out of mind." Recently I became aware that the need to forget does not apply to the *visibly* intact graves of my maternal grandparents who are buried in the town in which I was born. I experience their physical presence as a form of survival, and I visit their resting place every time I am in that town, whereas I have a horror at the thought of visiting any concentration camp, because of their total annihilation of memory, in the place of graves that would confirm the reality of history.

Survivors are always engaged in trauma prevention, which Krystal (1985, p. 152) rightly considers an important motivation in the lives of individuals who have suffered massive losses. Separations are extremely painful, and the refinding of the lost is henceforth fraught with anxiety. In order to go on living, the conscious reliving of memories of the past, including those of the persons we loved, has to be able to be obliterated. Until mourned, the lost are experienced as objects on which one cannot depend, but we can assume that the world we think of as lost comes back to us at night without our realizing it. Should we also accept that the need to detach from a useless past makes us complicit in its disappearance? Most likely this is true in everyday existence, but our mysterious unconscious processes render the past immortal.

References

Botella, C., & Botella, S. (2007). *La Figurabilité Psychique*. Paris: Editions in Press.

Freud, S. (1914a). Der Moses des Michelangelo. *Gesammelte Werke* (10:171–201). London: Imago, 1946.

Freud, S. (1914b). Remembering, repeating, and working through. Standard Edition, 12:145–156, London: Hogarth Press, 1956.

Freud, S. (1917). Mourning and melancholia. Standard Edition, 14:239–260, London: Hogarth Press, 1957.

Freud, S. (1920). Beyond the pleasure principle. Standard Edition, 18:3–66. London: Hogarth Press, 1955.

Gottlieb, R.M. (1997). Does the mind fall apart in multiple personality disorder? Some proposals based on a psychoanalytic case. *J. Amer. Psychoanal. Assn.*, 45:907–932.

Grubrich-Simitis, I. (2004). *Michelangelo's* Moses *und Freud's* Wagstück. Frankfurt: S. Fischer.

Klein, H., Biermann, C., & Nedelmann, C., eds (2003). *Überleben und Versuche der Wiederbelebung*. Stuttgart: Friedrich Fromann Verlag Günther Holzboog.

Krystal, H. (1985). Trauma and the stimulus barrier. *Psychoanal. Inq.*, 5:131–161.

Levi, P. (1988). *The Drowned and the Saved*. New York: Summit Books.

Loewald, H. (1962). Internalization, separation, mourning, and the superego. In: *The Essential Loewald Collected Papers and Monographs*, ed. N. Quist. Hagerstown, Maryland: University Publishing Group, 2000, pp. 257–276.

Oliner, M.M. (2010). Life is not a dream: The importance of being real. *J. Amer. Psychoanal. Assn.*, 58:1139–1157.

Oliner, M.M. (2012). *Psychic Reality in Context: Perspectives on Psychoanalysis, Personal History and Trauma*. London: Karnac.

Proust, M. (1913). *Remembrance of Things Past*, trans. C.K. Moncrieff & T. Killmartin. New York: The Modern Library, 2003.

Winnicott, D. (1960). The theory of the parent-infant relationship. *Internat. J. Psycho-Anal.*, 41:585–595.

Winnicott, D.W. (1969). The use of an object and relating through identification. In: *Playing and Reality*, New York: Basic Books, 1971, pp. 86–94.

8

THE FUNCTION OF MEMORIAL SPACES

Mourning Following Multiple Traumatic Losses

Anna Ornstein

Introduction

This paper was presented at a panel whose members were charged with the task of describing their personal experience of mourning the loss of an important individual in their lives.[1] I first attempted in 2008 to articulate what I had felt over the years about the loss of my father, two brothers, and most members of my extended family in the Holocaust (Ornstein, 2010). The writing and presentation of that paper was an important part of my mourning process. The wish to share my personal experience brought forth aspects of my mourning of which I was previously not aware. The present article is an effort to further reflect on this lifelong process.

As psychoanalysts, we concern ourselves with the *subjective experience* of mourning. However, in much of the psychoanalytic literature, these experiences are described in a highly abstract language, and individual differences are not taken into consideration. But abstract, metapsychological formulations do not provide guidelines for intervention; only a particular individual's subjective experience determines the severity and duration of the mourning process. When and how the process begins and how severely the bereaved is affected depends on a variety of factors: did the loss occur after a prolonged and painful illness, during which time mourning might have already begun? Or did the loss occur suddenly so that it will take some time before the reality of death can be accepted? Was it a parent who lost a child? Was it a grown child who lost an elderly parent? Or was it a spouse who was lost after a long and harmonious marriage, or a marriage that was fraught with ambivalence? It is in this last situation that mourning may be most heavily burdened by conscious and unconscious guilt and may become the source of a severe depression.

Joan Didion (2005) describes the difference in her reaction to the expected deaths of her elderly parents and to the deaths of her husband and only child.

Following the death of her parents, she felt sad, "regret for time gone by, for things unsaid," but the grief she felt upon the unexpected loss of her husband and child was different. "Grief," she wrote, "is not what we expect it to be, it comes in waves, paroxysms, sudden apprehensions that weaken the knees, and blind the eyes and obliterate the daily rhythm of life . . . (it) interferes with the ability to think and to eat" (pp. 26–27).

Mourning following multiple losses under traumatic conditions

In cases of multiple, traumatic losses, during which the bereaved themselves lived through potentially traumatizing situations, survivors of extreme conditions (genocide, mass killings, natural disasters) need time for physical and emotional recovery before they can engage in the painful process of mourning. At first, many of the defenses – primarily disavowal, the numbing of emotions, and a restricted vision of life – that were necessary to survive the traumatic situations have to be left in place until such time when the agony of acute grief can be experienced without the fear of becoming overwhelmed and rendered dysfunctional. Many survivors of the Holocaust were unable to mourn for many years; they avoided places that would trigger their memories, and with them, their unbearable grief. From a different theoretical perspective, but expressing essentially the same thing, Blum (2003) states that "numbing of affect and narrowing of thought may serve as a *temporary moratorium* during which the traumatized ego can begin to recover its usual organization and defensive constellation" (p. 426).

Bowlby (1961) considered the loss of a loved one to be one of the most painful experiences a human being can suffer. Other psychoanalysts described this pain in various ways: as the "agony of grief" (Hagman 1995, p. 190), as a narcissistic wound (Jacobson, 1965), as a feeling as if one had lost part of one's self (Parkes, 1972). And mourning needs "another": Furman (1974) made the observation that "mourning alone is an almost impossible task even for a mature adult" (p. 114). But Holocaust survivors dared not speak of their losses, nor could they feel free to share memories of their own traumatic experiences. Sharing memories was risky because of the fear of an indifferent or an incredulous response. Subjectively, the inability to share creates a sense of alienation from one's human environment. Memories of torture, of hunger, or of witnessing the slow death by starvation of a sister or a brother can only be shared with those we expect to listen with respect and understanding; indifference and dismissal or a quick reassurance reinforce the bereaved's sense of alienation. Alienation is also a familiar experience for those who suffered individual losses. Losing his young wife after a short illness, Stolorow (1999) described his sense of alienation as an "an unbridgeable gulf" that seemed to have opened up between him and his friends and colleagues (p. 465). He felt that they could never even begin to fathom his experience because he and they now lived in altogether different worlds.

A lessening of the sense of alienation may occur under unexpected circumstances. I had this experience while watching the film, *Schindler's List* (Spielberg, 1993). Many scenes of the movie were filmed in the camp where my mother and I worked in a stone quarry during the summer of 1944 (Fig. 8.1). Sharing at least

FIGURE 8.1 A former set for Steven Spielberg's *Schindler's List* in the Liban quarry, Poland, where Anna Ornstein and her mother worked while imprisoned by the Nazis. In the nearby Plaszów camp, built on the site of actual Jewish graveyards, prisoners were forced to excavate and use Jewish tombstones to build roads. This replica was made from cement casts of gravestones.

the location of horror with so many people, I felt that by watching the movie with me they were in a better position to understand what my mother and I had witnessed and survived. This made me feel closer to complete strangers in the audience.

Though there are many similarities in the process of mourning irrespective of the conditions under which the loss occurred, there are also fundamental differences between the process of mourning under ordinary circumstances and mourning following genocide. Under civilized conditions, the bereaved is usually surrounded by loved ones, children, friends and members of the community, but survivors of genocide are members of a group in which everyone has suffered the loss of family, home, and community. In an intact community, after the loss of an individual, ritual memorialization is taken for granted as this is commended by most religions and societies. In contrast, in mass tragedies where the bodies of the dead are lost on an ocean floor, in mass graves, or in a cloud of black smoke, these rituals cannot be observed. There are no funerals in which the finality of death can be acknowledged, an experience that facilitates the mourning process. There are no memorial services during which members of the community commemorate the virtues of the deceased. Survivors of the 9/11 tragedy said that not having a body to bury or to cremate affected their ability to mourn. The attack took not only the lives of their loved ones, it also took their deaths. In instances of genocide, whole communities, too, are destroyed and everyone who survives is bereaved. This, however, may become a source of solace for the survivors who develop special bonds and provide each other with what they need most at first: help in creating a community that supports their efforts to pick up the threads of their disrupted lives.

The Second World War ended in Europe in 1945, but written accounts of survivors' experiences and reflections on the magnitude of their losses began to appear only fifteen to twenty years later. It took me, personally, until 1962, that is, seventeen years after the war, to experience the pain of acute grief. I remember the experience vividly. By 1962, we were comfortably settled in a beautiful big house in Cincinnati and were enjoying the fruits of our studies as we became deeply engaged in our academic work and in our private practices. It was then, on a sunny morning in our living room, as I was watching our three children (ages nine, four, and two) playing together that I experienced for the first time a sharp, piercing pain around my heart and felt that I had to scream out laud in order to relieve the heaviness in my chest. I left the room and behind closed doors began to sob in a way I have not cried before. What happened here? As I was watching the children, my thoughts wandered to my father and my two brothers who could not witness this scene; it was then that a profound sense of acute grief and rage hit me with unexpected force.

Since then, I have heard not only from other survivors of the Holocaust, but also from those whose losses occurred under ordinary circumstances, that it is on happy occasions, especially when these are associated with their children or grandchildren, that their thoughts turn to the lost members of their families, and it is then their joy becomes mixed with grief.[2] I had learned to appreciate the significance that these emotions have for mourning, but how to conceptualize the simultaneous presence of two such contradictory emotions? I suggest that the establishment of new intimate relationships (such as building a new family) provides new selfobjects that are necessary to consolidate a survivor's traumatized self. Once the self is better integrated and firmed up, all kinds of affects, painful and joyful ones, can emerge safely without the threat of fragmentation. Such dramatic moments when profound joy "permits" the emergence of grief are most likely preceded by the internalization of idealized features of the lost members of one's original family.

I found confirmation of the relationship between mourning and the ability to experience joy in a short but significant paper by Freud (1916), titled *On Transience*. Freud described a conversation he imagined having had with the poet Rainer Maria Rilke and Lou Andreas Salome, in which the two expressed their inability to enjoy the beauty of the Alpine surround. Freud related this to Rilke's awareness that, in the end, all living things have to die. Although Freud could not dispute the transience of all living things, he did dispute the pessimistic view of the poet that transience diminishes nature's beauty. On the contrary, he writes, transience increases nature's beauty, because "transience value is scarcity value in time" (p. 305). He came to the conclusion that what spoiled Rilke's and Salome's "enjoyment of beauty must have been a revolt (resistance) against mourning" (p. 306). Freud considered the ability to mourn a precondition for the ability to experience joy; in his view, it is only after old attachments have been given up (decathected) could one invest joyfully again in life. I am suggesting that this process occurs in the *reverse* order: it is only after one's self is strengthened by the presence of empathically responsive others that the pain of acute grief can be fully experienced (Ornstein, 1985).

Freud considered the reparative function of mourning to be related to what he considered the final phase of this process, to the process of identification. My own observation and theoretical orientation favors what Kohut (1971, 1977) called "transmuting or micro-internalization processes." In this process, the functions that the lost "other" had for the mourner's self are broken down and internalized, especially those functions that have been relied on to repair, sustain, and regulate aspects of the self. What needs recognition, writes Hagman (1995, 1996), is that the compulsively recalled, innumerable memories of the dead are not simply

> static images from the past. They have a dynamic, selfobject function in the maintenance and restoration of the bereaved current self-state. Little by little, as these selfobject functions are revoked independent of the object's presence, many are microinternalized becoming part of the bereaved self-structure.
>
> [1995, p. 199]

This is in keeping with Kernberg's (2010) idea that mourning results in a structural change in the psyche. I believe that the process of internalization is enhanced by the idealization of the lost object(s). As the youngest of three siblings, I considered my two (three and five years older) brothers to be very bright. I was convinced that had they lived, they would have pursued academic careers. Though I always dreamed of becoming a physician, still, I think that my idealization of them and my internalization of their ambition were crucial in my decision to embark on an academic career.

Collective memorialization and the therapeutic action of "memorial spaces"

Finding it difficult to share their memories and their grief, many survivors began to write their memoirs shortly after the war. How writing, similar to a psychoanalytic dialogue, "liberates" affect and facilitates mourning is beautifully captured by David Grossman (2007), a writer whose son was killed in one of the Israeli wars:

> I write. In the wake of the death of my son Uri . . . the awareness of what happened has sunk into every cell of mine. The power of memory is indeed enormous and heavy, and at times has a paralyzing quality to it. Nevertheless, the act of writing itself at this time creates for me a type of "space," a mental territory that I had never experienced before, where death is not only the absolute and one dimensional negation of life. I write and I feel how the correct and precise use of words is like a remedy to an illness.
>
> [p. 30]

In the absence of culturally and/or religiously sanctioned mourning rituals, survivors of major trauma can find opportunities for *belated mourning* by writing or reading memoirs or poems, listening to memorial music, or attending art exhibitions that deal with the topic of loss. Memorial art, literature, sites, and structures offer opportunities for belated mourning because they themselves are efforts to complete the work of bereavement; they have the power to bring the past into the present in such a way that earlier feelings that had laid dormant for a long time can break through and retroactively reshape the present: they create an *après-coup* phenomenon. The *après-coup* phenomenon resides in the complex relationship between the work of art and its audience: "The dynamic psychological effects of artistic experience seem always to lie in the shared experiential space between the subjective reality of the individual viewer (reader or listener) and the artistic personality of the work's creator" (Rotenberg, 1988, p. 195). Memorial art and literature create what Bernstein terms a "memorial space," communicating affects that facilitate the emergence of similar feelings in the reader or listener.[3] A memorial space refers to an *experience*, not to a physical "place"; whether created by a site, through the act of reading a poem or a memoir, or by viewing a painting or sculpture, a memorial space is a mental "territory" in which "*the past is not simply remembered but is instead actively mourned*" (Bernstein, 2000, p. 347, emphasis mine).

My view, that survivors of the Holocaust were able to mourn their enormous losses belatedly and were able to live creative and productive lives, is not shared by many authors who wrote extensively about them (Barocas & Barocas, 1979; Bergman & Jucovy, 1982; Kestenberg, 1977; Krystal, 1968; Niederland, 1968). In the opinion of these authors, their inability to share their memories and their overwhelming survivor guilt creates an insurmountable resistance to mourning. I believe that this very pessimistic attitude may have deprived survivors who needed professional help of the opportunity to use their therapists and analysts as new selfobjects, allowing them to live life with renewed vigor and a capacity for joy.

In my view, in the absence, or only sporadic presence of professional help, most survivors found alternate ways of mourning. One such opportunity available for them was to write their memoirs. As Ogden (2000) has so aptly put it:

> I suggest that successful mourning centrally involves a demand that we make on ourselves to create something – whether it be a memory, a dream, a story, a response to a poem – that begins to meet, to be equal to, the full complexity of our relationship to what has been lost and to the experience of the loss itself.
>
> [p. 65]

Survivors also can use their relationships with fellow survivors to mourn; here, few words are needed to feel understood and to have the depth of their grief fully appreciated.

Summary

Since mourning is a highly individual matter, generalizations regarding the difference between mourning a single individual under civilized conditions and mourning multiple losses under traumatic conditions are not particularly helpful. There are a few features that set these two mourning processes apart: in mourning following a major disaster, the bereaved themselves lived through extreme conditions that require a period of recovery, which explains the delay in mourning. In cases of belated mourning, the capacity to experience acute grief is signaled by the appearance of intense affects – joy, grief, and rage. The pain of acute grief is then welcome because mourning is not about forgetting, but about remembering.

Multiple losses that occur under extremely traumatic conditions destroy the bodies of the deceased, which can also delay the grieving process. In addition, major disasters destroy whole communities and everyone who survives the calamity is bereaved. What may well be true for all mourners regardless of the circumstances under which they suffered their losses, is that all may create memorial spaces through their own creative activities and by responding to memorial art, literature, and sites of remembrance with reactivated grief. Memorial spaces are particularly helpful following multiple traumatic losses because they respond to a deeply felt need to articulate that which survivors of major tragedies experience as unspeakable and unsharable.

Notes

1 An earlier version of this paper was given at the panel, "Mourning, Identity, Creativity" at the American Psychoanalytic Association Meetings in New York, January 2013.
2 The juxtaposition of destruction and redemption is the oldest of Jewish paradigms. The commemoration of the Holocaust *(Yom H'Shoa)* is held on the day when the Warsaw

ghetto uprising began: the heroism of the ghetto fighters is celebrated along with the mourning of the destruction of Europe's Jewish population. This solemn day is then followed by the exuberant celebration of the establishment of the State of Israel.

3 I am using this concept in a different sense than did Shimon Attie (1994) when he projected photographic images onto buildings in Berlin where Jews used to live prior to WWII. He thus created potential *places* in which the past could come alive in the present. Memorial *spaces*, on the other hand, are created in response to memorial places and to a variety of memorial art.

References

Attie, S. (1994). *The Writing on the Wall: Projections in Berlin's Jewish Quarter*. Heidelberg: Edition Braus.

Barocas, H.A., & Barocas, C.B. (1979). Wounds of the fathers: The next generation of Holocaust victims. *Internat. Rev. Psycho-Anal.*, 6:331–340.

Bergmann, M.S., & Jucovy, M.E., eds (1982). *Generations of the Holocaust*. New York: Basic Books.

Bernstein, J.W. (2000). Making a memorial place: The photography of Shimon Attie. *Psychoanal. Dial.*, 10:347–370.

Blum, H.P. (2003). Psychic trauma and traumatic object loss. *J. Amer. Psychoanal. Assn.*, 51:415–431.

Bowlby, J. (1961). Processes of mourning. *Internat. J. Psycho-Anal.*, 42:317–340.

Didion, J. (2005). *The Year of Magical Thinking*. New York: Alfred Knopf.

Freud, S. (1916). *On transience*. Standard Edition, 14:303–307. London: Hogarth Press, 1950.

Furman, E. (1974). *A Child's Parent Dies: Studies in Childhood Bereavement*. New Haven: Yale University Press.

Grossman, D. (2007). Writing in the dark. *The New York Times*, May 13, 2007, pp. 28–31.

Hagman, G. (1995). Death of a selfobject: Toward a self psychology of the mourning process. *Prog. Self Psychol.*, 11:189–205.

Hagman, G. (1996). The role of the other in mourning. *Psychoanal. Q.*, 6:327–352.

Jacobson, E. (1965). The return of the lost parent. In: *Drives, Affects and Behavior, Volume Two: Essays in Memory of Marie Bonaparte*, ed. M. Schur. New York: International Universities Press.

Kernberg, O. (2010). Some observations on the process of mourning. *Internat. J. Psycho-anal.*, 91:601–619.

Kestenberg, J. (1977). The psychological consequences of punitive institutions. In: *Humanizing America: A Post-Holocaust Imperative*, ed. J. Knopp, National Institute on the Holocaust. Philadelphia: Temple University Press, pp. 204–219.

Kohut, H. (1971). *The Analysis of the Self*. New York: International Universities Press.

Kohut, H. (1977). *The Restoration of the Self*. New York: International Universities Press.

Krystal, H., ed. (1968). *Massive Psychic Trauma*. New York: International Universities Press.

Ogden, T.H. (2000). Borges and the art of mourning. *Psychoanal. Dial.*, 10:65–88.

Ornstein, A. (1985). Survival and recovery. *Psychoanal. Inq.*, 5:99–130.

Ornstein, A. (2010). The missing tombstone: Reflections on mourning and creativity. *J. Amer. Psychoanal. Assn.*, 58:631–648.

Niederland, W.G. (1968). Clinical observations on the "survivor syndrome." *Internat. J. Psycho-Anal.*, 49:313–315.

Parkes, C. (1972). *Bereavement: Studies of Grief in Adult Life*. New York: International Universities Press.

Rotenbreg, C. (1988). Selfobject theory and the artistic process. *Prog. Self Psych.*, 4:193–213.

Spielberg, S., dir. (1993). Schindler's List. Universal Pictures.

Stolorow, R. (1999). The phenomenology of trauma and the absolutisms of everyday life: Personal journey. *Psychoanal. Psych.*, 16:464–469.

9

THE LONG-TERM EFFECTS OF THE MOURNING PROCESS

Otto F. Kernberg

In an earlier paper (Kernberg, 2010), I pointed to some aspects of the mourning process that in my view had not been considered sufficiently in the literature. I proposed that mourning is a permanent process that has a profound impact on the structures of the mind, on object relations in general, and on the capacity to deepen the understanding of subjective experiences of self and others. In that previous effort, I wrote that the mourning process culminates in the consolidation of a permanent relationship with the lost object, while internalizing some aspects of the object's characteristics as part of the self-experience. This development points to the double process of identification: the incorporation of aspects of the lost object into the self, and the setting up of a permanent dyadic relation of a representation of self with the representation of the lost object. I proposed that these processes, occurring within the ego, also coincide with new developments in the functions of the ego ideal and modified superego as a result of the internalization of the life project of the lost object: the identification, within the ego ideal, with what the mourned beloved would have said or done, reacted to, or felt, expected to achieve in life, and hoped for the mourner to achieve. The organization of internalized value systems, and the integration of the mature superego, is thus modified and enriched.

Still, at the same time, the mourning process continues in the form of the repeated experience of grief over the loss, the lost object becoming a permanent, painful "absent presence," and, connected with this experience, the reactivation of guilt feelings over not having fully appreciated the loved one during life and the feeling of having failed them in other ways. The more ambivalent the past relation with the loved one, of course, the more intense are such guilt feelings, which when taken to a great extent results in the significant disturbance that characterizes *pathological mourning*. In this latter case, despair over the inability to repair real or fantasized guilt is reflected in depressive symptomatology that may include suicidal wishes, which express the underlying wish to expiate deep guilt feelings. Implicit dynamics may involve fantasies that self-elimination would permit the good parts of the self to survive, while simultaneously destroying the bad parts of the self – for example, the negative feelings, including the hatred of the lost object and the related unconscious introjection of the hated part of the object as part of the self. Under extreme circumstances, despair over the permanent nature of the loss coincides with the condemnation symbolized by the words inscribed over the entrance to Dante's inferno: "who enters here, abandon all hope."

But the purpose of this paper is to describe the process of mourning under more optimal conditions, in which ambivalence had not been so marked or extreme, and in which loss reactivates what Freud (1915–1917) and Melanie Klein (1940) describe as *normal mourning processes* – in Klein's view, the reactivation and reworking through of the depressive position, which she considered the central process of normal mourning.

Approximately five years after my initial contact with persons who had lost a spouse after decades of living together and had remarried and whom, as I described in my earlier contribution, I had been able to interview extensively, I revisited them with the question: *what further changes have taken place in them during the past five years?* I was able to reinterview a majority of these individuals, in addition to further reviewing more recent material from my patients and also my personal experience, having undergone similar vicissitudes in my own life at the same time.

In summary, five years hence, essentially the same observations I previously summarized continued to be made. Again, as in the original interviews, mourning reactions were reactivated by the interview process itself – perhaps somewhat attenuated in some cases. A majority of those interviewed reported an ongoing intense, lively upsurge of mourning and memories of past experiences that is suddenly triggered by present-day life situations. In addition, however, new elements emerged that, in my view, had not been so clearly evident five years before.

First of all, I found a generally changed attitude of these persons toward the potential of serious illness and death. They reported a decrease of the anxiety that might be elicited by the development of symptoms of a potentially serious illness and the possibility of death. The reduced fear of death and dying at times surprised the subjects of my inquiry themselves. They made comments such as, "if he was able to go through this, I shall be able to do it," revealing a sense of being *accompanied* by the lost beloved in the imagining of one's own process of dying, as well as fantasies of being reunited with them after one's own death, even in persons with no religious inclination or convictions in that regard. The sense of death as a *re-encounter* acquired the important function of helping to deal with the subjects' own death, particularly if the conviction of being loved by one's departed partner was very powerful. From an analytic perspective, this may be rooted both in oedipal and preoedipal experiences, at the most basic, that assure the permanence of the love of the internalized mother imago. In some of these subjects, as well as in certain patients with religious convictions who were dealing with similar issues, fantasies and questions emerged about what would happen to them if they confronted the competing love of two persons, the past and the present spouse or partner, were there some existence after death. This issue was explored by the Protestant theologian C.S. Lewis, who in his dramatic autobiographical essay, *A Grief Observed* (1961), solved that painful question for himself by assuming that in the presence of the love of God, all conflicts will be reconciled. Dynamically, one may speculate about the projection of oedipal triangulations into the fantasied world after death and the corresponding efforts of defensive denial or sublimatory resolution of conflicts around direct and reverse triangulation (Kernberg, 2012, pp. 263–264).

It impressed me that a more general, tolerant attitude toward conflict seemed characteristic of all the persons I interviewed, accompanied by a greater appreciation the viewpoints of those with whom they had previously experienced serious conflict, and an increased capability to forgive those who had disappointed them or treated them with hostility. This seemed to go hand-in-hand with heightened tolerance for the ambivalence of human relations in general, an increased curiosity and empathy about the experiences and motivations of others, and a greater sense of freedom to be of help to those undergoing a mourning process. While some of these changes might be attributed to the emotional maturation and deepening of self-reflection as an expression of the developmental process of essentially normal individuals, the particular intensity of this process in the subjects I am referring to seemed to *them* to be clearly related to the ongoing and subtle process of long-term mourning for a lost loved one.

This greater degree of tolerance may also be expressed in fantasies regarding the lost object. Where there are significant unresolved guilty feelings regarding the lost object, the mourned-for object may also be imagined as more tolerant and forgiving: the desired fantasy of reunion after the mourner's own death now may include encountering the desired, more benign, and totally forgiving lost object. The opposite may evolve in cases of *pathological mourning*: as part of depressive symptomatology, the patient may experience the frightening fantasy that he/she will instead be rejected in such an encounter, intensifying a panicky sense of abandonment.

Returning to the interviews, another experience shared by practically all persons was an increased degree of thoughts and reflection concerning earlier losses in their lives. Losses barely noticed at the time, as well as severely mourned losses of parents and siblings, and sometimes children, are revisited afresh in the context of the current loss. This reawakening of past mourning processes tended to be accompanied by the emergence of the lost loved ones, particularly one's parents, in the manifest content of dreams – very often in the context of scenes of early childhood or adolescence in which the dreamer is both a child and the present adult, relating to a live image of the lost one. In the very interactions dreamed about, old conflicts are revived and relived in combination, along with expressed new insights regarding these conflicts, so that the vivid repetition of the past, set in context of present day reflections, is condensed into the dream experience. Vivid dreams involving dramatically realistic *new* experiences with the lost partner are quite frequent, naturally followed by a painful awakening.

One subject told me that he felt that he lived in two worlds: one of daily reality, in which he felt immersed in the reality of his present human world, and one of his dream world, in which his deceased wife would appear as realistically linked to his current experiences and network of close relationships. A greater sensitivity to the nuances of present day intimate relations and friendships seems to evolve in parallel to the mourning processes referred to here – a combination of deeper understanding and a heightened valuation of intimate relations and the mutuality of friendship. That "friendships are the leaves of the tree of life," as one of my subjects paraphrased Octavio Paz, is reflected in the tangible enrichment of daily life.

While the acceleration of the experience of time is a generalizable aspect of the aging process, it is also seen in persons who have experienced the loss of long-standing, intimate relationships. The normal contrast – between the apparently stable external reality of childhood and early adulthood and the experience of the self as rapidly changing – is in later life replaced by the experience of changes in external reality that point to the transience of existence; this development is reinforced as a consequence of severe loss, inducing a higher sensitivity to change and a greater appreciation of the transitory nature of experience. One person stated succinctly that the relationship with the one they loved was the only stable reality in a world of constant change. That, in turn, intensifies the awareness of the value of enduring relationships and of the complex nature of one's own personality and those of others. Obviously personal conflicts, anxieties, and challenges determine the vast variety of reactions to the passage of time, but the awareness of this passage seems intensified to long-term processes of mourning.

For some of the persons interviewed, significant loss also deepened the experience of art and the search for permanent values in the aesthetical, as well as the ethical sphere. One person referred to Dali's famous sculpture of "time riding a horse," in which one of Dali's blanket-like, soft-surface clocks embraces the back of a tense and frightened running horse, a representation of the transitory aspect of life.

In contrast to the heightened awareness of the transitory nature of experiences and other aspects of external reality, several individuals I interviewed referred to unexpected reactions to objects concretely related to their mourned partner. These things – a particular object dear to the lost beloved, a piece of jewelry, a painting, a song, an object of art or literature closely related to the lost person's interests – gained an intensified meaningfulness and impact, triggering brief but deep mourning reactions. They seemed like memory "rocks," stable reminders in an ever-changing sea of reality. Most subjects were surprised by the intensity of the onset of sudden mourning reactions at the encounter of one of these objects. One person mentioned a drawing by Paul Klee of an angel, which his deceased wife had given him a few months before her death, and which the artist made during the late stages of his own illness. On the wall of his office, it functioned as a bridge to immediate contact with her, the memory of their conversations about Klee's art and life, and the silent communications between them.[1]

For psychoanalysts and psychoanalytic psychotherapists, the personal experience of profound mourning may increase their capacity to respond to that of their patients. It may enhance the understanding that patients need an open space in which to mourn, and thus the capacity of their therapist to fully tolerate, understand, and accompany them in their suffering, without premature reassurance or foreclosure of this process. The optimal way to help patients at this juncture is to permit them to share fully with the therapist their experience of the lost object, to allow the very presence of this absent person in the content of the hours. They become alive in the emotional experience of both participants, and the increasing awareness of their permanence in the mental life of the patient allows their memory to become a shared reality in the therapeutic encounter. The therapist's sensitivity to the patient's intolerance of the mourning process may facilitate the diagnosis of paranoid regressions – blaming others for the death and reacting with rage and wishes for revenge, and of pathological mourning reactions – severe, unrealistic guilt feelings and self-blame with depressive symptomatology and potentially suicidal impulses. The analytic resolution of such manifestations of the resistance to *normal mourning* may help the patient sustain and elaborate the process.

Perhaps the greatest therapeutic challenge in such circumstances is the dominance of the denial of mourning in narcissistic pathology. The patient's apparent indifference to what, from the outside, appears to be a dramatic and substantial loss may trigger strong negative countertransference feelings. However, the analyst's deep awareness that, by the unconscious devaluation of the lost object, the patient is not only defending against loss, but also impoverishing his own internal life, may increase the analyst's tolerance to this defense, and to the working through of their countertransference reaction. Radical indifference to loss, of course, should not be confused with the defensive hypomanic reaction to intolerable mourning, a denial of depression that seems easier to integrate and work through.

In conclusion, if all true learning is essentially painful, then that derived from the long-term process of mourning is especially so but nonetheless adds to the deepening understanding of intimate human relationships and their essential contribution to the richness of life. The underlying mechanisms involve the internalization of highly significant object relations into both ego and superego structures in the context of the dominance of love over hatred; the tolerance and working through of the depressive position, in contrast to the regressive defenses of narcissistic and paranoid structures and the guilt and depressive reactions of pathological mourning; and the reinstatement and deepening of the relationships with internalized good objects within the structure of one's mind.

Note

1 *Editor's note*: the reader will recognize objects such as the Klee drawing as sharing qualities in a normative sense with Volkan's "linking objects," as discussed by Ochsner, and, like the grave of Oliner's grandparents, as creating a "memorial space," a territory of mourning that Ornstein discusses (all, this volume)—*A. T.*

References

Freud, S. (1915–1917). Mourning and melancholia. Standard Edition, 14: 237–260. London: Hogarth Press (1957).

Kernberg, O.F. (2010). Some observations on the process of mourning. *Internat. J. Psychoanalysis*, 91:601–619.

———. (2012). *The Inseparable Nature of Love and Aggression*. Washington, DC: American Psychiatric Publishing.

Klein, M. (1940). Mourning and its relation to manic-depressive states. In: *Contributions to Psychoanalysis*, 1921–1945. London: Hogarth Press, pp. 311–338.

Lewis, C.S. (1961). *A Grief Observed*. San Francisco: Harper Collins.

10

MOURNING, DOUBLE REALITY, AND THE CULTURE OF REMEMBERING AND FORGIVING

A Very Personal Report[1]

Léon Wurmser

> *The worst is not.*
> *So long as we can say: "This is the worst"*
>
> —Shakespeare, *King Lear*[2]

Introduction

"Mourning is creative aliveness at the moment of loss," I read in a recent, very help-ful essay by Franz Wellendorf (2009, p. 35). I turned to that paper and the book in which it appeared when I was trying to regain ground under my feet in the middle of a vortex of overwhelming feelings sucking me down: after a long severe illness under my care and responsibility, my wife died, and at the same time I fell ill with cancer.

I am trying to describe my own experiences because my observations confirm Wellendorf's assertion about the complexity of reactions during the mourning pro-cess: that they go far beyond Freud's description of the detaching and dissolving of the links to the lost object during the process of mourning (Freud, 1917), but are rather more like what he himself had to live through in his own, never ceasing grief about his daughter Sophie and his grandchild Heinerle (as Adele Tutter describes somewhat more in the Prologue [this volume]). I had already seen this throughout my life in my own, never really ending mourning about what was lost in the Holo-caust, although I did not suffer any immediate personal losses.

My acute reaction to the loss of my wife revealed aspects of bereavement that also went beyond what I encountered in other psychoanalytic studies; at the same time, I wanted to write about the consolation I observed and found in the Jew-ish rituals of mourning. I believe that my observations may have broader validity: even during the write-up of these notes, after my wife's death, I worked with half a dozen patients and colleagues who had recently lost a parent or, in one instance,

FIGURE 10.1 A tender farewell: Zdeňka, Charlotte, and Léon at the Seder, 2009.

a friend whose son was ill with a metastatic brain tumor. The observations I made of myself were helpful in the psychotherapy and counseling of others, and thus I will present them as well as I can within the limits of discretion. This is itself like walking along a narrow ridge between two precipices: to be as unsparingly truthful, specific, and authentic as possible without falling into masochistic exhibitionism or the violation of the other's dignity. Authenticity in such an exploration is only possible when it is done with great and personal specificity.

"Basically I write in order to understand," says the Catalonian writer Maria Barbal (quoted in the afterword to the German edition of *Inner Land [País íntim]*, 2005, p. 398).

The farewell: The history of suffering and dying and the role of shared suffering (*Mit-Leiden*) and pain (*Mit-Schmerz*)

Years ago my wife Zdeňka started suffering from at first almost unnoticeably advancing symptoms of loss of memory and judgment, manifestations of Alzheimer's disease, which she vehemently denied until almost the end. Every help rendered to her was most intensely fought off and experienced by her as humiliating, intruding in her area of competence, and invasive; her deficits were ascribed to failures of others, especially mine. This caused a terrible, years-long struggle to take away from her the administration of my practice, the household, and the finances, which for almost five decades she had so very competently carried out, because it became more and more evident that for years, she had already been dangerously failing in those tasks. Moreover, there had been several car accidents, two with bodily injury. At the turn of the year 2008, a radical deterioration set in with massive weight loss, increasing, unbearable back pain, and an almost complete refusal of food and drink. It took almost three months until the diagnosis of pancreatic cancer, which I had from the beginning suspected, was confirmed.

Against all the prognoses of a speedy demise, Zdeňka survived the diagnosis by almost fifteen months. The struggle for her survival, which she and the family led, was fought against the illness, which in spite of her age of eighty-two was very virulent. For a while, chemotherapy proved for many months to be astonishingly successful; this had to be obtained, again and again, against the massive resistance of the physicians who wanted to deny her active treatment and tried to persuade her, and us, to give up on her. About ten times we desperately ran up against that sentence of death, until June 2009, when it became impossible to save her. In the meantime, in February 2009, I was operated on for bladder cancer.

My first and completely overwhelming reaction to the dying and death of my wife did not consist in the experience of loss, usually considered central, but in *the desperate participation in her terrible suffering* (German, *Mit-Leiden*), especially toward the end when I was overcome by remembering the bloody hole in her belly, the dreadful pains at every touch, pain that could only partly be assuaged with narcotics, the extreme weakness that more and more deprived her of audible and understandable speech, and the increasing râles. There was a very strong *identification* with her pain, and despair about my powerlessness in the face of her suffering.

Yes, there were feelings of *guilt* about the failure of all my efforts to help, some guilty feelings about my own survival, and especially ever-more obtrusive guilt feelings about all the pain I inflicted on her during fifty-six years of togetherness. One might say that a thwarted striving for omnipotence, a narcissistic claim, was asserting itself. Certainly it was such a striving for *omnipotence* that accompanied my battle for her survival against what I experienced at times as a horribly dehumanizing and unfeeling medical establishment, a battle in which I was not alone, but supported by family, by friends, caregivers, and also, more and more, by some of the physicians. Yet not every such fantasy of omnipotence must be by itself pathological. For example, circumstances may permit (and may even demand) such insistence in order to be effective in helping others, provided, however, that such insistence is not perverted by denial. I told the physicians, both those who supported my fight and those who opposed it, that "maybe I wanted to act heroically, but not foolishly."

There are other situations in which the fantasy of omnipotence is "normal," rather than pathological. As we know from analytic experience, the fantasy of *"omnipotence of responsibility"* so often used by the child as a response to early loss and traumatization is accompanied by correspondingly lifelong and pervasive feelings of guilt. I believe that very often, although certainly not always, the agony and death of a beloved person actualizes the *conflict between omnipotence of responsibility* and *implacable reality*, resulting in *strong feelings of guilt*. Later on I will have more to say on the topic of guilt feelings.

Still, I believe that the shared pain (*Mit-Schmerz*), this suffering-with (*Mit-Leiden*), cannot be simply explained by omnipotence, impotence, and guilt, but rather it also implicates a kind of *primordial solidarity* (*Ursolidarität*) – a *fundamental relationship with the loved other (Urbeziehung mit dem geliebten Du)*. Certainly, this basic relatedness is rooted in the original attachment to the closest others of early childhood, but it is renewed throughout life again and again and reactualized in relations of profound love, perhaps in the sense of what Wellendorf (2009) writes: "in grieving, *fidelity* manifests itself toward the object beyond its loss" (p. 30, my translation). Along the same lines, Beland (2009) cites Freud's letter to his friend Ludwig Binswanger after the suicide of Binswanger's son, in which he writes about his own, never overcome feelings of loss over his daughter (and implicitly, his grandchild):

> One knows that the acute mourning after such a loss will pass, but one will remain unconsoled, never find a substitute. Everything that moves into its place, even if it fills it completely, still it remains something else. And basically, it is alright so. It is the only way to continue the love which one does not want to give up.
>
> (p. 245, my translation)

As I emphasized in a paper on jealousy (Wurmser, 2007), such fidelity does not have to be at all exclusive: we are able at the same time (instead of the split infinitive) to love very deeply several persons and be faithful to them. On the contrary, the love for one person may rather deepen the love for another and the intimacy in that relationship. Love is no cake that is diminished by sharing; much more it is like a candle that is not diminished by lighting others, as the Kabbalist Abi Zimra said four hundred years ago. It is the opposition of a concretized experiencing of feelings and one that is symbolic, that is, mentalized.

My own deep attachment and basic solidarity in the *Mit-Leiden*, the "condolentia," had much to do not only with the ongoing, shared trauma, but also with the origins of our relationship: as a young woman, Zdeňka risked her life as a student in occupied, terribly violated Czechoslovakia, in the fight first against the Nazis and then against the Communists. Her solitary flight from impending arrest and likely death through the Bohemian forest resembled that of Adele Tutter's father and happened at about the same time (see Tutter's essay in this volume). For ten years, Zdeňka's parents did not know whether she had survived her flight. A good part of her identity consisted in the defiant stand against injustice, humiliation, and insincerity, which later on made our relationship often difficult. She was very shy and reclusive and only rarely spoke about her feelings or traumatic past; she was an unusually good and caring mother who did everything for her children and was always there for them, and she was an exceptionally effective, conscientious, industrious, and thrifty housewife who granted or claimed for herself only too little. Yet the shadow of severe traumatization hung over her life and resentment simmered under the surface. In other contexts I have talked about the parallels to my own life (Wurmser, 2005).

Multiplicity of issues of guilt, regret, and broken reality

Back to my own experience: in no way can guilt feelings be reduced (only) to the sense of thwarted omnipotence. Anybody with some psychoanalytic knowledge would, with Freud (1917), immediately point to profound *ambivalence*: to repressed and also not so unconscious *death wishes* against the deceased and understand the intense *Mit-Schmerz* as in part representing a reaction formation against such murderous fantasies and, as already mentioned, against all factually inflicted suffering. This connection was partly quite conscious, at least partly intellectually understood. Such death wishes kept emerging during a long marriage that lasted more than half a century, was often conflicted, and was strongly burdened by the traumata suffered by both of us; they were often very conscious, but mostly suppressed.

However, much more on the surface, there were feelings of the deepest and almost unrelieved *regret* about all the mutual understanding that had been missed over the decades. Guilt feelings, as well as the sense of irretrievable loss, both played a significant role in this profound regret. If it can be fully understood and reduced to this, I cannot say as yet, but I do not quite believe it. Disappointment and deep shame on both sides also certainly had a strong part in it.

I have noticed this deep regret about what had been missed in almost all those who mourn. "Why had I not kept in contact with him?" my youngest son said when a friend of his youth was unexpectedly found dead in his bed. "Why had I not called my old aunt anymore in the last few weeks?" my daughter-in-law asked – all this just a few days after my wife's passing. And I tormented myself: "Why had I not made more efforts to seek understanding and reconciliation?"

Part of the strategy of denial and forgetting against sorrow, helplessness, and weakness (Wellendorf, 2009, briefly refers to it, also impressively Verena Kast, 1982, 2006) consists of *wrath and anger*. I observe this in others, especially patients, as well as in myself. It struck me most strongly in our oldest granddaughter, Serena, at the time seven years of age. Already, during her grandmother's gradual decline, she kept herself much in the background during visits and shied away from touching her. She was present until shortly before her death and then at the funeral; she was restless, even boisterous in the funeral home and had outbursts of rage at home and in school during the weeks afterward. I think this was most likely a warding off of sadness and anxiety by turning it from passive to active, what some may call a manic defense. What may have appeared as a lack of empathy and remorse I would see as a protection against those overwhelming feelings, ultimately those caused by separation – a fight against grief.

Let us return to the complexity of guilt themes. I will describe an incident that presents the issue in concentrated form: on May 13, I came home from the office already quite upset because an intercurrent infection blocked the resumption of my own cancer therapy. My wife's caregiver left to go shopping immediately after Zdeňka went to the commode beside her bed. I kept offering her my help, and she refused it angrily. Only after two hours did she undertake to clean herself. When I tried to help her return to bed, she heavily fell from the edge of the bed to the ground. Afterward she poured out so much hatred and bitterness that it was hard for me to bear. The caregiver, who had returned, asked where all the bitterness against me came from. I said: "From a whole life." And then I had to be again alone with Zdeňka when the caregiver went to the pharmacy. I was horribly worried that she might have injured herself during the fall, particularly since her prothrombin time (a measure of clotting function) was highly prolonged. Everything was whirling in wild confusion, and I felt it was just too much for me (*überfordert*). Sometimes I thought I was going crazy. For her it had been a deep shame to be seen and served by me in her most intimate function, which was met on my side by an equally strong resistance, the more so since I had no fitting rubber gloves with which to clean her.

In my recollections, this scene does not leave me, because two days later her gastrostomy tube fell out, blood poured out of the wound, massive sepsis set in, and in a cascade of complications the process of dying became unstoppable: *with that fall the descent into death began.* Had it been my own impatience and disgust, my own anger, particularly at the caregiver, but probably also my own suppressed, strongly fought off death wishes against Zdeňka and myself that had precipitated the final catastrophe? This question kept haunting me into my sleep, and again and again I was (and still am at times) dreaming of reparation by reinserting tubes or resuscitating my dead wife.

One night I was kept awake for hours by the dreadful anxiety that Zdeňka had only seemed to be dead (*scheintot*) and could have been buried alive. As a matter of fact, no physician had come to verify her death, and the hospice nurse on call refused to make the long way to us in the middle of the night. We had to call the emergency police service for the pronouncement. But what astonished me about my later reaction was the *doubling of reality*: rationally, I knew that Zdeňka was truly dead. I myself had ascertained with my stethoscope that the beating of her heart and her breathing had ceased. Twelve hours later, immediately before the interment, I had kissed her on her icy forehead. And yet, I was kept awake by the torturing worry that she might have only seemed to be dead. Here too, in this double reality, in a kind of split and dissociation, the wish for reparation and atonement secretly lived on, together with a much greater guilt: "I have permitted my living wife to lie in a sealed coffin in the earth." Even without being psychotic, there exists such power of denial alongside the recognition of reality, the true meaning of what Freud marked as the splitting of the ego.

How do I understand this doubling? The first and simpler answer is: the dissociation and hence splitting of reality is an expression of the attempt to deny a great trauma that keeps repeating and irresistibly reinforcing itself – a trauma that reminds me incessantly of the traumata of the Holocaust that accompanied my youth: the transformation of a living person into a thing.

Superego split

Yet I ask myself whether, based on my clinical experience, I could not also understand this double reality – that my wife was still alive – as the result of a kind of superego split. It is not yet entirely clear to me: on the one hand, there is the invalidation and alleviation of one guilt (that I had not "caused" the fall and her subsequent death), and on the other hand, there is at the same time the accusation and punishment of a much greater guilt (that I had not protected her against being buried alive).

One split in the superego certainly originated from the fact that it had been an absolute commandment that I protect her life for as long as possible. In her extreme helplessness, her total exposure, I felt absolutely responsible for her life; at the same time, I felt absolutely responsible for ensuring that she would bear as little pain and suffering as possible. There existed no doubt that fighting against the false dichotomy of active, even aggressive treatment versus palliation of pain alone ("comfort"), we, my family and several physicians, enabled my wife to have one additional year of very valuable life with many beautiful moments: the birth of her sixth grandchild, family celebrations, a few short walks outside, once in the autumn forest – all, after her case had repeatedly been written off as hopeless and after we had been insistently told to cease treatment – *lebensunwertes Leben* ("life not worth living").

Even these two values: *maintenance of life* and *assuaging suffering* could enter into conflict with each other, in what I above called a false dichotomy, because they cannot always be reconciled. As I have already mentioned, this conflict was massively intensified by the recurrent demand from the medical establishment to render only palliative treatment, admonishing us that it would be inhuman to subject her to operative interventions or even just chemotherapy. Why would I not spare her so much pain and suffering by sending her to hospice care? Again and again, for fifteen months: hospice, hospice, hospice! Concealed behind this imposition, and sometimes very openly, were clear economic motivations; repeatedly she was discharged from the hospital in the gravest condition, even close to death, because Medicare refused to continue paying for her treatment. Still, the economic ratiocination was masked by a moral rationale, and the dilemma thus elevated to that of a superego conflict. Often I did not know what to do; toward the end, I struggled with the decision: should I push for a laparoscopy and actively treat the probable intestinal perforation and thrombosis of the upper mesenteric vein or let fate run its course, "fatally"? It is a conflict that haunted me for months afterward, a terrible superego conflict. I am now quite certain that it was this superego conflict that also engendered in me the split in the experience of reality, the double reality.

As a physician, all this also presented me with very painful questions about the *dehumanization of medicine*. More and more there exists a *split between the omnipotence of what is technical and the impotence of what is human*. Again, it is something that not only I have experienced, but also what I have heard from patients and friends alike, both in the USA and in Europe. For economic reasons, hospital care has greatly deteriorated. Bureaucratic rules decide over life or death. If I were not a physician,

I would have had to submit earlier to the authority of the system. Who will advocate for the patient if the medical doctor, more and more, represents other interests? Is this not a very great ethical and psychological problem that today decisively codetermines the entire mourning process?

However, this inner and much more external conflict can be looked at from a broader perspective. In connection with today's discussions about healthcare reform, in particular with the ever more gigantic costs of medical treatment, it is always emphasized how the care and medical services for the elderly drive the Medicare system and with it the community at large (and the states and nation) toward bankruptcy. Shouldn't care be rationed, as it already happens at some places? the question goes. The bioethicist Peter Singer (2009) entitled an article in the *New York Times Magazine*, "Why We Must Ration Health Care." Someone who, like Zdeňka, is fading away from Alzheimer's dementia and, moreover, suffers from incurable cancer and is rushing toward death, should be left alone, untreated, letting her die as comfortably and as soon as possible. The well-being and interests of the individual should be subordinated to that of the commonwealth (an argument strongly made to me by some Swiss friends advocating euthanasia, *Sterbehilfe*, as it is now called).

With that we approach, as hinted at before, the issue of life not worth living – "*lebensunwertes Leben*," or euthanasia – which, in a not-so-veiled form, several of the treating physicians urged me to consider during my desperate battle for Zdeňka's life, and which still gnaws at my conscience after her death.

It is certainly true that Alzheimer's disease was slowly destroying her personality. In that sense, loss and farewell was a very long, drawn-out experience. Yet core elements of her humanity, of her personality, were intact until the very end and called for loving protection, exactly as would a little child who is totally dependent upon our care and safekeeping. And almost until the end, as long as she was able to speak, she wished to fight for her life; at her core she was and remained a fighter who did not give up.

A few months before the end, she had a dream that I reconstruct now from my memory: pursued by a bear, she was struggling to get through ever-deeper snow to a log cabin in order to save the children there. The snow finally reached up to her neck. She did not know whether she would make it.

Two weeks before her death she held her youngest granddaughter in her arms and replied to her crying: "We have not yet had much of a chance to get to know each other, have we?" (Fig. 10.1).

Forgetting by denial

I return to my experience of broken reality. In addition to the superego split, there is something simpler: the *denial* (one form of forgetting) not only of the traumata, but of *the many layers of guilt feelings* for all that had not been lived, not been said, not been loved over the decades of our relationship; for the death wishes, now mostly unconscious, yet in earlier times intruding into consciousness;

for the failure, with regard to the omnipotence of responsibility to preserve her life as long and as humanely as possible. The fear of being buried alive is a basic anxiety for me, reaching far back into childhood, and which is now revived by the inner judge in this double form: that this fate has struck Zdeňka and will one day strike me as well.

In a milder form, I have repeatedly experienced this double reality since Zdeňka's death, although only in short moments: that she really was not dead, as the tradition suggests, during the seven days of deep mourning, that her soul has not yet left the familiar rooms and the lives of those closest to her. I am conscious of the symbolism of this myth, but the concrete experience of it has flitted through my consciousness.

With several of my patients, I have been astonished by the massive denial of the death of their closest relatives: the event of the death of mother or father is, as it were, bracketed out from the flow of narration in psychotherapy. In the case of one patient, the affect of sadness and the fear of loss were entirely displaced onto me because of my own, by now recurrent, operations for cancer, while her mother's death, which occurred at the same time, was barely mentioned. This "art of forgetting" is, I believe, of dubious value. Yet my attempt to dislodge it largely failed; the ambivalence of her relationship to the deceased was too profound. It is, parenthetically, an example of the extent to which the transference to the therapist may serve as defense against external actuality.

Identification, pathological mourning, and melancholia

An additional thought about *Ursolidarität* and the *double identification* with the lost person and with the lost relationship (Kernberg, 2010; this volume): our identity is rooted in such primary solidarity; the deeper the bond, the stronger our identification. Where we love, we admire; where we admire, we want to be similar. And in turn: shame occurs when we feel contempt from whom we admire and by whom we wish to be admired, as Aristotle stated (*The Art of Rhetoric*, 1926, II.VI.1383b).

Can pathological mourning, and with it massive depression ("melancholia"), be largely understood as an inability to give up the ambivalently invested object, a denial of loss?[3] Succinctly put by Freud:

> Of the three preconditions of melancholia – loss of the object, ambivalence, and regression of libido into the ego [we would rather say self] – the first two are also found in the obsessional self-reproaches arising after a death has occurred. In these cases it is unquestionably the ambivalence which is the motive force of the conflict, and observation shows that after the conflict has come to an end there is nothing left over in the nature of the triumph of a manic state of mind. We are thus led to the third factor as the only one responsible for the result.

[1917, p. 258]

He explains further this third aspect: "by taking flight into the ego [self] love escapes extinction. After this regression of the libido the process can become conscious, and it is represented to consciousness as a conflict between one part of the ego and the critical agency" (p. 257) – or, as he would later formulate it, between the ego and the superego. We might even expand this conflict as between the superego and the rest of the self, whereby, as Freud described before in this essay, the hatred against the object is now displaced, vested in the superego, and directed against the self: the shadow of the lost object has fallen on the self (as I paraphrase Freud).

My view broadens Freud's understanding and explanation of severe depression. As Freud writes in later papers, the difference between mourning and severe pathology lies in the pathological relationship of the self to the archaic superego, but I might now add that the latter constellation can be understood less as the perpetuation of a pathological object relationship and its loss and more as a profound transformation in reaction, generally speaking, to trauma (Wurmser, 2007; 2012). How can we describe the connection between severe traumatization and the archaic superego?

We can define trauma as an overwhelming, unsolvable external conflict between self and environment, which leads to a conscious, unsolvable inner conflict. The affects battling each other overwhelm the capacity of the ego to master them, a failure that leads to what Freud in *Studies on Hysteria* called a split between the groups of ideas, the act of making the connections between them unconscious (Breuer & Freud, 1893-1895). Dissociation and even hypnoid states remain important concepts for the understanding of the traumatic genesis of the severe neuroses.

In severe, repeated traumatization, every emotional experience resonates as if the trauma is recurring. This leads to the (usually partial) standstill of affective development: the differentiation, verbalization, and desomatization of the emotions are blocked. Thus in traumatization, by definition, feelings, once roused, can very rapidly become overwhelming and out of control: they are *global* ("dedifferentiated"), *beyond symbolization* ("deverbalized"), and are experienced as if *physical* ("resomatized"). According to Krystal (1988; 1998), these three concepts – dedifferentiation, deverbalization or hyposymbolization, and resomatization – comprise *affect regression*.

But there is something else of great importance, especially in the recurrent traumatization in childhood: these affects tend to appear in sexualized form. Sexualization is an archaic defense set up to regulate affect, a transformation of anxiety and pain into pleasurable excitement that can then be "discharged": "lust instead of dread, power instead of helplessness, love instead of torment" (Wurmser, 1989; 1993; 2000; 2007). The flooding of affect, combined with the primordial defense of sexualization, leads in turn to an overwhelming sense of humiliation and embarrassment: not to have any control over one's own emotional life is potentially at least as shameful as the loss of sphincter control, if not more so. *Aggressive* wishes are then used to reestablish control, a further form of archaic defense to deal preventively with the spiraling out of control, an important way of *turning passive into active*. In this connection it is also very important to see not only the passivity toward the outside, but, at least as essential, the *ego's passivity* vis-à-vis the affects, the drives, and the lashings by the superego (Rappaport, 1953).

The result of the severe disturbance of affect regulation in trauma is an archaic constellation we typically encounter in the intensive, long-term treatment of the severe neuroses. The following five states and contents are associated (see also Shengold, 1989). Each of the five may be an entrance point into the equation:

1. overstimulation from outside forces that is experienced as traumatic, as intolerable, and to which one feels helplessly, passively exposed;
2. overwhelming, but usually contradictory feelings, the traumatic state of inner passivity and the sense of bursting – "I cannot stand it anymore";
3. the sense of devouring, consuming forces, for example, threatening imagery of orality, such as rapacious animals or elements (fire, floods);
4. sexual excitement;
5. fantasies of aggression and of violence, even cruelty.

The archaic constellation of traumatogenic affective storms, sexualization and aggression is in turn again very deeply frightening and humiliating and calls for equally global defenses to assert control: in particular, massive counteractions by the superego in the form of pervasive and global forms of guilt and shame. A very central part of such an overweening superego is the omnipotence of responsibility: "It is in my power to prevent all these disasters. If I am entirely good, nothing horrible will happen again. If the horrors recur, it is my guilt, I am totally bad." These may be conscious or unconscious, with a strong sadistic (i.e., sexualized) component. As Charlotte Brontë wrote in *Jane Eyre* (1847), "conscience, turned tyrant, held passion by the throat" (p. 254).

The more unconscious these processes are, the more pathological and the more repetitive, stereotypical, and compulsive they may be, as Kubie explained in many papers and books many years ago. The reverse is also true: the more unconscious conflicts have been dealt with, the more inner freedom and the more liberated the sense of creativity may be. On the other hand, "creativity" in response to, or as part of, mourning may itself reflect a pathological rumination rather than an overcoming of the loss; it is not *eo ipso* "normal," "nonneurotic" (see Kubie, 1958, and Tutter's Prologue, this volume).

Is remembrance a denial of loss? I do not think so. I see it as a bridging between acknowledgment of the outer loss and the preservation of the inner person, the living "inner object." Thus it is a compromise formation. It is, as Adele Tutter made me aware, a profoundly creative part of the work of mourning. James Atlas (2000) writes in his biography of Saul Bellow, "Mourning isn't only a tribute to the dead; it's an acknowledgment of their power over the living – a form of commitment" (p. 235). Thus perhaps remembrance represents the continuation of that fidelity, our "primal solidarity" with our loved ones into the present and future.

This brings me to the second leading topic: the emotional significance that the Jewish mourning rituals had for me. This effect was unexpectedly strong and deep and lasting.

About the culture of remembering and forgiving

"After the twelve months of mourning . . . one must accompany the mention of one's dead father or one's dead mother with the words:'May his memory be a blessing for life in the world to come'" (Wieseltier, 1998, p. xi).

Elsewhere I have repeatedly spoken about how Judaism is very strongly a culture of memory, but also one in which forgiveness between person and person and at the same time between person and God plays a decisively important role (Wurmser, 2001; see also Jan Assmann's contribution to this volume, "Rituals of Memory.") The commandment "*Zakhor!*" ("Remember!") accompanies Bible and liturgy. "In Jewish history, writing is often a form of rescue," states Wieseltier (1998, p. 513).

And it is a culture of teaching and learning as a counterforce to death. I quote more from Wieseltier's very helpful and for me quite supportive book:

> In the Wisdom of Ben Sira: "The man who teaches his son will make his enemy jealous and exult over him before his friends. When his father dies, it is as though he were not dead, for he leaves behind him one like himself." And I have found the same thought in the rabbinical canon: . . . He who has a son toiling in the Torah, it is as if he did not die.
>
> [pp. 198–199]

Wieseltier criticizes the full submersion of the son's identity in his father's (we would speak of "primary identification," see Eickhoff, 2011) and the denial of death manifested in it. The opposite assertion, he says, is just as valid: "He who lives exactly as his father lived, it is as if he did not live"; "the finality of the difference between the father and the son must also not be denied" (pp. 198–199).

And yet, "Hold fast to the Torah because it is a tree of life," we say in the liturgy: in fact, "in Jewish law, the obligation to honor one's teacher takes precedence over the obligation to honor one's father and mother" (Wieseltier, 1998, p. 254).

Thoughts about sitting Shiv'a

A few days before the death of my wife, the rabbi of the home hospice program visited us and spoke, after a longer dialogue about dying and transcendence, the Hebrew prayer before dying, with the "*Widdui*," the confession of sins, while I held Zdeňka's hand in mine. "When thy judgment is to let me come under the shadows of thy wings envelop my soul into the cloak, the *tallith*, of light!"

It is well known that, according to Jewish law, the body should be buried within twenty-four hours, and during the interval before, should always be watched over. One of the ancient ideas is that the soul only gradually, step by step, abandons the earth and that we help her with this (soul is in the major languages feminine: *anima, psyche, neshama, Seele*). Thus the *shomer*, or guard, stays with her in prayer so that her body and the remaining soul will never be left alone, but remained connected with the community.[4]

For us, it was less than twelve hours before we gathered in the funeral chapel of a very small congregation. Immediately before, the *Kria* took place, the (ritual) cutting and tearing of our clothes. The rabbi read a summary of Zdeňka's life and sang the prayers, and then all three of our sons spoke in deeply moving ways about their mother; I added a few words of thanks to Zdeňka. In a small convoy of cars, we drove far out into the countryside to the cemetery. Led by the rabbi, we four carried the simple pine wood coffin from the hearse. Three times the rabbi silently stopped the procession in order to testify to the stopping of time; the delay of the final good-bye; and the honor given to the dead.

I include here some comments from the Talmud that are germane. In tractate Megillah, p. 23 b1, there is a brief statement that, during funerals, if there are at least ten people present (a *minyan*, in Orthodox congregations, at least ten men, in others also women), the leader of the procession repeatedly halts the procession and says: *amdu, yeqarim, amodu; shwu, yeqarim, shwu!* —"Stand, dear ones, stand! Sit, dear ones, sit! In the translation:

> On the way to a burial, it was the custom to halt the procession to bemoan the loss of the deceased, and deliver eulogies. The procedure was as follows: The leader would tell the people: 'Sit, dear ones, sit!' They would sit and weep while listening to eulogies. He would then tell them: 'Stand, dear ones, stand!' After proceeding a short distance, the procession would again be halted as before. This procedure was repeated at least seven times.[5]

At the edge of the open grave, the four of us spoke an extended *Kaddish*, the prayer for the dead, which is nothing other than a sanctification and praise of God and his justice and an Aramaic prayer for peace and forgiveness.

Then the rabbi was the first to throw with upturned shovel some glebes into the grave, upturned for the same reason as the stopping of the procession, not to show any haste; and then we relatives and friends filled the grave with earth. Friends remained present until the grave was sealed.

Almost immediately after the funeral, the seven days of Shiv'a sitting began. Shiv'a is the number seven. The biblical basis for this is the period of mourning observed by Joseph for his father Jacob: *evel Shiv'at yamim* (Genesis, 50.10; Wieseltier, 1998, p. 365). We observed this for five days at my middle son's house. On Shabbat, the day of joy, the period of mourning was interrupted. The seventh and last day I was with my youngest son's family in a suburb of New York. During these seven days it is customary not to shave or make oneself up. The immediate family sit for several hours every day on low chairs and relatives and friends come to visit. Usually they bring food, the *se'udat havra'ah*, the "meal of healing" or recovery. In the first few days (or at least on the first one), those most directly affected by the death should not have to prepare any food for themselves.

What personally impressed me the most was the custom that conversation should be devoted to recollections of the dead, in a true dialogue led by the closest mourners. A number of visitors remained for several hours, others for less time, and it was mainly our sons who were asked in much detail about their mother's life, and they responded by describing her very fateful life story, rich in substance and ideas, and the complexity of her personality. I was surprised and shaken when I heard about sides of my wife that had been almost entirely unknown to me: her artistic ability in the service to her children; her inexhaustible, but mostly quiet help in advice and deed; her reputation as a hero in the resistance, a prominent fighter for justice and freedom prior to her flight – a fame about which I had been almost entirely ignorant, but about which one of our sons had learned by chance. The discussions reached far into the history of past and present, the more so since a number of friends hold important positions in government. The talks were usually interrupted for the afternoon and evening prayers, and they were again finished by the Kaddish of the mourners.

Every morning my sons joined a *minyan* in order to recite the Kaddish, because this should only be said in such a sizable group. And it is the task of the community to make sure that there always are at least ten people present to form a *minyan*; again, this togetherness and belonging carries the mourner, greatly counteracting the feeling of being abandoned and helpless by providing some substitute completeness, and the consolation of not being alone. "Mourning is also remembering, dialogue, dealing with what has occurred, mostly within a community."[6]

Verena Kast (1982; 2006) distinguishes four phases of the process of grieving: 1. denial, 2. erupting emotions, 3. speaking and separating, and 4. the establishment of a new relation to self and world. The ritual of Kaddish creates the time and space to admit to and stand by our wounded state and human weakness, explains my son David.

The stopping of time

But now some psychoanalytic thoughts about this: the shared remembering of my wife's personality, the honoring interest in her, had both a very upsetting and an incredibly and lasting consoling effect. The ideas about death vary in Judaism very broadly. One interpretation of the Shiv'a time is that the soul of the deceased is still dwelling in these days among the living, and hence still present. Metaphorically, i.e., symbolically, this is very understandable: in the dialogue the other lives on; as Lao Tzu said, true immortality is being remembered. Another interpretation of the seven days of Shiv'a is that the soul is grieving the loss of her body and of those near to her and that we are thus in solidarity with her grief: we identify ourselves with her loss. One is with all of this very strongly *bound up into the community*. Shared suffering is half the suffering, says the German proverb, and an Aramaic saying in the Talmud testifies to it: *O chevruta o mituta* – either community (togetherness) or death. This saying refers to the legend of Choni haMa'agal, the Circle drawer, who fell into a seventy-year sleep. After he woke up, nobody recognized him as who he was, and all ridiculed his claim that he was Choni, whom they knew as an ancient scholar and miracle man. Shunned, shamed, and lonely, he died after a few days. Without love and respect and belonging, life becomes meaningless and dead.

Several of the rites signify, like Choni's story, the stopping of time, just as now time has ceased for the dead person: not shaving, not caring about food, the halting step during the funeral procession, and yes, even the dwelling in the discourse upon the life of the deceased. One mark of all of this is the stopping of life: one interrupts most daily tasks for this period. After the death, but before the burial, even regular prayers and blessings are omitted. Equally, on the day after burial, no *tefillin*, phylacteries, are put on. The mirrors are veiled (see below). Time stops for one week: one should not do anything active, yet gradually return to everyday life, to normality. That one sits close to the ground, and that jacket and shirt are torn, is to show solidarity with the dead, who is now given over to destruction and dissolution. All this taken together fits very well to the defense *of turning passive to active*, vis-à-vis the *trauma of death*, and at the same with the *identification in lasting love* with the one who has left us. Such identification and solidarity should help overcome the ambivalence toward the deceased.

There is also the custom at the end of the Shiv'a sitting that one wanders through the house of mourning and then accompanies the departing soul on her way.

Wieseltier (1998) takes up a thought of the medieval scholar HaMe'iri (Provence, fourteenth century) about the temptation of totality and absoluteness in the effect of grief: "when a man finds himself happy, in any of the varieties of happiness, it is not fitting that he should settle himself in his happiness. No, he must recall the times of trouble." Thus it should be in reverse during the time of trouble: "the good and the bad are two points on a line." Wieseltier continues:

> Is there a more totalizing emotion than the emotion of sorrow? It sees nothing but its object and the universe that stole its object away. It regards the world from the standpoint of its wound, and thereby simplifies it. And here is HaMe'iri, with a word of caution. Mourner! Do not mistake a season for a law.
>
> [pp. 228–229]

More on the "meal of healing," the theme of equalizing justice, and the Kaddish and forgiveness

Interesting traditions point to the power of metaphor in the "meal of healing": the first food of the mourning period should consist of lentils or boiled eggs. Why? Because both have "no mouth," no opening, just as the mourner is without words because he silently accepts the judgment of Heaven; and because they are round, like fate, "like the turning wheel of the world" – just as mourning surrounds all the living (Wieseltier, 1998, pp. 312–317). The meal of lentils that Jacob prepared for his father Isaak and which then his brother Esau bought for the right of the firstborn was the "meal of consolation" after the death of Abraham, his grandfather. Thus lentils and eggs also have the power of consolation. This custom was unknown to me prior to my reading Wieseltier's book, *Kaddish*, and thus for us it did not play a role.

Could not the "mouthless" food also symbolize nameless grief, the overwhelming nature of sorrow?[7]

But Wieseltier reports more about social justice during the mourning rituals, quoting from the Talmud:

> The rich used to bring food to the house of the mourner in baskets of silver and gold, and the poor in baskets of peeled willow twigs, but the poor were ashamed, and so the rabbis instituted that everyone should bring their food in baskets of peeled willow twigs, out of respect of the poor. The rich used to serve drinks in the house of the mourner in vessels of white glass, and the poor in vessels of colored glass, but the poor were ashamed, and so the rabbis instituted that everyone should serve drinks in vessels of colored glass, out of respect of the poor. The rich [in mourning] used to uncover their faces, and the poor [in mourning] used to cover their faces, since their faces were blackened by the years of [working in] drafts, but the poor were ashamed, and so the rabbis instituted that everyone should cover their faces, out of respect of the poor. The rich used to be carried to burial on a grand bed, and the poor in a box, but the poor were ashamed, and so the rabbis instituted that everyone should be carried to burial in a box.
>
> [1998, pp. 316–317]

Now to the origin of the Kaddish, as explained by the eleventh century prayer book that took its name from the French city, Machzor Vitry:

> A tale of Rabbi Akiva (the great scholar of the first and second century). He was walking in a cemetery by the side of the road and encountered there a naked man, black as coal, carrying a large burden of wood on his head. He seemed to be alive and was running under the load like a horse. Rabbi Akiva ordered him to stop. 'How comes it that a man does such hard work?' he asked. 'If you are a servant and your master is doing this to you, then I will redeem you from him. If you are poor and people are avoiding you, then I will give you money.' 'Please, sir!' the man replied. 'Do not detain me because my superiors will be angry.' 'Who are you,' Rabbi Akiva asked, 'and what have you done?' The man said: 'The man whom you are addressing is a dead man. Every day they send me out to chop wood.' 'My son, what was your work in the world from which you came?' 'I was a tax collector, and I would favor the rich and kill the poor.' 'Have your superiors told you nothing about how might relieve your condition?' 'Please, sir, do not detain me, for you will irritate my tormentors. For such a man [as I], there can be no relief. Though I did hear them say something – but no, it is impossible. They said that if this poor man had a son, and his son were to stand before the congregation and recite [the prayer] "Blessed the Lord who is blessed!" and the congregation were to answer amen, and the son were also to say "May the Great Name be blessed!" [a sentence from the Kaddish], they would release him from his

punishment. But this man never had a son. He left his wife pregnant, and he did not know whether the child was a boy. And if she gave birth to a boy, who would teach the boy Torah? For this man does not have a friend in the world.' Immediately Rabbi Akiva took upon himself the task of discovering whether this man had fathered a son, so that he might teach the son Torah and install him at the head of the congregation. 'What is your name?' he asked. 'Akiva,' the man answered. 'And the name of your wife?' 'Shoshnia.' 'And the name of your town?' 'Lodkiya' [i.e. Laodicea/Latakia, in Syria]. Rabbi Akiva was deeply troubled by all this and went to make his inquiries. When he came to that town, he asked about the man he had met, and the townspeople replied: 'May his bones be ground to dust!' He asked about the man's wife, and he was told: 'May her memory be erased from the world!' He asked about the man's son, and he was told: 'He is a heathen – we did not even bother to circumcise him!' Rabbi Akiva promptly circumcised him and sat him down before a book. But the boy refused to receive Torah. Rabbi Akiva fasted for forty days. A heavenly voice was heard to say: 'For this you mortify yourself?' 'But Lord of the Universe,' Rabbi Akiva replied, 'it is for You that I am preparing him.' Suddenly the Holy One, Blessed Be He, opened the boy's heart. Rabbi Akiva taught him Torah and 'Hear, O Israel!' and the benediction after meals. He presented the boy to the congregation and the boy recited [the prayer] 'Bless the Lord who is blessed!' and they answered, 'May the Great Name be blessed!' At that very moment the man was released from his punishment. The man immediately came to Rabbi Akiva in a dream, and said: 'May it be the will of the Lord that your soul will find delight in the Garden of Eden, for you have saved me from the sentence of Gehenna.' Rabbi Akiva declared: 'Your Name, O Lord, endures forever, and the memory of You through all the generations!' For this reason, it became customary that the evening prayers on the night after the Sabbath are led by a man who does not have a father or a mother, so that he can say Kaddish and 'Bless the Lord who is blessed!'

[Wieseltier, 1998, pp. 41–43]

Here again is the great importance given to learning and teaching as part of the process of forgiving – the culture of remembering as well as the culture of forgiving! The legend of the man Akiva also reminds me of Staretz Zosima in *The Brothers Karamazov* (Dostoyevsky, 1879): "I ask myself: 'What is Hell?' And I answer thus: 'The suffering of no longer being able to love'" (*shto jest' ad? . . . Stradaniye o tom, shto nel'za uzhe bolyeye lyubit;* p. 322; p. 349).[8]

But I would like to reflect as a psychoanalyst upon yet another aspect of this story: the doubling of the name Akiva, in the rabbi and the "heathen." Could we not see this also as some form of double consciousness, double personality, or split identity just as we observed it clinically? Is it a myth about doubleness that expresses the conflict within our conscience with regards to death—the burden of guilt in life, and the shame over the utter and total dehumanization inherent in death, as embodied by the naked and degraded black man? The doubleness of guilt and shame is only overcome by the atoning power of teaching, studying, and acceptance by the community, and by the mandate of forgiveness, which also applies to the mourner, who must forgive himself.

Much later in his book, Wieseltier (1998) cites the opinion of an otherwise little known Rabbi Ovadia from the fifteenth century, that

> the kaddish is not a prayer for something. It is a proof of something. The son does not request that his father be granted a good fate. The son demonstrates why his father deserves to be granted a good fate. The son is not the advocate, the son is the evidence. . . . Examine me and forgive him. He taught me to be here, and here I am. It is the dead who are responsible for the Kaddish for the dead. . . . The Kaddish is not a prayer for the dead. It is an achievement of the dead.
>
> [pp. 420–421]

Mirror magic and the death-giving eye

Why the *veiling of the mirrors?* I have received several answers to this question. The traditional explanation I obtained is this:

- During Shiv'a, a mourner strives to ignore his/her own physicality and vanity in order to concentrate on the reality of being a soul.
- A mirror represents social acceptance through the enhancement of one's appearance. Jewish mourning is supposed to be lonely, silent; dwelling on one's personal loss. Covering the mirrors symbolizes this withdrawal from society's gaze.
- Prayer services, commonly held in the Shiv'a house, cannot take place in front of a mirror. When we pray, we focus on God and not on ourselves.
- Physical relations between a husband and wife are suspended during the week of Shiv'a, and thus the need for physical beauty is removed.[9]

But the explanation that seems closest to consciousness and hence most persuasive is that the mirror opens the boundaries to the world of the uncanny, the beyond, the demoniac. The mirror symbolizes the transition into another world: the beloved person has stepped through this portal, and we cannot follow her there. One patient reported a dream (or fantasy?): "Behind broken glass and a damaged picture a mirror was hanging. Through it I could pass and enter another world. It was at the same time uncanny and I was curious. It meant change, and I kept stepping through the mirror." Thus the mirror can be a symbol of the most profound transformation.

Seligmann (1921, p. 288) quotes similar interpretations: "One is afraid that during this time the evil spirits dance their circles and want to look at themselves in the mirror"; and, "the mirror image which is identified with the soul of that person could be carried along by the departing soul"; but he adds that these interpretations fall short. He suspects that the central motive for this custom, also widespread around infants, women who have given birth, and those who are ill, may be the fear of the dangerous "rays of the gaze" ("*verderblichen Augenstrahlen*"): the rays emanating from the eyes of the dead might be absorbed by mourners, in a form of the *"evil eye."*

In certain cultures, it is believed that the image in the mirror is in fact one's soul; Elkisch (1957) writes that "the idea of death with regard to mirroring or reflecting one's image in the water is essentially connected with the idea of losing one's soul"; Elkisch further explains that the sight or the dream of one's reflection in the mirror is commonly thought to portend death.

The mirror also opens up the portal to another alternate reality, the world of the unconscious. Thus the veiling and turning around of the mirror may be a way to defend against the feared envy, jealousy, and judgment coming from the ghost of the dead—the projection of one's guilt over survival and hostile wishes against the dead, and the threat of punishment for them (Freud, 1912). And for that, one has to inwardly ask the dead for much forgiveness.

Another possibility is that the closing of the eyes of the dead and as the covering of the mirrors is again a turning of passive into active: in death, the aliveness and attentiveness of the eye has now stopped, has become rigid and frozen.[10] In veiling the mirrors, the process of arrested sight is actively reenacted, restaged, as it were.

However, it is the following interpretation that makes the most sense to me: a friend and colleague, Marion Oliner (see her contribution to this volume), describes how, after the deportation and murder of her parents in Auschwitz, she avoided looking at herself in the mirror that hung in a corridor of the children's home where she had, for some time, found refuge:

> I apparently did not look at myself in the mirror after I reached the "home" to which I was sent in 1942. The reason that I know this so precisely was that I passed a mirror on the way to bed every night, and one night I was shocked to see myself, which can only mean that I had not seen myself for a period of time. I thought that it meant that the loss you sustain when someone dies is also a loss of yourself. For me it was not part of a ritual but rather something that happened spontaneously. As you know, there was no period of mourning otherwise.
>
> [Oliner, personal communication]

Could not this have also been some kind of survival shame?

More generally, the entire ritual of the mirrors seems to me to hint at a *deep connection between death, grief, and shame.* Death and mortality are for all of us a deep slight of our self-image; and the total dehumanization of the corpse, the absolute transition from the person into a thing, touches upon something that we might call *primary shame (Urscham)*, similar to the "petrification" or "mortification" in the experience of shame itself and in the myths of the transformation of people into rocks (for example, Circe, Rapunzel).[11] Toward the end of his book, Wieseltier (1998) quotes an English writer of the seventeenth century: "I am not so much afraid of death, as ashamed thereof." Wieseltier adds: "Here was a man for whom human mortality was a contradiction to human dignity" (p. 583).

But always back to the essential: *remembering one means keeping them alive*. Someone quoted to me Elie Wiesel: "Who remembers lives twice." Yet, as Wieseltier laments: what about those untold human beings who perished in the Shoah and who have nobody, no children, who will remember them? Who will say the Kaddish for them and keep Yahrzeit for them?

The pressure of the world of things

> *Das aber kann ich nicht ertragen,*
> *Daß so wie sonst die Sonne lacht;*
> *Daß wie in deinen Lebenstagen*
> *Die Uhren gehn, die Glocken schlagen*
> *Einförmig wechselnd Tag und Nacht.*

Theodor Storm, Einer Toten[12]

A third circle of themes that has great weight in the process of mourning today, and likely always has, is the burden of practical tasks that falls upon us almost immediately after a death. I mean by this all the urgent notifications, changes in titles, transfer of accounts, all the necessary registrations and changes, implications for the taxes, answering questions and letters, preparations for the tombstone, sorting and clearing out of the belongings, the clothes, the papers.

We had thought that we had for years already done the necessary preparatory work, but it turned out that all these tasks assailed us like a pitiless storm surge immediately after the Shiv'a sitting. Suddenly, everything was so much more complicated than anticipated. In addition to the deep sadness, I felt and still often feel a huge fatigue: "Are not suffering, death, and loss already enough? How can I deal with these new burdens?" Of course, these are all demands that invade from the outside and amplify those from within (superego commands and narcissistic wounds!) Sometimes I was gripped by a great anger for not being left alone. Everything demanded my decision.

Something similar happens with all the urgent tasks in the house of illness and death, the need to now rid it of all the accumulated things, to go through what has been left behind, and to sift through and start ordering what I myself had left lying around, unfinished and disordered, over several years of emergencies and caring, of terror and grief. The entire household had to be revamped. Again, this is a series of superego demands that also belong to the process of mourning, to the work of grief, the "*Trauerarbeit*," as Freud called it (1917). I ask myself: why has this been omitted from psychoanalytic writings (at least as far I know them)?

At the same time, this process of sifting and ordering forces more and more the leave taking from things that had to do with my wife, reminding me very much of the process of detachment so impressively described by Freud. This forced and oppressing separation from many objects, from things, stands symbolically for the great loss of somebody very close to me. It is so for the whole world at home: the house, the blooming and wonderfully fragrant bushes she had planted, the flowers she had put into the earth, the trees in the shadow of which I sit and which she had set as little, promising sprouts into the lawn, the stone plates she had laid, the little swimming pool with its mosaic mural (*mosaikmuster*) that she had built for the children, the walls she had artfully painted, the paintings she had hung . . . With all these I think now of the final farewell from her, and that hurts very much. Have I valued her throughout life? By far not enough!

I do not like to talk about the death of the other person as "object loss" though; the human being is no object, except when we dehumanize him. It is precisely not an object that we mourn, but the most valuable fellow being (*Mitmensch*) – not an It (*Es*), but a You (*Du*; Buber, 1947).

The grieving psychotherapist

What are the consequences for my psychotherapeutic and supervisory activity now? (Unfortunately, from 2006 to until recently, I conducted no psychoanalyses in the proper or classical sense.)

It is inevitable that my wife's long course of illness and death, and periods of the severest anxiety and sadness, had continually intruded (and had to intrude) into psychotherapy and supervision. The "frame" was repeatedly, radically blown apart. Already at the time of her progressively decompensating Alzheimer's disease, and more so with the many life-threatening crises related to her cancer and again for my own operations and other medical interventions, it was often necessary to cancel sessions at short notice and, rarely, to interrupt them in the middle. It was therefore also ineluctable to respond to questions and reveal much about my current situation. Most of what were telephone sessions could be held at home, so that between them I could be with my wife and assist her. In addition, although we had, for the last year of her life, around-the-clock caregivers, as my wife could never be left alone, still it was I who for legal reasons had to give her most of her medications, especially the narcotics. There were weeks where I had to cease my work almost completely, especially when I had to wait in the hospital for rounding physicians and consultants, and of course during the Shiv'a week.

Is psychotherapy or supervision under these circumstances still feasible and useful? I certainly would say yes. It was necessary both for the continuity of work and the relationship to patients and colleagues and also for myself, as a hold on reality and for meaning in life – quite apart from the fact that treatment and care were very expensive and made my income important. Naturally, with all of this, the *real relationship* moved strongly into the foreground; but even this opened the possibility to work on *new transference conflicts*, and, in particular, on *revived traumata*. The latter appears to have become more and more important. Patients and colleagues who have gone or are going through traumatic experiences of shared suffering ("*Mit-Leiden*") and loss, but have partly denied or disavowed them, have been encouraged to turn to them and admit some "forgotten" affects. So much of this living through becomes a shared experience. We are talking in a common language in a way that would have been impossible before: about sadness of course and deep sorrow, but also layers of guilt, conflicts in the superego, anger and wrath about the lack of understanding and coldness of others, questions of deep doubt about still-necessary medical decisions, and most of all, again and again, great anxiety, even panic. Still, shared shame is half the shame; shared suffering is half the suffering.

A colleague and friend shares with me how hard it is for him to do things his gravely ill son is now not able to do anymore: reading, watching television, exercise. For him it is also a deep solidarity, a "suffering-with" (*Mit-Leiden*): "I do not think that I could ever wake up and be happy again ... My interest in finding meaning is destroyed." He wants to take his son's suffering off his shoulders and put it entirely upon his own, with the fantasy of magically removing his son's brain tumor by vicarious suffering.

And yet the often great fatigue and sense of paralysis is part of the working through of a very deep woundedness, and it has to be accepted that it may be repeatedly imperative to lie down and rest. In other words: *regression in the service of working through the pain* should not be rejected and suppressed as something shameful. Occasionally it may be good to cry together. Shared humanness has something healing for both. At the same time, it is the awareness of the work ethic, in other words, the picture of the father who continues his work or quickly resumes it, that may lend one's patients strong inner support and trusting steadiness during a severe storm. Anonymity and "indifference" turn into dubious factors: could at times this attitude, which was and is significant, even indispensable (especially in the historical development of psychoanalysis) protection against the analyst's acting out, be enlisted as a fetish to repudiate mourning, hindering optimal work? "The sorrow which has no vent in tears may make other organs weep" (Maudsley, 1895, p. 138).

Also, the cognitive regression that I described in myself as a split reality is a manifestation of dissociation, but should in no way be mistaken as psychotic (a great, yet very frequent error, adding to the hyperbole and diagnostic inflation ravaging our field). Quite independently from the work of mourning, I have often witnessed with dismay and anger how colleagues are incredibly quick to regard it, in fact, almost everything that has to do with regression, as psychotic and to reduce it to a so-called psychotic core. I am reminded of Schiller's word: "*und sie treiben mit Entsetzen Spott*" (they deal with horrors disdainfully or cavalierly). With such exaggerations of pathology, one blocks human empathy and understanding of the other's genuine distress.

What I have found especially difficult is working with people who show very little sympathy and interest; for example, colleagues in supervision who rarely, if ever, inquire, but always burst into sessions with their material as if their reality were the only important thing, or from whom even the occasional question did not seem genuine, but perfunctory. "I come to you to deal with our tasks, not with your problems." This I have hardly experienced with patients. Moreover it is also very delicate to bring this into the dialogue, because such a remark would be immediately experienced as a strong reproof. And this is true as well.

Made aware of this by reading this essay, one candidate explains to me how uncertain he had been, and afraid that he could "violate invisible boundaries":

These conscious conflicts certainly covered deeper layers, defense against my own traumata, my own sadness and feelings of guilt in connection with the illnesses and dying of my mother . . . The difficulty in showing sympathy toward you perhaps reflects how difficult it is [to express it] toward myself, then and certainly to a large part even today.

The opposite can also become a problem: when the hours, particularly in supervision, become completely consumed by sympathy. Besides the strong and sincere participation and humanity, there may be some displacement of the supervised's own worries and personal sorrows and pain, and I try then, earlier rather than later, to come to those. This return to their own issues is of course even more relevant in their work with patients.

Sadness, pain, guilt, and splitting of reality are always tightly connected with problems of aggression, especially that which is directed against one's own self. Also, thwarted wishes for omnipotence and immortality and the deep threat to self-esteem and self-image in the therapist, as well as in patients and colleagues in supervision, play an underground role, largely unconsciously, as a kind of counterpoint. These conflicts can in particular be approached only with a great deal of tact, so that their interpretation are not experienced as veiled reproach and a form of acting out of the superego in the countertransference (generally an enormously important and vastly underreflected problem). Insight into the underlying conflicts *within* the superego, not *with* the superego can here help farther.

My own mortality and existential vulnerability has also become a burning issue for me. *Understanding is consoling.* But the greatest consolation is "the *sympathy*, the *shared suffering (das Mit-Leiden)* in the strictest sense" (Meuli, 1975, p. 423), the dialogue:

> When there is anguish in a person's mind, let him talk it out, and a good word will make him glad (or "give him joy": *de'agá belev-ish jasschénna, wedavár tov jesammechénna*").
>
> —Proverbs/*Mishlei*, 12.25

> Give sorrow words; the grief that does not speak
> Whispers the o'er-fraught heart and bids it break.
>
> —William Shakespeare[13]

Notes

1 This essay owes much to the dialogue with Dr. Heidrun Jarass, Regensburg, especially to the support she gave me from 2005 to 2009 on an almost daily basis during the very difficult time of the severe suffering and fatal illnesses of my wife. I also want to thank very much those who assisted my wife and I during these painful years with much sympathy and life-prolonging help: Drs. Joel Ross, Daniel Laheru, David Hutcheon, Everett Siegel, Robert Shochet; Mrs. Ella-Mae Burke and Andora Shinabarger; Rabbi Gershon Blackmore, and Rabbi Ross Singer for his very thoughtful *hesped*. This paper was given at the American Psychoanalytic Association Meetings in Washington DC, June 6, 2010, and as a plenary address at the German Psychotherapy Weeks in Lindau, April 29, 2010.

2 *King Lear*, IV.I, Shakespeare, 1994, p. 1294.
3 This is in accord with John Steiner (2005), who observes that intense identification with the lost object can serve as a potential means to *avoid* the recognition of loss, interfering with, rather than facilitating the process of mourning – *ed*. [AT].
4 Similar beliefs and rituals are found in other cultures, as was widely publicized after Nelson Mandela's death. Fellow members of the Thembu clan of the Xhosa tribe accompanied Mandela's body until the burial, speaking to him, explaining what was happening, and reassuring him that everything was being carried out correctly – *ed*. [AT].
5 I am very grateful for Mr. Ron Mitnick's help in locating this passage for me.
6 F. Markert, 2010, personal communication: *Sadness and Depression – Understood as Stuck Mourning* (draft).
7 I will take up the topic of "nameless grief" further in the Epilogue.
8 "*shto jest' ad? . . . Stradaniye o tom, shto nel'za uzhe bolyeye lyubit'*"
9 Mr. Ron Mitnick, Rabbi Ari Enkin, personal communication.
10 This was suggested by Dr. Alf Gerlach.
11 The ancient myth of Niobe also comes to mind; she was turned into a stone and condemned to mourn for her children, who were slaughtered to punish their mother's hubris and vanity – *ed*. [AT].
12 "This I cannot bear: that the sun keeps smiling as always, that as during your life's days the clocks still go and the bells toll, monotonously alternating day and night." Theodor Storm, "For a dead woman," quoted in Meuli, 1975, p. 422.
13 *Macbeth* 4.3, Shakespeare, 1994, p. 1330; I thank Dr. Zvi Lothane for bringing this quote to my attention.

References

Aristotle (1926). *Art of Rhetoric*. Loeb Classical Library, trans. J.H. Freese. Cambridge, MA & London: Harvard University Press, 1975.

Atlas, J. (2000). *Saul Bellow: A Biography*. New York: Modern Library.

Barbal, M. (2005). *Inneres Land: Roman*, trans. H. Nottebaum. Berlin: Transit Buchverlag, 2008.

Beland, H. (2009). Kollektive Trauer – Wer oder was befreit ein Kollektiv zu seiner Trauer? Annäherung an die Trauer des Selbstverlustes über den Vergleich mit Freuds Empirie und Theoriegeschichte des Trauerns. In: *Über die (Un)Möglichkeit zu trauern*, eds. F. Wellendorf & T. Wesle, Stuttgart: Klett/Cotta, 2009, pp. 243–262.

Breuer, J., & Freud, S. (1893–1895). Studies on Hysteria. Standard Edition, 2:1-305. London: Hogarth Press, 1955.

Brontë, C. (1847). *Jane Eyre* (Norton Critical Edition), ed. R.J. Dunn. New York: W.W. Norton & Company, 2000.

Buber, M. (1947). *Between Man and Man*, trans. R.G. Smith. London: Kegan Paul, 1947.

Dostoyevsky, F.M. (1879). *The Brothers Karamazov*. Russian edition, Moscow: Chudozhestvennaja literatura, 1988; English edition, trans. R. & and L. Volokhonsky. San Francisco: North Point Press, 1990.

Eickhoff, F.-W. (2011). Ein Plädoyer für das umstrittene Konzept der primären Identifizierung. *Psyche – Zeitschrift für Psychoanalyse*, 65:63–83.

Elkisch, P. (1957). The psychological significance of the mirror. *J. Amer. Psychoanal. Assn.*, 5:235–244.

Freud, S. (1912). Totem and taboo. Standard Edition, 13:1–161. London: Hogarth Press, 1955.

_____. (1917). Mourning and melancholia. Standard Edition, 14:237–258. London: Hogarth Press, 1957.

Kast, V. (1982). *Trauern. Phasen und Chancen des psychischen Prozesses*. Stuttgart: Kreuz Verlag.

_____. (2006). *Zeit der Trauer*. Freiburg: Kreuz Verlag.

Kernberg, O. (2010). Some observations on the process of mourning. *Internat. J. Psycho-Anal.*, 91: 601–619.

Krystal, H. (1988). *Integration and self-healing: Affect, trauma, alexithymia*. Hillsdale, NJ: Analytic Press.

_____. (1998). Desomatization and the consequences of infantile trauma. *Psychoanalytic Inq.*, 17:126–150.

Kubie, L.S. (1958). *Neurotic Distortion of the Creative Process*. New York: Noonday Press.

Maudsley, H. (1895). *The Pathology of Mind: A Study of its Distempers, Deformities, and Disorders*. London and New York: Macmillan & Co.

Meuli, K. (1975). *Gesammelte Schriften* (2 Bände). Basel/Stuttgart: Schwabe.

Rappaport, D. (1953). Some metapsychological considerations concerning activity and passivity. In: *The Collected Papers of David Rappaport*, ed. M.M. Gill. New York: Basic Books, 1967, pp. 530–568.

Seligmann, S. (1921). *Die Zauberkraft des Auges und das Berufen*. Hamburg: Verlag J. Couvreu.

Shakespeare, W. (1994). *The Oxford Shakespeare, Vol III. The Tragedies*, ed. S. Wells. New York: Oxford University Press, USA.

Shengold, L. (1989). *Soul Murder: The Effects of Child Abuse and Deprivation*. New Haven: Yale University Press.

Singer, P. (2009). Why we must ration health care. *The New York Times Magazine*, July 19th 2009, pp. 38–43.

Steiner, J. (2005). The conflict between mourning and melancholia. *Psychoanal. Q.*, 74:83–104.

Talmud Bavli. Schottenstein Edition of the Babylonian Talmud. Brooklyn: Artscroll (1935–1952).

Wellendorf, F. (2009). Verletzbar durch Verlust und Endlichkeit –Trauern und Überleben. In: *Über die (Un)Möglichkeit zu trauern*, eds. F. Wellendorf & T. Wesle. Stuttgart: Klett/Cotta, pp. 21–36.

Wieseltier, L. (1998). *Kaddish*. New York: Random/Vintage.

Wurmser, L. (1989). *Die zerbrochene Wirklichkeit: Psychoanalyse als das Studium von Konflikt und Komplementarität*. Berlin: Springer.

_____. (1993). *Das Rätsel des Masochismus*. Berlin: Springer.

_____. (2000). *The Power of the Inner Judge: Psychodynamic treatment of the Severe Neuroses* (German: *Flucht vor dem Gewissen: Analyse von Über-Ich und Abwehr bei schweren Neurosen*). Northvale, NJ: Jason Aronson.

_____. (2001). *Ideen- und Wertewelt des Judentums: Eine psychoanalytische Sicht*. Göttingen: Vandenhoeck & Ruprecht.

_____. (2005/2013). *Getting To The Heart of Things–An Attempt at an Autobiography*, trans. M. Ott, unpublished manuscript.

_____. (2007). *Torment Me, But Don't Abandon Me: Psychoanalysis of the Severe Neuroses in a New Key*. Northvale, NJ: Jason Aronson.

_____. (2012). Archaic heritage, the self-contradiction in Monotheism, and the Jewish ethos of *Menschlichkeit*: Thoughts of a psychoanalyst about a triple centenary. *Amer. Imago*, 69:401–429.

Wurmser, L. & Jarass, H. (2007). Pathological jealousy: The perversion of love. In: *Envy and Jealousy: New Views About Two Powerful Feelings*, eds. L. Wurmser & H. Jarass. London: Routledge.

11

DISCUSSION OF PART II

Nothing gold can stay?

Jeanine M. Vivona

In four powerful papers, Oliner, Ornstein, Kernberg, and Wurmser draw on their personal experiences of losing loved ones as a basis for reconsidering central tenets of the psychoanalytic theory of mourning. These authors focus on common aspects of the processes of mourning following the death of a significant other, while taking into account the individual circumstances and dynamics that undoubtedly shape and sometimes forestall the mourning process. Kernberg and Wurmser reflect on the experience of losing a beloved spouse after decades of life together; Oliner and Ornstein consider the more extraordinary situation, the lifelong aftermath of losing family members, home, community, and a sense of safety as a result of war and genocide.

Here I draw out a few of the many threads that weave through the individual contributions, juxtaposing and synthesizing the authors' different conceptualizations of normative mourning and its transformative potentials. I also bring in ideas generated during the discussion among Kernberg, Ornstein, and Wurmser, panelists at the session, "Mourning, Identity, Creativity," the impetus for their contributions to the present volume.[1] My remarks are organized around five questions that permeate the papers: 1) What is the normative nature of mourning? 2) What is loss and what is trauma? 3) What are the transformative or creative potentials of mourning? 4) What lies beyond analysts' personal experiences of loss and mourning? 5) What is necessary for a bereaved person to engage in adaptive mourning?

What is the normative nature of mourning?

Mourning involves immense suffering. Accepting that deep and prolonged anguish is inherent in mourning, Wurmser, Ornstein, Oliner, and Kernberg do not consider recurring painful feelings toward and memories of the lost person to be pathological. The acuteness and character of this suffering, and the felt need of mourners to share it, is not captured in the literature, as Oliner observes, yet we are inevitably moved by it. The remarkable response Oliner evoked from her audience in Berlin strikes me as similar to the response I observed during our panel presentation in New York as the audience listened to the stories of loss with stricken faces, ashen or red with sadness, eyes moist, cheeks wet with tears, clearly visible to us on the stage. We all know some version of this pain.

Wurmser depicts the mourner's suffering powerfully and poignantly. Examining his experience of his wife's illness and death, he considers guilt, regret, and shame as consequences of both the identification with the departed person, and the loss of fantasies of omnipotence, which the reality of death destroys. Regarding the suffering of his interviewees, Kernberg notes the persistence as well as the value of painful memories, dreams, wishes, and conscious reflection centered on the lost spouse. Reflecting on her own losses during the Holocaust, Ornstein notes an adaptive function in the experience of unbidden, deeply painful memories of the deceased person. Although it may have a compulsive, driven quality, and may be colored with guilt or shame, Ornstein conceptualizes such episodic remembering not as pathological, but as an adaptive way to maintain and restore the bereaved person's self. Thus, for these authors, painful remembering, as well as guilt, regret, and concomitant desires for reparation, is intrinsic to all mourning, both adaptive and pathological. Yet Oliner reminds us that such remembering requires that the mourner relinquish crucial defenses, which may be possible only gradually, with time, and that looking forward may for a time take precedence over looking back, especially when losses occur in the context of trauma.

The authors are united in disagreement with Freud's theory that the ties to the lost object are given up or decathected normatively in mourning. To be sure, reality requires the lost one be given up as an external presence. Yet adaptive mourning, according to these authors, requires the lost one be maintained as an internal presence, which is sometimes profoundly felt and influential on the thoughts, feelings, and actions of the bereaved. Precipitated by losses of both the external other and those aspects of self connected to that lost person – the husband, daughter, friend that one was to him or her – adaptive mourning brings the lost loved one into the self in new ways.

Kernberg and Wurmser in particular speak of the ongoing object relationship to the departed spouse, conveying the bereaved person's poignant desire to maintain the connection to the lost loved one, to remain faithful to the spouse, and to continue living in a way consistent with the wishes and plans of the deceased person. In fact, Kernberg and Wurmser believe that maintenance of an inner relationship that memorializes the deceased person is characteristic of normal mourning, and thus depathologizes the persistent cathexis of that relationship, perhaps implying that relinquishment of the inner relationship, which Freud considered normative, may instead be a process of pathological or incomplete mourning. Indeed, Wurmser believes "Love is no cake that is diminished by sharing" (this volume); nor is love an energy of limited quantity. Moreover, the equation of fidelity with exclusivity is a relic of earlier development, rather than an inherent demand of faithfulness to a loved person.

Kernberg offered a similar idea during our discussion of this issue on the panel. He suggested that the ongoing presence of the inner relationship to the lost love may facilitate the ability to love another spouse (see also Kernberg, 2010), whereas refusal to engage in new love relationships may reflect an inability to mourn fully.

Ornstein does not merely reject Freud's belief that decathexis of the lost object is necessary for the bereaved person to reengage in life and relationships; she reverses this relation, asserting that selfobject relationships make mourning possible, not the other way around. If the tie to the departed person is eventually relinquished, it is because new selfobject relationships have taken over the functions of the tie. Like Ornstein, Kernberg and Wurmser conceptualize the form of the internalized tie to the deceased person to be a *relationship*, although each uses somewhat different terms for this relationship; yet for none of them is it a cathected *object*.

Consistent with these views, Oliner contrasts Loewald's theory of mourning with Freud's and finds particularly useful Loewald's idea that identification with the lost object enlarges the ego, such that mourning *and* loving again become possible. Indeed, in his paper on the superego and mourning, Loewald (1962) repeatedly refers to "relinquishment and internalization," this phrase serving to underscore the interdependent and simultaneous operation of these processes in mourning: the external object is relinquished *and* internalized. It is in this way, perhaps, that the transformed ego is capable of new relationships that are enriched by the first love, as also described by Kernberg. For Loewald, as for the authors here, the preserved relationship persists as structure.

Loewald considers internalization to be a lifelong process of development; notably, it is a mechanism of therapeutic action by which the relationship with the analyst facilitates change in the analysand. Consistent with this idea, and putting aside the important question about the nature of identification/internalization prior to the oedipal period, it is clear that the authors believe that love relationships are internalized in the process of living. For instance, during our discussion of the question of decathexis on the panel, Ornstein articulated that the deceased loved one had already been a source of selfobject functions during life, and thus his or her death is experienced as a loss of self, as well as a loss of an object. Of course, this must be so; a loss is felt as significant to the extent that the lost one has occupied a place of importance in the inner world of the bereaved person, and thus has formed that world. Yet when we follow Freud in drawing an analogy between mourning a death and resolving the oedipal complex, as he does in the well-known "shadow of the object" passage that Oliner quotes, we consider the internalized lost object as though it is only a new object in the mind, just as the superego is a new structure in the mind of the oedipal child.

I agree we can better understand the suffering of mourners and the compelling ongoing presence of the inner tie to the departed loved one by remembering that the relationship to the loved one was already internalized before the death and remains a presence in the mind. That internal relationship is neither relinquished, as each of these authors attests, nor is it created anew in mourning. Instead, death of the loved one *reveals* the internalized relationship, which now exists in painful contrast to the external absence of the deceased person, whose former presence obscured it. This painful contrast between inner and outer reality is a source of the acute suffering that centers one's emotional life on the deceased person and the experience of loss, at least for a time, as Wurmser describes so poignantly. This self-focused suffering was what Freud wished to explain in "Mourning and Melancholia" and what he, I believe, correctly thought begins to resolve when the mourner becomes able to invest in relationships with others again.

Thus Ornstein, Oliner, Kernberg, and Wurmser all believe that some accepted hallmarks of pathological mourning, in particular the maintenance of the inner relationship with the deceased person and persisting painful memories and feelings of guilt and regret, are in fact characteristics of *all* mourning. I asked Ornstein, Kernberg, and Wurmser, how they distinguish pathological from normative mourning. Drawing on the views of Freud and Melanie Klein, Kernberg believes pathological mourning is characterized by depression, guilt, and sometimes suicidal wishes, symptoms which suggest an inability to make reparation for one's inherent hatred of the loved one, who is now deceased. Such dynamics can manifest in the transference, for instance, when the patient rejects the analyst's empathy. Ornstein believes that the compulsive need to repeat rather than remember signals pathological mourning, which is motivated by the felt need to protect against overwhelming grief. Similarly, Wurmser believes pathological mourning is evinced by rigidity and fixity as compared to openness and responsiveness. In contrast, Oliner notes that a particular type of rigidity, that is, the persistent defensive dissociation of internal and external world, is sometimes a necessary preparation for mourning, rather than a sign of pathology.

What is loss and what is trauma?

Oliner and Ornstein reflect on the death of loved ones who were murdered during a time when war, torture, and dislocation resulted in the violent destruction of their known world, including its cherished relationships, customs, and beliefs, as well as its material aspects. Oliner escaped the concentration camps yet lost both parents and her home; Ornstein was interred with her mother, who also survived, while her father and brothers were killed. Both women lost their homes, communities, and sense of safety during childhood. No one would question the traumatic nature of such experiences. Yet Oliner finds that most psychoanalytic theorizing on trauma (with the exception of Krystal's work) fits poorly with her experiences and their aftermath and finds relatively more value in the psychoanalytic literature on object loss and mourning, in particular the works of Loewald. In situations such as Oliner and Ornstein describe, the deaths of loved family members cannot be separated from their traumatizing context. Thus both women consider their experiences to be *traumatic losses*, and they underscore the prolonged importance of defenses such as denial, disavowal, numbing, and emotional constriction and the delay of mourning until a sense of safety is in part restored. Indeed, Oliner asserts the importance of denial and dissociation, which may be evinced in depression and emotional constriction, to protect the bereaved person from the full force of his or her losses by keeping memories of these traumas at least partly at bay. The self-protective function of delayed mourning is not prominent in the theorizing of Kernberg and Wurmser.

Yet Wurmser, too, centers his understanding of mourning around trauma, citing Krystal's work, as Oliner does. Wurmser offers a psychoanalytic definition of trauma that encompasses the experiences of Ornstein and Oliner as well as his own: "we can define trauma as an overwhelming, unsolvable external conflict between self and environment, that leads to a conscious, but unsolvable inner conflict" (this volume). Compared to the more objective definition of trauma as an experience that threatens life or bodily integrity, his is a subjective definition of trauma, in that what is experienced as overwhelming and unsolvable depends on the person. Wurmser articulates that his long marriage and his experience of his wife's illness and death were shaped by their joint and separate histories, including their experiences during the Holocaust. Against the backdrop of early traumatic losses, the death of a spouse, particularly a prolonged and painful one involving contention with medical professionals, would likely ignite overwhelming, seemingly irresolvable conflicts.

In his prior work on this subject, Kernberg (2010) states, "mourning, of course, always implies a traumatic loss" (p. 616). Thus he identifies traumatic loss not by the attributes of the circumstances surrounding the loss or by its subjective meanings to the bereaved person, but by its psychological outcome, that is, the process of mourning itself. His construction of trauma here parallels a medical definition of trauma as an experience that causes (physical) injury. For Kernberg, trauma is an experience that causes psychical injury.

Indeed, none of the authors distinguishes between trauma and loss. Yet perhaps this is apt. The loss of a beloved person is a type of trauma, and trauma is a type of loss. *Traumatic loss*, then, underscores the simultaneous experiences of loss and trauma in those who lose a loved one felt to be essential to one's being and existence; mourning is its expression.

What are the transformative or creative potentials of mourning?

The creative potential of mourning is addressed explicitly by Kernberg, Ornstein, and Wurmser, and implicitly by Oliner. Examples of the creative stimulus of mourning, their papers themselves evince the desire of mourners to transcend personal suffering through the creation of new works that may do good for others. These authors agree that the death of a loved one changes you; you are never the same again. To go back to the way things were would be to deny the loss and foreclose the possibilities for growth that mourning offers. On the other hand, Wurmser observes that creativity in mourning may at times reflect pathology, and Kernberg and Ornstein concur that artistic endeavors are sometimes fueled by repetitive or compulsive responses to loss; thus the creation of art is not in and of itself evidence of adaptive, normative mourning.

Each author conceptualizes creative change in mourning as occurring at various loci – in the intrapsychic realm, through the creation of a new internal object relation or identity or moral code; in the interpersonal realm, through the creation of a new life or a new kind of interpersonal relationship; and in the wider world, through creative acts of all kinds, notably the creation of works of art that both derive from one's personal mourning and facilitate the mourning of those who experience that art.

Yet each author uses distinct language to describe the processes of change in mourning. Ornstein uses the language of self-psychology and understands the expansion of the self in mourning to include providing for oneself the selfobject functions previously provided by the deceased person, as well as the expansion of identity through identifications with the lost object. Kernberg uses the language of object relations and the structural model, and in particular he describes the enrichment of the superego and the ego ideal in ways that reflect ongoing adaptations to the loss of the loved one and to the existential truths that loss engenders in the bereaved person. Oliner and Wurmser use the language of ego defense and adaptation; Wurmser notes the reorganization of infantile fantasies that occur when the bereaved person is confronted with the reality of death and his or her personal failings, perceived or actual, toward the loved one.

During the panel, I was struck by this use of different theoretical languages to formulate apparently similar observations and interpretations, and I continue to wonder about the extent to which Kernberg, Ornstein, and Wurmser truly differ in their conceptualizations of the transformations wrought by adaptive mourning. At the time, I asked the panelists to reflect on the degree to which they believe they have articulated a consistent set of observations and ideas, despite their different theoretical lenses and terminology. Their responses to this query were more notable in tone than in content. While retaining their individual languages, the panelists downplayed their differences and seemed to desire both consensus and commonality, to consider their underlying ideas and experiences as essentially similar, despite the different terms they continued to use. This was true even between Kernberg and Ornstein, whose positions were theoretically the most distinct and historically most contentious. To witness these panelists unprecedentedly relinquish their theoretical differences in this way was both surprising and moving. Differences in theory, however important, were eclipsed, however temporarily, by the palpable power of shared suffering and grief. Indeed, although only Ornstein spoke about the Holocaust, a question from an audience member brought forth that each panelist had experienced those events of their generation in direct and personal, if different, ways. Speculatively, the panelists may have engaged in something akin to creative mourning as they found new ways to relate to one another in the context of discussing and experiencing their grief, in particular evidencing tolerance of differences with others, a process noted by Kernberg, and emphasis on current, present relationships, an outcome noted by Wurmser.

What lies beyond analysts' personal experiences of loss and mourning?

The very personal nature of these writings is their strength and their limitation, the latter particularly with respect to the authors' goal of revising psychoanalytic theories of mourning. For this purpose, we must acknowledge the limits of personal experience, even more than of professional experience with patients. Regarding representativeness of the authors' observations, the mourning process is complexly shaped by the characteristics and history of the individual who experiences the death of a loved one, the relationship to the deceased person, the context in which the loss occurs, and the experiences that surround and follow it. For instance, the experience of mourning is affected by the relationship to the deceased person (e.g., spouse, parent, child), the type of death (e.g., expected, tragic, traumatic), and the setting (e.g., war, peace, home, exile). Is there a general experience of mourning that unites these different circumstances? The authors think so, despite fully recognizing the complexity and variety of mourning experiences. Indeed, Oliner observes, "in psychoanalytic thinking there are very few, if any, absolutes" (this volume). Consequently, answering such a question requires studying the experience of many types of people and many types of losses.

Despite differences in their personal attributes, Wurmser and Kernberg describe the similar experience of mourning a spouse of many years. Kernberg notices common dynamics in some of his patients and in a group of interviewees, whose characteristics he does not mention except to note that all have been remarried. The observation of common features is a reasonable starting point for theory development, as Kernberg (2010) notes, yet his observations do not capture even this particular mourning experience in sufficient variety; missing, to give one example, are the experiences of those who do not remarry after the death of a spouse, an important omission given the various functions that remarriage may serve in the context of mourning. Moreover, the authors (and perhaps some of Kernberg's interviewees) as analysts and their patients constitute particular groups whose mourning experiences are distinct by virtue of their vocation and status as patients and their shared inclination toward psychoanalytic therapy, with its valuing of reflection, remembering, and emoting. Finally, as mentioned earlier, the authors share generational and personal experiences of the Holocaust, and all agree that such early experiences of loss are reawakened by and shape the experience of subsequent loss. A general psychoanalytic theory of mourning must be informed by observations of people who have not suffered early traumatic loss.

Moreover, as noted earlier, the mourning experience is altered when loss occurs in the context of trauma and hardship. Ornstein asserts that mourning is compromised when there is no body to bury and when the surviving community of mourners are themselves bereaved and traumatized. Indeed, when we juxtapose the experiences of Kernberg and Wurmser, who lost their beloved spouses, with the experiences of Oliner and Ornstein, who as children lost parents and other beloved family members as well as country, community, and identity, we are better able to appreciate both the differences and the similarities in the experience of bereaved people and the mourning process that the loss of loved ones precipitates.

Of course, in any person's life, the precise pattern of influences is inscrutable, inevitably moot. Thus theoretically important relationships among factors or processes cannot be definitively discerned within an individual case or even in a group of cases presented to support a theory. These limitations of the case study are well known. To give one example with respect to the theory of mourning, Wurmser and Kernberg theorize about a kind of loss that is inherent in life, part of development itself, and thus inexorably entwined with it. Consequently, the changes wrought by experiencing the death of a beloved spouse of many years cannot be easily separated from the insights that come from living and aging, quite apart from the consequences of losing loved ones to death and the internalizations and transformations that may follow. Kernberg reports that his interviewees attributed their changed attitudes toward both death and life to the loss of the spouse in particular. Conviction aside, this is not something one can conclude with any objective certainty.

Finally, I am struck by the optimistic color of some of the theorizing. Not only is there an idealization of the departed loved one, as Ornstein mentions, but also an idealization of the process of mourning itself. For instance, Kernberg focuses on expansions of the superego as the bereaved person takes on aspects of the life project of the deceased spouse, and he does not mention the complementary constrictions that may also occur in terms of the bereaved person's separate wishes and life plans. Are there defensive processes at play that foster a valorization of the creative and expansive aspects of mourning while occluding the compromises mourning may entail or potentiate? Wurmser acknowledges the potentially defensive aspects of mourning, which are naturally difficult to detect in one's own experience without the assistance of psychoanalysis. For a psychoanalytic theory of mourning, which must take account of the operation of unconscious processes and meanings, important questions such as these remain unanswered.

Despite these limitations, the authors' experiences and observations contribute to our literature a broader picture of mourning, as well as new theoretical notions for our consideration. Although we do not know whether these observations will help to reveal the normative nature of mourning, our literature is enriched by an expanded view of mourning responses that may be adaptive, at least some of the time. For instance, we do not know whether delayed mourning in response to traumatic losses is common, yet Ornstein and Oliner argue cogently that the delay was adaptive for them. Similarly, although the internal bond to the departed person may be relinquished in some cases, all of the authors demonstrate the adaptive value of a persisting internal bond to the departed person in their own lives.

What is necessary for a bereaved person to engage in adaptive mourning?

Wurmser demonstrates the wisdom of Jewish funeral rituals that initiate a mourning process that potentiates creative change by providing time and space for communal mourning, encouraging a feeling of solidarity with the departed person and acknowledgment of the reality of the death, and creating opportunities for mourners to share memories verbally. These practices acknowledge the importance of others, whose presence combats the bereaved person's sense of being abandoned and helpless. Talking about the departed person is important and painful, but ultimately consoling; such remembering also assists the bereaved in maintaining the relationship to the deceased loved one as an internal presence. Because talking is both sharing and symbolization, it helps to connect (and reconnect) the mourner to the community. For Oliner, too, such rituals offer to replenish the bereaved person. On the other hand, both Oliner and Ornstein describe how mourning can be obstructed when memories of the departed cannot be shared, when deaths are not marked with graves and rituals, and thus cannot be grieved publicly and in words. Like Wurmser, Ornstein believes one cannot mourn alone.

Moreover, Ornstein identifies other internal and external obstacles to the sharing of grief. Internally, there is the fear of collapse in the face of unbearable grief; externally, there is the realistic fear that others will not share in the experience of grief, but will instead turn away. The result is alienation, both internal and external. In such cases, memorial art facilitates mourning in some of the same ways funeral rituals do, by acknowledging death and the need to grieve and by offering a space in which that grieving can take place. The artist who creates memorial art and those who experience it, such as the strangers in the movie theater with Ornstein for the viewing of *Schindler's List*, do not turn away, but wish to show, to see, and to share. At the same time, the bit of distance between the aesthetic representation and the specifics of the mourner's personal experience may protect the mourner from experiencing unbearable grief.

Clinically, recognizing the normative characteristics of mourning, particularly the maintenance of the inner relationship with the deceased person, implies that we should not aim to loosen this persisting tie or to interpret defenses that purportedly maintain it. Instead, Ornstein advises that we understand compulsive repetition as motivated by a need to protect against overwhelming grief and that we support the bereaved person in the dreaded, painful task of remembering the lost person. Both Wurmser and Oliner agree, implying that the bereaved patient may be prone to self-protective rigidity and thus may benefit from exploring defensive obstacles to being open to new experiences in the world, particularly to those that may evoke memories of the lost loved one and the life and self shared with that person. Kernberg suggests that helping the bereaved patient tolerate ambivalence toward the deceased loved one may facilitate mourning and that such ambivalence may be enacted in the transference around the experience of the analyst's empathy. Wurmser believes regression may be healing for the bereaved person when the analyst empathizes with, rather than pathologizes, this way of expressing and managing genuine distress.

Wurmser shares the challenges for the grieving analyst, and for the patients and supervisees of the analyst whose grief and loss are inevitably revealed through visible distress and absences from work and which necessitate a degree of self-disclosure the analyst might not otherwise entertain. This experience of the "real relationship" with the analyst awakens patients' prior experiences of loss and death, potentiating shared suffering as well as affording the opportunity to observe their responses to the grieving of other important people in their lives.

Wurmser alone mentions that bereavement confronts the analyst with his own mortality. The death of a loved one shatters the illusion of immortality and thwarts the universal wish to deny death; it leaves bare the painful existential truth that everyone dies, that death can occur without warning or reason, that there comes a day after which there is no tomorrow, no next time, no second chance. Living without this protective illusion must influence one's work with patients, particularly those who are grieving.

In sum, Wurmser, Ornstein, Oliner, and Kernberg together offer us a poignant, textured, sensitive, and clinically useful understanding of the experience of mourning. Despite their different theoretical lenses and personal experiences, they are united in a view of mourning as painful, difficult, protracted, and yet potentially transformative. In particular, they shed light on the persisting yet changing nature of the tie to the departed person, which may be an ongoing source of comfort and creativity, as well as pain. Their theorizing, although certainly preliminary, promises to enhance our clinical work with diverse bereaved patients.

In recognition of the interest in the union of mourning and creativity that inspired the original panel and occasioned this new theorizing, I end with a poem by Robert Frost (1923) that expresses the inevitability of death and awakens the experience of mourning. Frost wrote this short poem at the age of forty-eight, by which time he had experienced the deaths of both parents, two of his young children, and his closest friend.

Nothing gold can stay

> Nature's first green is gold,
> Her hardest hue to hold.
> Her early leaf's a flower;
> But only so an hour.
> Then leaf subsides to leaf.
> So Eden sank to grief,
> So dawn goes down to day.
> Nothing gold can stay. [p. 84]

Expressed here is the anguished suffering of the bereaved person as well as the hidden hope that the early leaf, the golden flower, while gone from the world, remains in memory, where it can stay.

Note

1 The author was the discussant of presentations by Kernberg, Ornstein, and Wurmser at the panel session chaired by Adele Tutter, "Mourning, Identity, Creativity" at the Winter Meetings of the American Psychoanalytic Association, January 2013 (see full report in Nimroody, 2014).

References

Frost, R. (1923). *New Hampshire: A Poem with Notes and Grace Notes*. New York: Henry Holt & Co.

Kernberg, O. (2010). Some observations on the process of mourning. *Internat. J. Psycho-Anal.*, 91:601–619.

Loewald, H.W. (1962). Internalization, separation, mourning, and the super-ego. *Psychoanal. Quart.*, 31:483504.

Nimroody, T. (2014). Panel report: Mourning, identity, creativity. *J. Amer. Psychoanal. Assoc.*, 62:313–321.

PART III

History, Ancestry, Memory

12

LOST WAX TO LOST FATHERS

Installations by British sculptor Jane McAdam Freud

Jane McAdam Freud in conversation with Adele Tutter

Over the past several years, artist and Fellow of the Royal Society of British Sculptors Jane McAdam Freud has created a remarkable series of drawings and sculptures that explore and memorialize her relationship with her father, Lucian Freud – painter, son of Ernst Freud, and grandson of Sigmund Freud – who passed away in 2011 (Fig. 12.1). A few years earlier, as artist-in-residence at the Sigmund Freud Museum in London from 2005–2006, McAdam Freud generated a body of work inspired by her great-grandfather's collection of art and objects, which she handled and studied for twenty months. She relates her thoughts about this work in conversation with Adele Tutter, coeditor of this volume.

Adele Tutter:	Jane McAdam Freud, you've talked about the role that much of your recent work plays in your process of mourning your father. In your words, the sculpture *THISHERE* (Fig. 12.2, left) "contains in it the words HIS/ HER and the words HE/ SHE and also IS/HE, creating questions/notions of a presence – greater presence or ancestral presence perhaps." Can you elaborate on this notion of a presence? Might it have something to do with memory?
Jane McAdam Freud:	It is to do with memory and also to do with god-like figures. The first death of a god-like figure for me was the death of Father Christmas. My first traumatic memory was the confirmation from my mother that there is no Father Christmas. The IS/HE is very much linked up with identifying Father Christmas as someone who would be there to look after me in the face of the knowledge that both my parents were quite irresponsible and could barely look after themselves.
AT:	Usually children continue to idealize their parents long after giving up their belief in Father Christmas. Your story makes

FIGURE 12.1 Three generations of Freuds. Clockwise, starting from upper left, Jane McAdam Freud on Sigmund Freud's couch in the Freud Museum, London; *Reflection (Self-portrait)*, Lucian Freud, 1985; *Self-Portrait*, McAdam Freud, 1998–99; Sigmund Freud and his portrait sculpture by Oscar Nemon (composite photo), 1931; and McAdam Freud, with her portrait sculpture of Lucian Freud, *Earthstone Triptych*.

	the overlapping of HIS/HER, HE/SHE with the fraught question – *IS/HE?* – especially poignant. How old were you at the time?
JMF:	I was eight years old at the time and we had just moved home away from my father in Central London to South West London. I discovered from the other children that my beliefs in Father Christmas were "out of sync" with theirs.

FIGURE 12.2 *THISHERE*, 2008; right, *Wax Works/Preserved Matter,* 1990–present (lower), *On the Other Hand, 2010.* All work in this and subsequent figures are created by Jane McAdam Freud unless otherwise specified.

AT: The words are engraved on a slab that looks like a tombstone, with a piece of turf on the top, as if it had pushed itself up out of the ground. Can you tell us about the choice of this form?

JMF: I think it was around this time that I turned to art (something I had always enjoyed and found transformative) and imbued it with these care-taking and magical qualities that I had mixed up with notions of God (through transference of my mother's quasi-ambivalence to religion, from being a non-practicing Catholic who was nevertheless indoctrinated through her convent school upbringing, contrasted against art school in the 1960s). Art emerged as my religion. All the magic I invested into my Father Christmas figure was now spread out amongst the other present but absent significant god-like figures, like my great-grandfather Sigmund and my father Lucian. The tombstone-like forms, I like to think of as signifying great power of life in death or absence through myth and memory. I think it is very apt that you see it as pushed out of the ground as there was a type of resurrecting of the past going on at the time I made *THISHERE*.

AT:	The series *Wax Works* (Fig. 12.2, right) is made from the wax that your father obtained for you to work with together. You have remarked that these pieces were kept in a refrigerator to keep them from melting until they were cast in bronze, but that you "sort of forgot about them." I'm assuming that the process of casting would involve melting, and thus destroying the wax. Was the refrigeration an inadvertent way of preserving the material with which you worked with your father?
JMF:	How right you are, not that I consciously thought about in that way but it seems obvious as you say it now. However the wax does not necessarily have to be melted, as a mold can be taken and then the wax preserved (in the fridge).
AT:	Can you tell us about the sculpted forms themselves?
JMF:	The forms are of male and female nudes. What I've said about these figures is that they consider the premise that man's (and woman's) typical state is clothed, so they are posed in positions where it might be more natural to be nude, i.e., bathing, sun bathing, masturbating, etc. In hindsight I think they are an allusion to my father's nudes, which I couldn't then see as relevant conceptually in terms of contemporary art. Not something I voiced but quite clearly something that manifested through these fridge works. The figures were in dialogue to my father's nudes, a conversation (one which I would have been too afraid to have with my father) about the relevance of life drawing in contemporary art.
AT:	Yes: this seems to echo the relationship between the physical presence of the wax forms in the fridge below the mirror, and their implicit absence in the empty cast or mold.
JMF:	I like to look at the positive. However, the mold was also absent in the case of these waxes as I worked directly in wax and molds from those waxes had not been made. I have now, since the exhibition of this work, made molds and cast some of the works using the "lost wax method."
AT:	Is the mirror above the refrigerator part of the piece?
JMF:	The mirror, a separate work of mine, displayed on the fridge shows one handprint reflected to form the pair and it is called *On the Other Hand*. I found it interesting that one hand is there and the other appears as an absent presence – an illusion (neither two- nor three-dimensional), an illusory pairing symbolic of a sacred pairing – an earthly being paired with spiritual being.

I am instinctively drawn toward something between atavism and animism, which could be called *Ata-mism*. My understanding of the term animism is a personal one derived from the Italian word *anima*, suggesting to me the aura of a person which carries something of the aura of their ancestors. Atavism for me carries within it the idea of bringing the past to the present. The work *On the Other Hand* operates as a contemplation of the ancestors who operate from within us biologically, influencing everything from our appearance to our manner.

AT: For the terracotta relief portrait of your father, *Plaque* (Fig. 12.3, left), you used a higher firing temperature to bring "the look of the material back to its raw state where it is alive and malleable as opposed to fired and inert." It is quite a beautiful piece – it appears burnished, almost like actual aged skin. Might this portrait comment on what seems like a process of animation?

JMF: I think it can and I think the ultimate is the self-portrait, which I am working on as a subject now. While immersed it gives me the feeling that I am getting to know myself and am finding answers. I once read that Leonardo said "all the answers are in the mirror."

AT: Last summer, in Příbor, the Czech Republic, we spoke about the notion of relief sculpture as a bridge between your father's two-dimensional painting and your three-dimensional sculpture – another sort of dialogue.

JMF: There are quite clear dialogues going on between the process of painting and the process of relief: the way he modeled his paint, layering it on to emphasize the three-dimensional illusions and the way I build up clay or wax to emphasize the same three-dimensional illusion.

AT: *Earthstone Triptych* (Fig. 12.3, right) is a relief sculpture in which one face has an open eye, and the other, a closed eye. The two faces can't be seen simultaneously unless there is a mirror, as shown in the installation view with *Shadow*. You've explained that *Shadow* is cut into fifteen parts, and that this number has special significance to your family. Many questions could be asked about this evocative piece; for starters, can you tell us more about the relationship between the two standing, two-faced sculpture and the shadow? And the open/closed eye?

FIGURE 12.3 Left, *Plaque*, 2012; right, *Earthstone Triptych* (left) and *Shadow* (right), both, 2011.

JMF: All art is about life and death as is all life in some sense. Acceptance of life is to accept death. One cannot be had without the other. The closed eye represents death and the open eye represents life. Many of my works are made in relief and deal with this beautifully simple equation like the two sides of a coin that contain each other and are mutually dependent.

Shadow came about from the paper template that lay on the floor while I erected *Earthstone Triptych* from clay. When the clay sculpture was finished, I tidied the studio but missed the presence of the template, and so decided to make the template in its lying-down form in clay as part of the installation, and have it operating as a three-dimensional shadow, cut into parts representing present and absent siblings.

My forms most often engage the two-dimensional/three-dimensional illusion, from the two-sided pick-up pieces to the large-scale forms. It is the process that I am most drawn to as it lies between painting/drawing and sculpture and contains the illusory and physical qualities of both.

AT: *Portrait of My Father* (Fig. 12.4, left) is exquisitely textured and conveys a sense of age. Unlike your relief sculptures of your father, it is fully dimensional. You mention "needing permission" to sculpt your father; did he give this, and did he sit for the work, or was it made after his death?

JMF: Often in terms of process, after a period of working solely with relief I am driven to re-engage with forms in the round. Permission is something quite childlike but that's what I felt I needed and got, as I did

FIGURE 12.4 Left, *Portrait of My Father*, 2012; right, *Mm & Mm*, 2010.

not want to imbue the piece with any negative thoughts, intentions or memories. My father sat for the sketches from which I made the sculpture. I started on the large relief sculpture, *Earthstone Triptych*, and showed him the tentative beginnings. I completed this and several sculptures very quickly soon after my father's death when he could no longer sit, in a sort of race against time to get the marks down from his image, so clear in my mind.

AT: In a personal essay published in *The Telegraph on* Aug. 2, 2011, soon after your father passed away, you wrote, "the last time I saw my father was a couple of weeks ago, when I finished the sketches of him. I'm now using them to make a large portrait sculpture. It helps me to keep him alive." Is this the sculpture?

JMF: Yes, *Earthstone Triptych* is the sculpture I referred to at that time, and I made *Portrait of My Father* soon after.

AT: *Mm & Mm* (Fig. 12.4, right) is a sculpture with two faces, which you've identified as Moses and Mary. It expresses (at least) two dualities – Catholic/Jewish, male/female. How do you understand the pervasive representation of duality in your work?

JMF: Well I think we all live with an unconscious resonance of our reflective symmetry, in that we are divisible vertically into two parts. Some internal organs defy this rule but we can't see those. Our sensory selves live in a state of balance between the two sides of our bodies and there is always the conscious unconscious duality.

I am now also thinking about aging and physical impacts on the bodily experience, where working with one's hands takes its toll, for example, repetitive strain injury where the loss of flexibility of one side means learning an asymmetrical way of negotiating our movements around it. This also carries a sense of loss/mourning on a visceral bodily level.

The dualism we live with is also evident in that we know we are living in the second millennium: I see it as the very time of the "two."

We have two parents and live in a two-gender world and we each contain a bit of both genders hormonally. I suppose my work is very visceral and as much driven on a body level as on a rational level, so I play out these compounded sets of pairings through my works.

AT: At the risk of being obvious, might joining together the Catholic and Jewish aspects of your heritage suggest a representation of your parents and their marriage, and a mourning of their relationship – remembering them together, as distinct from mourning them separately?

JMF: I describe the images as based on the icons Mary and Moses and I agree there is that aspect of unification at a deep level and the joining of the two icons with all their differences represents the joining of my parents, which is quite comforting.

FIGURE 12.5 Upper, Freud contemplating a figure, possibly Javanese, London, 1937. Lower, *Allora, Circles and Cycles*, 2006.

AT: You were artist-in-residence in the Sigmund Freud Museum, London, between 2005 and 2006 (Fig. 12.5, upper). Two busts from your *Allora* cycle (Fig. 12.5, lower) take after marble busts in your great-grandfather's collection. The word *allora*, with its double meaning of "now" and "then," implies a continuity – a contiguity, even, between past and present. In so beautifully replicating these sculptures, you are bringing some of your great-grandfather's things with you: in your words, "it is, as though, with the words, *now then*, we are collecting the past and bringing it to the now so that we can proceed with the next." Is it possible to articulate how bringing these things – inanimate but very real "things" – of your great-grandfather, of your ancestry, into the present, help you to "proceed with the next"?

JMF: It is through the tactile that I find my inspiration and creative outlet so handling these objects that my great-grandfather handled was my way of understanding him: through his aesthetic and tactile appreciation I am able to recognize my own, able to trace its precedent. This gave me a sense of family links and heredity. I traced my predilection for sculpture back to my great-grandfather Sigmund.

AT: You've explained with regard to the reverse of the "medal ode to my father," *Truth* (Fig. 12.6, left), that the word **TRUT**H is carved into the surface featuring at its center the word *rut* – "an annual period of sexual activity in deer and some other mammals, during which the males fight each other for access to the females." Another definition is "a sunken track or groove where vehicles get stuck."

FIGURE 12.6 Upper, *Truth*, obverse and reverse sides, 2011/2012; lower, *E art H*, 2011.

Could you comment further on these references?

JMF: The assumption with the concept of truth is that there are truths to be discovered or created, however in my experience the deeper we go the more complicated things seem. One of the meanings of rut refers to a groove in the road where one is able to go a couple of inches forward or backward but nowhere else. For me it is a little like the notion of truth.

My use of the word *truth* also has a personal meaning in reference to my father, for whom art was his truth, in that it was the only thing he 'truly' wanted to do. Knowing this created its own sense of rut.

AT: You are clearly interested in embedded meanings – "rut" in *Truth*, and the number of meanings contained in *THISHERE*. Clearly, much meaning is embedded in this two-sided medal – art is part of your truth, too, and so this medal must contain parts of your truth. Without having to go into specifics, did the making of this piece help you to "excavate" some of those meanings? If so, did it seem to serve a different sort of purpose from the other representations of your father? Does another piece with an embedded signifier, *E art h* (Fig. 12.6, right), do something similar?

JMF: The medal *Truth* helped me to accept my father's behavior as containing something positive and perhaps spiritual, therefore allowing me to keep him as an inspiration rather than someone to react against which is of course the other side of acceptance. As you imply, perhaps it also helped me to accept myself.

Very interesting also that the words *truth* and *rut* add up to eight letters and the words *THISHERE* contain eight letters. My father was born on the eighth of December and eight was his favored 'lucky' number (in gambling).

E art h, a large installation made from grit and salt with *art* at its center, also helps me to understand my father as *art* was at the center of his life: also expressing my relationship to materials, earth, sand, salt, grit, etc. (Sand was my first love in terms of materials, which dates back to the sand pit in nursery school).

AT: When you hung *Sigmund's Marbles* next to *Dad Drawing* (Fig. 12.7), you juxtaposed a drawing of a bust in your Sigmund Freud's collection, with a drawing of your father: one a Hellenic ideal, and the other a familiar, very realistic portrayal of your father. I am struck by the affective similarity between these otherwise two very different drawings – a tender feeling of intimacy and reflection. You've stated that:

Jenny Leeburn reminded me of something I said in a presentation about Sigmund and Lucian using the same processes, i.e., seeing several people a day at a regular time, studying them in depth (on the couch) and getting to know them extremely well – and "never giving them an idea of how long it was going to take," she furthered. This is the more extraordinary as my father always proclaimed not to be interested in Sigmund and psychoanalysis and

FIGURE 12.7 Left, *Sigmund's Marbles*, 2006; right, *Dad Drawing*, 2011.

Sigmund professed not to be interested in art but he loved and collected ancient art.

Is it possible that in drawing these pictures of your father, and your great-grandfather's art, you, too, were "getting to know" your subject? Might this exercise of drawing them, and then joining the drawings, in some way express and/or represent your linkage, your connection, to them?

JMF: As well as my connection to them, it might also express my connection to my ancient colleagues, the artists who made these marbles, etc.

"Sigmund's Marbles, Dad Drawings" also has a nice implication about Sigmund's mind, questioning his (as is the case with anyone) ability to totally objectify his subjective self. When I say subjective I mean in terms of his tastes, particularly in reference to his collected antiquities and the reasons he collected them and his appreciation of them as works of art/sculpture. (The pairing was actually the idea of the curator Nicola Angerame for my exhibition *3Generations* at Whitelabs Gallery in Milan.)

However, as you say, drawing one of Freud's marble sculptures and drawing my father and then exhibiting them as a pair unites Sigmund and Lucian through my interest in art/sculpture. In that respect it is a sort of triptych with the third object as an absent presence, being my hand/authorship of the art, my art as a sort of usurper of both. Oh dear, I hadn't really considered this aspect of Duchampian appropriation in this work too! I have used the idea consciously in another work *Dead or Alive*, a short film merging Sigmund's antiquities with my own works, frame by frame.

Life's unconscious competition is however for life itself and as we grow older we are increasingly aware of our proximity to the end. The inherent competition is between the young and the old, and between life and death.

The ultimate competition is with ourselves after all, for life itself and every artist wants also to be immortal. Lucian has achieved this in the shadow of Sigmund.
I like exceptions to rules and keep in mind what Brancusi said to Rodin when
Rodin asked him to work in his studio, "small shoots do not flourish under the
shadow of great trees," noting that Lucian flourished under Sigmund all the same.

AT: *Stalemate* (Fig. 12.8, left), a series of vinyl drawings, expresses the competitive dimension of Lucian Freud's relationship with Francis Bacon (Fig. 12.8,
lower). You've quoted your father as saying that his friend had "gone off," in
other words, gone "stale." I'm wondering about the influence of Bacon –
your father's "mate," but also his competitor, the two ranking as perhaps the
most important figurative painters of the twentieth century – on your own
work. Isn't a silhouette of one of your sculptures, from the series *After Bacon*,
in one of the units?

FIGURE 12.8 Upper, Francis Bacon and Lucian Freud, Dean Street, Soho, 1972. Lower
left, *Stalemate*, 2012; lower right, *Head and Heart*, from the *After Bacon* series, 1993.

JMF: Yes, well observed! In fact all my *After Bacon* sculptures (Fig. 12.8, upper right) appear in silhouette in *Stalemate*. Bacon was as much of an influence on my generation of art students including me, as was Lucian Freud. Bacon's influence was easier to handle and process than my father's influence. Of the two, it is easier to talk about and admire the work of Bacon, as there is more distance.

AT: I can't help but ask what it means for you – as an artist and as a daughter – to watch Francis Bacon's *Triptych*, a 1969 portrait of your father, Lucian Freud, become the most expensive work of art ever sold at auction [November 12, 2013, Christie's NY, $142.4 million]. In a "stalemate," no one wins, but no one loses. Is this a sort of solution, or compromise, to competition?

JMF: Well my father wasn't really interested in money and he spent a lot of time without any, while the dealers, etc., were making heaps from his work. Things got better later, but with a gambling addiction, he still needed to borrow. Personally, I don't believe art and money have anything to do with each other. It is interesting that the competition was won on a financial level by Bacon but the winning image is of Freud.

As a sculptor, I don't feel competitive with painters. I feel more interested and competitive with people in the same field as me, i.e. sculpture. However, in light of Sigmund's interest in sculpture (through his collection) and the above glimpse into my continued "Duchampian appropriation," I may be unconsciously negotiating a 'stalemate' stance myself.

AT: The notion of the sculpture whose different faces cannot be seen simultaneously comes into play in *Star* (Fig. 12.9, upper). Can you comment on the images on the various segments that comprise *Star*? What is their relationship to one another?

JMF: The images come from a series of my paintings using the Rorschach test process. I wanted the images to be freestanding as with sculpture not flat on a wall like painting. One of the images is Sigmund's glasses.

AT: So you have the tension between flat and form again. Form become flat in *Stalemate*, and flat becomes form in *Star*.

JMF: Interesting that you noted this. I sometimes like to reference the aesthetic conflict in my works, perhaps more obvious in works like my sand installation, *76 Degrees, One Sunny Day* (Fig. 12.9, lower).

AT: I'm curious about *76 Degrees*. Was there something particular about the day/time/season when you created it? A particular memory about the sand (the beach)? Or is there a reference here to the "angle of repose" (the greatest angle a given material can achieve with a flat surface)?

JMF: The work was made for a venue on the coast in Italy, in Andora, so the sand is local and *76 Degrees* does in fact refer to the angle of repose when the sand is poured. I was thinking of the pairing of two applications of the word repose, that is, to sunbath (repose) on sand on a hot day and the way the sand rests at a specific angle of repose. The title merges the meanings.

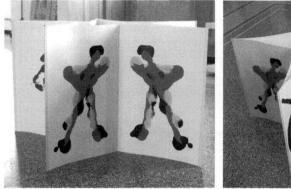

FIGURE 12.9 Upper, *Star*, 2012; lower, *76 Degrees - One Sunny Day*, 2013.

AT: You've identified sand as your "first inspiration." Was it also your first sculptural experience, as a child? Or did it inspire you to create things in other medium?

JMF: Sand was my first inspirational 'tactile' experience. It was then that I knew what I wanted to do, and who I was, even. Putting my hands in the sandpit, aged three or four, through the water into the sand, first transported me to that very same timeless place I go to now when I model works in clay and I still feel the certainty that I am doing exactly what I am meant to be doing. It was a sensation that spoke to me of the meaning of life in terms of sensory experience and was a defining moment. I didn't know the term for getting to know and manipulate materials. I didn't know then that it was called sculpture, but I knew it was part of who I am and what I wanted for my life.

I also think of *76 Degrees* as a large breast, again as a manifestation of the aesthetic conflict, which may drive my two-dimensional, three-dimensional interest. My first inspiration – the nursery school sandpit experience (feeling sand through water) – reflects on my first tactile sensations, that is, the feel on my fingers of the milky wet silky flesh of the feeding breast.

FIGURE 12.10 *Us*, 2011.

AT: *Us* achieves the gradual transformation of your father's face into yours (Fig. 12.10). It's really uncanny how this exercise demonstrates the likeness.

JMF: So many people tell me I look like my father and the likeness is something I know. It was so evident to me in those two photos so I went with it. Everything just fitted into place with no photo editing manipulations. It was one of the most fun, straightforward and painless works I have ever made.

AT: Most people find the inheritance and sharing of physical features something of a comfort when the people that we love and are related to die. Is this the case for you? Or is your physical likeness more of a metaphor, in terms of your identification with your father, as a person, as an artist?

JMF: Yes it was very comforting working with my dad's image, especially so putting us together, having him all for me in that sense. In the image he appears as me/mine, and so not shared.

AT: There's an inherent ambiguity in your evocative statement, *"I always find myself returning to Earth, sand and clay when contemplative, the materials to which we return."* It could mean that these are the materials to which we return in the studio, or the materials to which we return when we die and decompose – a stark contrast, in juxtaposition with the notion of sand as the birth of your inspiration, as the feeding breast, a sort of alpha and omega. Does this link to mourning your lost ones, who have "gone into the ground"? Or is it more of an abstract meditation about the eternal?

JMF: I like the alpha–omega contrast. Yes, earth is and means all those things concerning life and death, the stuff of art and being, the stuff of love and loss.

13

SUDEK, JANÁČEK, HUKVALDY, AND ME

Notes on Art, Loss, and Nationalism Under Political Oppression

Adele Tutter

We act in a manner similar to the people of Pæstum who dwell in the Tyrrhenian Gulf; for it happened to them, though they were originally Greeks, to have become at last completely barbarised, becoming Tyrrhenians or Romans, and to have changed their language, and all the rest of their national habits. But one Greek festival they do celebrate even to the present day, in which they meet and recollect all their ancient names and customs, and bewail their loss to one another, and then, when they have wept for them, they go home. 'And so,' says [Aristoxenus], 'we also, since the theatres have become completely barbarised, and since music has become entirely ruined and vulgar, we, being but a few, will recall to our minds, sitting by ourselves, what music once was

— Athenaeus[1]

But it is pre-eminently as the deepest layer of my mental soil, as firm sites on which I still may build, that I regard the Méséglise and Guermantes 'ways.'... Whether it be that the faith which creates has ceased to exist in me, or that reality will take shape in the memory alone, the flowers that people show me nowadays for the first time never seem to me to be true flowers. The 'Méséglise way' with its lilacs, its hawthorns, its cornflowers, its poppies, its apple-trees, the 'Guermantes way' with its river full of tadpoles, its water-lilies, and its buttercups have constituted for me for all time the picture of the land in which I fain would pass my life ... the cornflowers, the hawthorns, the apple-trees which I may happen, when I go walking, to encounter in the fields, because they are situated at the same depth, on the level of my past life, at once establish contact with my heart

— Proust[2]

Oh Orpheus sings! Oh great tree of sound!

— Rilke[3]

There is no sound that is broken away from the tree of life

— Janáček[4]

1.

A few years ago, I bought tickets to hear the Emerson String Quartet perform the two string quartets of Leos Janáček (1854–1928; Table 13.1) at Lincoln Center. Hoping to enrich my children's awareness of their Czech heritage, I sought to reacquaint myself with the composer's biography before the concert. But my Internet search did not yield the expected Wikipedia entry, but a set of instantly familiar thumbnail images of Prague.

As my confusion slowly cleared, I realized that they were the work of the Czech photographer, Josef Sudek (1896–1976), as beloved to me as Janáček. Unknowingly, I had searched for "Sudek" instead of "Janáček," and although I vaguely knew that there

TABLE 13.1 Timeline of the lives of Leoš Janacek, Josef Sudek, Antonín Tutter, and the Czechoslovak Republic

Leoš Janáček born	*1854*	
Janáček sent to monastery school in Brno	1865	
Janáček's father dies	1866	
Prussian army garrisoned in Brno		
Janáček's sister Rosalie dies	1868	
Janáček marries Zdeňka Schultzová	1881	
Olga Janáčková born	1882	
Vladimir Janáček born	1888	
Vladimir dies at age 2	1890	
	1896	Josef Sudek born
	1899	Sudek's father dies when Sudek is 2
Olga dies, age 21	1903	
WW I begins	1914	
	1916	Sudek wounded by shraphnel
	1917	Sudek's right arm amputated
WW I ends	1918	
Czecho-Slovak Republic established		
	1920	*Antonín Tutter born*
Janáček writes *Capriccio for Piano Left Hand*	1926	
Janáček dies	1928	Sudek completes the first *Svatý Vít* cycle
Sudetenland ceded to Hitler at Munich	1938	
Germany invades Czechoslovakia	1939	Sudek returns to *Svatý Vít*
	1941	*Tutter remanded to slave labor*
WW II ends; Russia liberates Prague	1945	*Tutter's mother dies*
Communist Party coup d'etat	1948	Sudek begins trips to Hukvaldy
		Tutter escapes Czechoslovakia
Soviet Union invades Czechoslovakia	1968	
	1971	Sudek publishes *Janáček-Hukvaldy*
		Tutter returns to Czechoslovakia
	1976	Sudek dies
Velvet Revolution	1989	

was some connection between them, I could not remember the details. I then searched for "Janáček Sudek," and the word *Hukvaldy* leapt out at me. And it all flooded back.

Of course! Sudek had taken photographs of Janáček's home and environs in the tiny Moravian village of Hukvaldy. In particular, I remembered a graceful picture of a chair behind a lace curtain, lit by the sun.

FIGURE 13.1 Upper, Josef Sudek: left, on the Karlův most (Charles Bridge), c. mid 1930s; right, Prague, 1969. Lower, Leoš Janáček: left, 1881; right, c. late 1920s.

2.

This uncanny experience prompted me to take a closer look at these two men, who on the surface could not have been more different (Fig. 13.1).[5] Sudek was self-effacing, unassuming, and humble: a gentle, sweet man who had close and enduring relationships, but no romantic ones. Janáček was a temperamental man of fierce passion, at times choleric and belligerent, at other times affectionate and tender; a man of few friends, he had numerous love affairs, at his wife's expense. But in other ways, Sudek and Janáček were very similar: both were intensely devoted to their art; both had a great love of nature and their homeland. Moreover, both suffered significant childhood loss.

In a previous effort, I argue that multiple traumas powered Sudek's work, and that his oeuvre functioned as a transcendent means of mourning (Tutter, 2013). As

FIGURE 13.2 Four centuries of political domination of the Czech lands. The Hapsburgs, 1526 to 1918: upper left, Holy Roman Emperor Ferdinand I (1526–1564); lower left, Crown Emperor Karl I and Emperor Franz Josef (combined rule, 1848–1918). Upper right, Hitler, 1939–1945. Lower right, the Soviet-sponsored Communism, 1948-1989. In the background of this photograph taken in Bratislava during the 1968 Warsaw Pact invasion of Czechoslovakia are the offices of Univerzita Komenského, named after Jan Amos Komenský, religious refugee, educator, and Czech national hero.

a nineteen-year-old conscript in the Austria-Hungarian army, he was injured in the right arm during the First World War, fighting for the very forces that had for three centuries deprived the Czech people of self-rule (Fig. 13.2, left). After four years and several surgeries, his gangrenous arm finally required amputation at the shoulder. While Sudek minimized the impact of this grave forfeiture, he vowed to never leave home again. He had already suffered the significant trauma of losing his father to pneumonia when he was only two years old – and would endure even more. He lived to witness the Nazi invasion of Czechoslovakia in 1938 that ended the twenty-year life of the first Czech Republic (Fig. 13.2, upper right); the Soviet-engineered 1948 Communist Party coup d'etat, which ushered in an era of privation and paranoia; and the Warsaw Pact invasion of 1968, which effectively crushed the Prague Spring and its peaceful demands for democracy and basic freedoms (Fig. 13.2, lower right).

After the 1948 coup, Sudek for the first time broke his self-imposed moratorium on travel and journeyed to the eastern frontier of Moravia, a remote land of unspoiled natural beauty and rich with folk tradition, to visit the birthplace of one of his favorite composers. Thereafter, and until 1970, Sudek would make annual pilgrimages to Janáček's home in Hukvaldy. But he was in no hurry to publish the photographs he made there. On the contrary: as Jaroslav Šeda explains in his preface to *Janáček-Hukvaldy* (Sudek, 1971), the eventual volume, Sudek's last –

> [Sudek's] visits to Hukvaldy went on for twenty years before his collection of photographs numbered several hundred . . . He explored every inch of the country knowing it intimately as a lover knows the graceful body of his mistress. No, he could never give up this particular countryside – yet, somehow it still was not "perfect" or "ready." Not long ago, after a lapse of many years I looked again at those peaceful photographs of Janáček's house with his chair and writing stand and the curtain figured with a poetic arabesque of sun rays and shadows. Gently there came to me the sound of the passionate and then somewhat sad *Adagio* from his *Intimate Letters* [the second string quartet]. And the decision was made. We went to see him and announced firmly: You can't hide them any longer, Mr. Sudek. People must see them. Make a book of the Hukvaldy photographs.
>
> [Šeda, 1971, unpaginated]

Just as surely as Sudek's pictures of Hukvaldy took Šeda to Janáček's music, Janáček's music took me to Sudek's pictures of Hukvaldy.

3.

The Czech National Revival was crystallized in the crucible of nineteenth century European nationalism and catalyzed by three centuries of domination by Austria-Hungary. Raised during a time of feverish national pride, or *národnost* (a term only imperfectly translated as "nationalism," and closer in meaning to *Volkszugehörigkeit*, or "folk allegiance"; see Wein, 2009), both Sudek and Janáček made work expressive of a primordial love of their homeland.[6] Janáček worshiped

Bedrič Smetana and Antonín Dvořák, revered creators of the new "Czech classical music" granted the status of national heroes. But while Smetana and Dvořák introduced largely Bohemian folk melodies into German Romantic and Classical forms, Janacek structured his music from the unfamiliar rhythms and tonalities of Moravian folk music: a most "rustic, colorful, virile, and yet at the same time tender art" (Hollander, 1955, p. 173).[7] If Dvořák's cycle, *Songs My Father Taught Me*, speaks to the enduring bond between Czech folk song and family, Janáček (1989) deepens the equation: "in folk song," he writes, "there is the whole man: body, soul, landscape, all of it, all" (p. 60).[8]

Beckerman (1986) explains that by

> basing musical works on folk material, Czech composers automatically accepted a particular type of rhythmic organization that is a pre-fixed reflection of the Czech language. Thus, the typically Czech first-beat accent is but one step removed from the accent patterns of Czech speech.
>
> [p. 70]

Janáček took this a step further, constantly listening for and notating phrases of spoken Czech language – which he termed "speech melodies" – on scraps of paper, and replicating their distinctive syncopation and inflections in his musical phrasing.[9] In his view, speech melody reflected "the speaker's inner life," joining it with the "environment in which it is spoken"; "the seat of the emotional furnace," speech melody lay (pp. 42–43).

4.

Janáček's incorporation of the Czech language into his music is all the more meaningful, given that its systematic suppression was the principal means of the Habsburg politics of cultural erasure. By the time young Leoš went to school in Hukvaldy, German was the official language of the bourgeoisie, academy, and government, and Czech was the derogated language of the servant and peasant class. German-speaking citizens were a relative minority in rural towns like Hukvaldy, but accounted for more than half of the cosmopolitan population of Brno, where Janáček lived from adolescence.

A dominated, powerless culture can assert its legitimacy and separate identity through language: "people with no power . . . will draw linguistic lines explaining who they really are" (Urciuoli, 1995, p. 535).[10] It is no wonder that Janáček's signature genre was opera, a form that blends language with all the other components of culture – music, dance, and literature. Thus John Tyrrell (2006), author of the definitive Janáček biography, notes that "as a Czech composer, it was virtually one's patriotic duty to contribute to the genre" (p. 772). Vilem Tausky, Janáček's student, agrees, asserting that the "whole of [Janáček's] life's work reflects his nations' centuries-old struggle for material freedom and a cultural identity" (1982, p. 6) – a nation that until 1881 did not have its own National Theatre, only a German one.

FIGURE 13.3 Photographs by Sudek: left, Svatý Vít, statue of the Holy Roman Emperor Karel IV, coronated in Prague in 1347; right, the spires of Svatý Vít (St Vitus), and in the distance, Národní divadlo (Czech National Theatre).

5.

While rooted to a great extent in language, the notion of *nation* was – and remains – a profoundly physical one for the Czechs, many of whom still embrace a deeply rooted Franciscan animism: a transcendent, sensual identification with nature. As Sudek's sympathetic, even reverential photographs of the Bohemian and Moravian countryside (Tutter, 2013) amply demonstrate, "love of country meant love of lakes, the arrangement of the fields, rivers, towns, and villages, as well as historical, political, and linguistic factors" (Beckerman, 1986, p. 67).

To commemorate the tenth anniversary of the first Czech Republic in 1928, Sudek published a superb folio of photographs of the cathedral of Svatý Vít – the crown jewel of Hradčany (the Prague castle complex) and principal iconographic signifier of Prague that had stood unfinished for six hundred years. Underscoring its history as well as its vulnerability, Sudek's radical images document the construction that was hastily brought to a conclusion in time for the Tenth Jubilee (Tutter, 2013)

Eleven years later, after Hitler invaded Czechoslovakia, Sudek returned to Svatý Vít for another cycle of pictures that meticulously itemize its contents and surrounds, including a stone relief of Karel IV, King of Bohemia and Holy Roman Emperor, who inaugurated the construction of Svatý Vít and founded Karlova Univerzita (Charles University) of Prague, the oldest university in Europe (Fig. 13.3, left). In Sudek's lens, this *Pater patriae* (Czech, *Otec vlastí*) of the Czech lands smiles, surveying the finished cathedral he had envisioned. Blind to the eyes of the viewer – and, perhaps, what the viewer knows – his profile merges with the Moravian Eagle, heraldic symbol of the old Czech and Moravian kingdoms.[11] In another image, the cathedral's fine Gothic spires frame the still relatively new Czech National Theatre, its massive mansard roof surprisingly delicate, surrounded by trees as if guarded by them (Fig. 13.3, right). With their ageless designation of place and privileging of unequivocal national signifiers, these iconic images of Prague were proof and promise of the survival, against all odds, of Sudek's sovereign country. If Janáček honored and preserved his country's spoken language in his music, then Sudek honored and preserved his country's visual, physical language – its monuments and saints, fields and forests – in his images.

6.

My father, Antonín Tutter, was from Nová Cerekev, a small Bohemian village about the size of Hukvaldy, seventy-five miles south of Prague. Born in 1920, he was a child of the First Republic, raised in a buoyant atmosphere of hope and potentiality (Table 13.1). Abraham Lincoln was his idol.

As a law student at the Karlova Univerzita in the years before World War II, my father took part in antifascist demonstrations against Hitler until the Nazis closed the university and sent him, along with many other young men, to a slave labor camp in Germany. For the duration of the war, he worked in construction and on the trains, sabotaging the signals just infrequently enough to avoid being shot. At the war's end, the Allies targeted the train routes in Germany intensively. Only six decades later did my father tell me, as he lay dying, how he and his comrades would cheer on the bombers they could hear in the distance, even as they feared for their lives. Only then did I understand his long-standing aversion to sirens, and why he could not sleep in any bed except his own.

When the war was over, my father found an motorcycle abandoned at the side of the road. Grateful for its full tank of gas, he sped home in a hurry, as he had had word that his mother was not well. Arriving at the house where he was born, he saw his brother's face in the window, and was from his expression given to understand that their mother was dead.

7.

The pictures that Sudek took in Janáček's home in Hukvaldy are of ordinary things; yet in some ways, they are not ordinary at all. The chair, for instance, is a special object, shaped and impressed by the body it holds, as intimate as a garment. I have proposed that, much like a chair, Sudek's art functioned as a concretized, aesthetic version of Anzieu's (1985/1989) construct, le moi-peau – "the skin-ego" – able to circumscribe and contain a self fractured by trauma and tasked with navigating a precarious, if not apocalyptic, world. So, too, might Sudek's allegiance to his country and contract to stay within its boundaries have functioned to strengthen the boundaries of his own self, and the boundaries of the country with which that self was identified, binding, organizing, and stabilizing them (Tutter, 2013).

Did Sudek's relationship to Janáček have a similar role? Although the composer was dead twenty years when Sudek broke his oath against travel and first visited Hukvaldy, I suggest that for Sudek, he was nevertheless very much alive.

The image of the chair in Janáček's living room that both Šeda and I remembered is in fact part of a series: Sudek photographed the chair, or an identical one at least three times. In each image, the window lace acts as a scrim for the play of light and shadow on the vacated seat. In 1948, the chair is to the right of the harmonium at which Janáček composed, by the window that frames what would have been his daily, familiar view (Fig. 13.4, upper left). Photographed at a different window in 1960 (Fig. 13.4, lower left), the chair is back at the harmonium in the image made during Sudek's last trip in 1970 – in sharper focus now, leaving no doubt that everything in Janáček's house is still in order, and that all remains as it once was, and will always be (Fig. 13.4, upper right). But if one looks carefully through the window of the last image, one can see that something has indeed changed: one tree has become two.

If we search through Sudek's large oeuvre, we find a very similar chair in his own home (Fig. 13.4, lower right).

Perhaps his editor's entreaties were not the only reason that Sudek agreed to publish the Hukvaldy pictures; he finally acquiesced only after the 1968 Soviet invasion shattered any remaining illusions of liberty and safety (Fig. 13.2). *Janáček-Hukvaldy*, Sudek's last and clearly very private project, was, I propose, a concerted gesture of dissent in response to this latest assertion of Soviet hege-mony – just as he traveled to Hukvaldy in response to the first, just as he returned to Svatý Vít in response to Nazi aggression. In *Janáček-Hukvaldy*, Sudek provides physical evidence that Janáček's home – and, I will suggest, in a material, mystical sense, his own – still stood.

8.

Janáček also had his share of catastrophic loss. Until the age of eleven, he lived in abject poverty in Hukvaldy, his father the village teacher (*kantor*), so poorly paid that he could neither repair the roof of the two-room school in which his family also lived, nor sufficiently heat its damp rooms. Three infant siblings perished in succession before Leoš was born; two others, a brother and sister, were lost between his sixth and seventh years.

In those times, the *kantor* was responsible for educating village children and providing music for church services; thus, all the Janáček children received instruction in several instruments, and played and sang at weekly Mass. Music became Leoš's joy and passion. He benefited from the example of his talented parents: his father was a most stringent instructor, and he would later recall in particular his mother's fine singing voice. At the age of eleven, Janáček's obvious musical gifts earned him a scholarship to the prestigious school for choirboys at the Augustinian Abbey in Brno. This represented a sizable financial reprieve for his family, there being too many children to clothe and feed, but it was a decided tragedy for young Leoš: music, the thing he loved most, had turned on him, depriving him of his home in his beloved Hukvaldy, and his mother's voice.

FIGURE 13.4 From Sudek, *Janáček-Hukvaldy:* upper left, 1948; upper right, 1970; lower left, 1960; lower right, Sudek, undated.

All life as he knew it came to an end. After he said good-bye to his mother, who left him in the urban square outside the monastery, nourishing warmth and softness gave way to the vacuum of ascetic loneliness:

> My mother left me at the Klášterní náměstí [cloister square] with a heavy step. Me in tears, she too.

All alone. Foreign people, not warm-hearted; foreign school, hard bed, bread even harder. No cuddles.

My world, exclusively mine, is founded. Everything fell into it.

[Tyrrell, 2006, p. 49]

The elite choirboys of Brno, who formed their own orchestra and played at important religious and civic occasions, were known as "The Bluebirds." It is a happy enough name, but Janáček was singled out by virtue of his poverty and, at least for the first several years, his poor knowledge of German. He felt imprisoned in the monastery's harsh environment, and depleted by its intense musical and academic curriculum.[12] It would be more than four years before this caged bluebird could return to Hukvaldy, a prohibitively expensive two days' journey by carriage from Brno. Worse still, was to never see his father again: within a year of his arrival in Brno, Janáček learned of his death from rheumatic fever – an "unimagined cruelty" (p. 49). Not two years later, there was more cruel news: his favorite sister Rosalie, who had been like a mother to him, was taken by typhus. Like my father's, his home had become marred by absence.

9.

Temporally associated with the privation and discipline of the monastery, Janáček's losses were also linked to foreign oppression. A few months after his father's death, the Austro-Prussian war reached Moravia: the Prussian army was stationed in Brno for a month en route to the Austrian front, and troops were garrisoned at the monastery. Janáček was the sole student too poor to leave for the relative safety of home. His later comments on this time consist of only a musical memory: he recalled the Prussian soldiers performing their military exercises in the main square "like swarms of black ants" (Janáček, 1982, p. 41); "the tin drums rolled and above them the high piccolos squealed. Predatory music. Even today it lingers and buzzes" (Tyrrell, 2006, p. 52). Like the German air-raid sirens, the sounds of the enemy are irradicable.

The historian Catarina Kinnval (2004) explains that oppressed and otherwise vulnerable groups seek security and affirmation within collective identities such as nationalism.

The strength of nationalism and religion as powerful identity-signifiers lies in their ability to convey unity, security, and inclusiveness in times of crisis . . . [the] idea of the nation as providing an inside is intimately connected to the idea of the family. It is associated with home, the place where the door will always be open for you, where a fire will be lit upon arrival, and where you will receive the warmth of your mother's care.

[pp. 761–763]

In *Civilization and its Discontents*, Freud (1929) makes a somewhat analagous comment about a city with a particularly reassuring sense of permanence and endurance, "Mother Rome":

Let us, by a flight of imagination, suppose that Rome is not a human habitation but a psychical entity . . . an entity, that is to say, in which nothing that has once come into existence will have passed away and all the earlier phases of development continue to exist alongside the latest one.

[p. 70]

If nationalism and its civic identifiers can stand for mother, a repository of safety, shelter, and memory, then it stands to reason that those lacking in security and support will tend to cling to them all the more. Abandoned by his family to the severity and deprivation of the a monastery; having lost his home, his father, and his sister; and having endured a forcible military occupation – all, before his adolescent identity was fully consolidated – Janáček identified ever more strongly with his father's vehement *národnost*. Henceforth, his people would be his family, and his personal survival would hinge on the survival of his culture and of the nascent Czech state. Perhaps the survival of his house would come to serve the same purpose for Sudek.

Vamik Volkan (1997) likens individual identity to a close fitting garment, and national and ethnic group identity to a loosely fitted, large communal "garment" or "tent" that envelops, shelters, and coheres its members (p. 27): a collective analog of the skin-ego. Indeed, within weeks of his father's death, the twelve-year-old Leoš begged the uncle now charged with his care, "I have one request for you, dearest uncle: Please buy me a Slavonic suit" (Tyrrell, 2006, p. 59). Cut from the cloth of his homeland, Janáček's nationalism was fitted, like a garment, on his body (Weiss, 2001).

10.

Janáček disliked Brno, engraved as it was with homesickness, grief, and war. His feelings for Hukvaldy were an entirely different matter. With awe and rapture, he describes its wonders in a postcard to his late-life love and muse, Kamila Stösslová, imploring her to visit.

You can see for yourself on the postcard that it's more beautiful here than in Luhačovice [the spa village where they met] . . . Close to the castle there's a game park and in it herds of fallow deer. You can go up to within a few steps of them. They have antlers like shovels . . . Walks to the "old castle," sitting on the peak (not high!) is magnificent. The sun, when it comes out, gives warmth here as if quite near. And the air! it smells of resin . . . The water is from a spring; they call it "the holy [spring]" . . . Down below the castle flows the mountain stream, the Ondrejinice; perhaps I'll get acquainted with the trout which gambol in it. There'll be lots of fruit here; they still have corn in the fields . . . Today my forester brought in a head of cabbage from the field; cleaned, it weighed seven kilos . . .

[letter of August 5, 1918, Janáček, 1994, p. 21]

Janáček rejoiced when at last he was able to purchase a house in Hukvaldy, and was thereafter perpetually impatient to spend time there. Again, to Kamila, he announced:

> What do you say to this: I have bought a nice little house with four rooms, a garden, stables, and a field. It belonged to my sister-in-law. I wasn't keen to see that family property passing into foreign hands . . . It's in beautiful Hukvaldy . . .
>
> [letter of 24 October 1921, Janáček, 1994, p. 34]

11.

Sudek shared Janacek's profound affinity for music. He was known for his "Musical Tuesday" gatherings, at which he played for his friends selections from his vast collection of classical music recordings. His love of music is evident in a respectful image of a monument to one of Prague's celebrated citizens, Wolfgang Amadeus Mozart, his bust embraced by the horse-chestnut tree so beloved to Czechs (Fig. 13.5, left).

Like Janáček's mother, Sudek's mother also liked to sing. One of Sudek's earliest memories is of his mother singing as she hung the washing to dry. Taken from the window of his studio, his mysterious studies of hanging laundry transform a

FIGURE 13.5 Photographs by Sudek: left, *Mozart Monument, Villa Bertramka*, where Mozart often stayed when in Prague. Janáček was a frequent visitor to Villa Bertramka and advocated for its preservation. Right, from the series *The Window of My Studio* (1940–1954).

humble task into a shrouded evocation of a tender musical moment, at once intimate, and distant (Fig. 13.5, right).

In my first memory – I was three years old – I am sitting on an overgrown lawn with my mother under a towering pine tree. The sun is behind my father as he approaches us, and happily tells us that this place is now ours.

In 1965, my father took us on a trip. Our family of four left our three rooms in Brooklyn and drove upstate to the Catskill Mountains, whose rounded green hills and fields of hay and corn bear an uncanny resemblance to southern Bohemia. We were told that an old dairy farm deep in a valley was for sale. Its farmhouse and overshot barn overlooked a brook and pastures, all backed by a steep hill planted with pine that reminded my father of the sloping evergreen forests his family logged – so much so that he bought the property on the spot. I spent summers on those one hundred acres of meadow and forest until I was sixteen, and went away to school.

12.

Many have made the case that the Czechs were complicit in accepting Soviet domination, the Communist Party enjoying a strong popular base in the First Republic. However, as Applebaum (2012) meticulously documents, the Soviets had already begun to lay the foundation for the 1948 coup during the war years, gradually expanding their influence in the weakened Czech nation. Perhaps their most powerful leverage was the propagandistic message that future self-rule would be possible only through the Communist Party and strong ties to Russia. This ploy cynically exploited Czech nationalism (associated for many Czechs, Janáček included, to a romantic pan-Slavism which fancied Russia as the "mother" of all Slavs), as well as simmering Czech hatred of their prior German-speaking oppressors, Austria-Hungary and Nazi Germany. Looking to the East made sense to a small country with no standing army; after all, the West had abandoned them at Munich.

After the war, my father finished his law degree and worked as a public defender in Cheb, a town on the German border in western Bohemia. Stoking anti-German resentment was by then a common means of bolstering loyalty to Russia – especially in a Sudentenland town that had once given Hitler an enthusiastic hero's welcome. Just a few months after the 1948 coup d'etat, my father was appointed to represent a Czech woman accused of Nazi collaboration. It was meant to be a show trial, and he was directed to lose the case. Not about to help convict an innocent woman – emblematic, perhaps, of his innocent country – he fought the case and won. He returned home uncharacteristically late that night and found the building in which he kept rooms in flames.

It was rumored that a local storekeeper belonged to the resistance and could get people over the border emergently. My father rushed into his shop and pleaded for help, but the storekeeper shook his head, repeatedly insisting that he had no such role. My increasingly agitated father vowed to "eat his shoe" to prove his sincerity, and went so far as to remove one of his shoes and gnaw on its leather sole until the storekeeper relented and quickly got together a lantern, some food, and a map. My father fled that night and crossed the border to the barking of patrol dogs. Needing the light of the moon to navigate, he also feared being exposed by it; the dense forest was a refuge. He made his way to a German DP camp; a few years and a few countries later, his ship sailed into the New York harbor.

13.

The Saints Cyril and Methodius are heroic figures in Slavic countries. Emissaries from Byzantium in Moravia, these two brothers are historically credited with creating the precursor to the Cyrillic alphabet, the Glagolitic alphabet, which in 826 enabled them to translate the Bible and the liturgy into Old Slavonic. The two saints are typically portrayed with Glagolitic scrolls; note how in Fig. 13.6 (left), the pattern of crosses decorating their vestments echoes the blocky forms of their alphabet.

Although the equation of language and state is a modern ideological construct, its passion was fanned by nineteenth-century nationalism (Woolard & Schiefellin, 1994); consequently, "language and nationalism were intrinsically interwoven throughout the early modern and modern period" (Wein, 2009, p. 80). For the Czechs, culturally significant texts and the Czech language itself became important national signifiers, linked to the appealing vision of a sovereign Czech nation-state that promised not just autonomy but also the idealized legacy of the old kingdoms of Bohemia and Moravia. Tyrrell (2006) explains that the 1826 millennial anniversary

FIGURE 13.6 Left, icon of Sts Cyril and Methodius, c. fourteenth century. Note the scrolls with Glagolitic script and how the motif of the cross is used as a quasi-calligraphic decoration of the vestments. Right, statue of St Methodius, nineteenth century copy after a c.1750 original, Kostel Narození Panny Marie (Church of the Birth of Saint Mary), Příbor.

of the creation of the Glagolitic alphabet revived an awareness of the history that located

> Moravia at the hub of a vast Slavonic empire . . . that could stand up to its vigorous German-speaking neighbors. This was the vision of Moravianness that Janáček embraced as a young boy, one that would inflect his views and his music up to the end of his life.
>
> [p. 10]

No doubt the statue of St. Methodius that guards the Church of the Birth of Saint Mary in Příbor (where Leoš was born and lived for several years before his family relocated to Hukvaldy, six kilometers away) only enhanced Janáček's regard for the heroic saints of Moravia (Fig. 13.6, right). With great excitement, the fifteen-year-old "Lev" Janáček anticipated the celebration of the 1869 millennial anniversary of the death of St. Cyril, breathlessly writing his uncle from the monastery:

> You don't know how much I'm looking forward to the sacred ground [Velehrad], where once great Svatopluk [a ruler of Great Moravia] and the Slavonic apostles Ciryl [Cyril] and Metod [Methodius] had their post, that I will see it; I am not worthy to tread in their footsteps . . .
>
> [Tyrrell, 2006, p. 59]

And thus it is no wonder that the proponents of the Czech language that boldly resisted the near-successful attempt to extinguish it are virtually canonized by Czechs – for example, Josef Jungmann (1773–1847), who introduced the notion of linguistic nationalism and who followed his groundbreaking *History of Czech Literature* (1825) with the first Czech dictionary (1834–39; Tucker, 1996).[13]

"Language is the mirror of culture," wrote Edward Sapir (1949, p. 162). For Janáček, however, *culture was the mirror of language.* Among other things, he was convinced that the melodies and rhythms of folk song originally derived from the melodies and rhythms of spoken language itself. Did he identify with the champions of the Czech language by formulating a Czech "musical alphabet" from which one could make authentic Czech music, freed from the imposition of conventional, "foreign" (i.e., German) forms? Such a notion is encouraged by his radical experimentation – eliminating the aria from his operas, adopting the abruptly changeable rhythms of folk music, and employing exotic modal tonalities that evoke the ancient church music of the once great Czech kingdoms. In honor of the tenth anniversary of the First Republic, Janáček composed the utterly otherworldly *Glagolitic Mass*; set in Old Slavonic, its resplendent brass fanfares and echoing timpani are expressly intended to conjure "the whole atmosphere of Cyril and Methodius!" (Janáček, 1989, p. 122).

14.

My father was the only member of his family to escape Czechoslovakia in the crisis of 1948, the circumstances earning him the status of political dissident. Once he had left, he was barred from returning, despite annual and increasingly desperate pleas for a visa. Only once, in 1971 – the year *Janáček-Hukvaldy* was published – did he inexplicably receive permission to visit Czechoslovakia, perhaps because of temporary relaxation of constraints on travel, one of the short-lived capitulations to international pressure after the crisis of 1968. But after this brief reprieve, the Iron Curtain – so distant from the States, yet an oppressive, heavy reality in my home – drew closed again. Letters that arrived from far away – how well we knew those crinkly gray glassine envelopes with the blue and red border, curious handwriting, and exotic stamps – were heavily censored with black marker or scissors. When unfolded, their weightless, nearly transparent contents sometimes reminded me of the paper that we cut, in school, into snowflakes.

15.

Janáček's defense of his marginalized language was more than a musical conceit and a political protest against enforced linguistic colonization: it was a personal way of life. His antipathy toward all things German was fierce. "Ah, dear Uncle," he wrote at age fifteen,

> you don't know how I love these Czechs, you won't believe how I hate these Germans, these Germans who don't have their own homeland, who came into our beautiful Czech lands, to take our beautiful homeland away from us, attach it to themselves and then Germanize us ...
>
> [Tyrrell, 2006, p. 61]

The child who was mocked at school for not knowing German grew into a man who refused to ride the German-owned trams in Brno, boycotted the German theater in Prague, and crossed out German names on postcards and replaced them with Czech ones. He proudly donned a traditional Moravian coat (*čamara*) when in 1881 he married Zdeňka Schultzová, a young girl and former student from a prosperous, German-speaking family of Brno's bourgeoisie (Fig. 13.7). Quite the insouciant figure, the defiant composer further shocked his unexpecting in-laws by insisting that the wedding mass be held in Czech. And, although Janacek by then spoke fluent German, in apparent identification with the aggressor, after the wedding he only spoke Czech to his new bride, who barely knew the language, and who would soon learn that her new husband was in fact penniless.

Surely deep-seated shame around the degrading poverty of his origins factored into Janáček's bristling hostility toward authority, his fractious nationalism, and idealization of peasant culture and traditions. The vigorous passion and intensity

FIGURE 13.7 Left, Leoš Janáček, in traditional Moravian attire, and Zdeňka Schultzová, at the time of their wedding, 1881; upper right, Olga Janáčková, c. 1900-1902; lower right, Vladimir Janáček, 1890.

with which Janáček and Sudek alike invested all of their pursuits recalls the defensive, "muscular" qualities that Ester Bick termed a "second skin" (1968), which functions to counter an underlying fragility and tremendous, frustrated need. From a different perspective, if Sudek's visual imagery functioned as an organizing scaffold and auxiliary "skin-ego," then Janáček's fanatical attachment to the Czech language and folk music may have likewise served as an aural analog of the "skin ego," *l'enveloppe sonore* ("audio-phonic skin"; Anzieu, 1979, p. 23). Recalling their similar memories of their mothers singing, Anzieu posits that the original *l'enveloppe sonore* is in fact the mother's containing voice, which can receive and metabolize a child's violent projections. The rhymes and rhythms of song are particularly holding, as is the iteration of chorus and verse. Of note, while Janáček's music is more famously connected to Czech speech and folk song, it is uniquely formally distinguished by the repetition of abbreviated musical fragments, a novel development in classical music that anticipates later trends.

In his learned discussion, Barale (2009) explicates the theories of the philosopher Theodor Lipps, who held that rhythm "expands and takes on a much more general significance, until it becomes equated with the general conditions of psychic experience, or of intentionality – or, as Lipps puts it, of the movement 'of the mind as it stretches out to the object'" (p. 43).[14] Similarly, Stein (2004) offers that music offers powerful consolation, "temporarily relieving or diminishing feelings of pain by providing an illusory response ensconced in rhythm and sound to the dominant wish of the bereaved – reunion with the lost object" (p. 807).

From a different perspective, the sung or spoken word can be "taken in," in varying contexts, as "milk or stones" (Baranger & Baranger, 2008, p. 821). Julia Kristeva (1982) offers that by the very virtue of its orality, the spoken word gratifies and thereby mitigates mother-hunger: "through the mouth that I fill with my words instead of my mother whom I miss from now on more than ever, I elaborate that want, and the aggressivity that accompanies it, by *saying* . . ." (p. 41, emphasis and ellipses original). Janáček insisted on drawing his own staves, and his florid, "muscular" notation (a vexation to copyists, whose inevitable errors drove the composer to distraction) is practically calligraphic, his scores resembling wildly impatient cursive scrip – written furiously, lavishly, as if indicating a greedy hunger for expression, for speech, for language itself (Fig. 13.8).[15]

FIGURE 13.8 Autograph score, Janáček, fanfare from *Sinfonietta*; note the handwritten staves and cursive-like notation.

16.

Unexpectedly, in the middle of delivering my first paper on Sudek in 2013, I became momentarily overwhelmed and unable to continue after speaking the following words:

> in 1968 the Soviets used tanks to crush the nonviolent reform movement so hopefully known as the "Prague Spring"

During the discussion that followed the talk, I realized that I had connected with intense grief relating to long-buried memories of August 1968 – the feelings of a six-year-old child that had managed to remain dormant, and completely detached from their source, even during the course of a long analysis. I still remember almost nothing about the 1968 invasion, only the idea that my father was gone for a time; I do not know for how long, or whether he had actually left. Yet I have a belief, maybe a conviction, that he did in fact disappear, an idea edged like so many of my early memories with a aura of unreality. In looking back, however, I do think that in some way, part of him died that day. Only when I spoke about Sudek and shared *his* experience of 1968 with my community did my own feelings about our shared history emerge. As Léon Wurmser notes, shared suffering – *Mit-Leiden* – "is half the suffering" (this volume). I have not been able to recover those feelings since; nor did I include this story in these notes until they were almost finished. Quite unconsciously, I forgot it. The story, like the feelings that accompanied it, had quietly gone back underground.

When I tried to understand why the words so hopefully known as the "Prague Spring" precipitated such a powerful release of grief, I lingered on the words *so hopefully*, and their tinge of ruined innocence. They brought me to the memory of anticipating the annual shattering of my father's unremitting hope that *this* year he would get a visa to his homeland. One year, my father was overjoyed to learn that if, for a certain fee, he would surrender his Czech citizenship, he would get a visa (he paid; he did not). More money was extorted; nervous visits were made to the Czech Embassy; letters were written to congressmen. We received a reply from Senator Moynihan:

> unfortunately we have no influence or jurisdiction over these matters.

Now, I understand my father's inexhaustible, seemingly irrational hope as his guard against the powerlessness and despair that pervaded Communist Czechoslovakia – and our home, which at times felt like a tiny satellite of the Eastern bloc. But at the time, my father's implacable optimism seemed self-indulgent, and I resented his refusal to reconcile himself to his inevitable exile and thus relieve us of the weird half-light in which we lived. But he could not. How could he? And so we lived the life of the exile, existing, as Edward Said (1994) describes,

> in a median state, neither completely at one with the new setting, nor fully disencumbered of the old; beset with half-involvements and half-detachments;

nostalgic and sentimental on one level, an adept mimic or a secret outcast on another.

[p. 149]

When I was a child, I asked my father why he didn't wear a hat, like other men. He told me that during his flight through the forest a branch caught his hat, and he

FIGURE 13.9 Sudek, *Forgotten Hat*, from the cycle *A Walk in the Magic Garden*.

was afraid to lose time going back to retrieve it. From that time on, he refused to wear one: "I left my hat there," he said. I supposed he was still waiting to get it back. Only when much older did he relent; but even then, he would only wear a knitted hat or a cap. In first writing about Sudek, I described the photograph, *Forgotten Hat* (Fig. 13.9), in which "a straw boater like the one from Sudek's youth lies on the ground, as if left behind during a hasty departure" (Tutter, 2013, p. 144). But I did not remember my father's story about his own hasty departure – let alone recognize the association. It only came to me well after I considered this essay finished.

Dostoevsky's novel, *The House of the Dead* (2004), tells the stories of prisoners in a Siberian gulag, who maintain a "strange, impatient and intense hope . . . at times so wild as to be almost like delirium, and what was most striking of all, often persisting in men of the greatest common sense" (p. 208). This reminds me of Max Brod's description of Janáček: "His glance bewitched me. Still more his words, whose holy naïvety moves me still today" (Tyrrell, 2006, p. 3).[16] *Holy naïvety*: what a perfect description of my father, whose "strange, impatient and intense hope" to return to his homeland did not reflect "hope" as I knew it, but a delirious, grasping instinct – an utterly naïve, holy faith. I myself had no reason to have faith in hope, and had long lost hope in faith. But for my father, relinquishing faith would have meant relinquishing not only hope, but also his home, and perhaps even his soul.

17.

Janáček's children did not survive him. Virtually separated from Zdeňka by the time their daughter Olga was born in 1882, he begrudged the extra care and expense required of his sickly infant daughter (Fig. 13.7). By the time Vladimir was born six years later, things had improved; Janáček had reconciled with his wife, and was moreover delighted to have a son, especially one who showed early signs of musical talent (Fig. 13.7). But at the age of two, Vladimir contracted scarlet fever and died, devastating his father, who reacted by plunging himself every more fervently into his work, particularly his survey of folk song in the field. Janáček was also comforted by his frail Olga, whom he had grown to love; she had a beautiful contralto voice and identified with her father's vigorous Russophilia. Like her grandfather before her, her heart, too, was weakened by rheumatic fever. A decade after Janáček lost his son, he lost his daughter, who was only twenty-one.

Wracked with grief, Janáček composed the ravishingly beautiful opera, *Jenůfa*, during the last stages of Olga's illness. He adapted the libretto himself from a play by Gabriela Preissová, *Její pastorkyňa* ("Her Foster-Daughter"), whose protagonist, Jenůfa, secretly gives birth to an illegitimate baby boy. Her foster-mother drowns the infant – ostensibly to protect Jenůfa's honor and future prospects, but also to protect her own. By the opera's end, Jenůfa is able to forgive this and other crimes. In performance in Brno at the time that Janáček's son died, the play caused an uproar; critics protested that its depiction of rural infanticide could not be realistic. Janáček knew better. We know that he carried a heavy burden of remorse around his initial rejection of his daughter; he may have also felt guilt over surviving his children, recapitulating his survival of his infant brother and sister (and the siblings that died before he was born, and whom he replaced) during the desperate circumstances of his youth. He played *Jenůfa's* "searingly radiant" closing passages of forgiveness and redemption to Olga on her deathbed, and dedicated it to her (Tyrrell, 2007, pp. 810).

A letter written to the soprano Gabriela Horvátová, one of many lovers, allows a glimpse of Janáček's feelings of desolation and grief, bitterly alive, ten years after Olga's death, and the implicit hope that his music would not "forget me," but carry forth his legacy in lieu of his children.

> By now my family consists of nothing but [musical] notes. They have got heads and feet. They can run, play, bring forth tears or happiness. They are difficult to catch, and to understand them – they took a long time. And what a number of them in a line! At least they won't forget me; they won't deny me – we are Janáček's. Is that happiness enough?
>
> [letter of January 7, 1918, Vogel, 1962, pp. 27–28]

18.

Janáček's horizons brightened considerably when at the age of sixty-three he met Kamila Stösslová, who at twenty-six was only a few years older than his daughter Olga lived to be. Although Kamila neither wanted nor planned to leave her husband, Janáček's terrible longing to marry her and father her child persisted. He wrote her that the *Glagolitic Mass* would be their "wedding service," and his beloved countryside the metaphorical "cathedral" that it describes:

> Today I wrote a few lines about how I see my cathedral . . . And that cathedral is high – reaching right to the vault of the sky. And the candles that burn there, they are the tall pine trees, and at the top they have lighted stars. And the bells in the cathedral, they're from the flock of sheep . . . Into that cathedral two people enter, they walk ceremonially . . . And these two want to be married . . . So, priest, come at last! Nightingales, thrushes, ducks, geese make music!
>
> [letter of November 24–25, 1927; Janáček, 1994, p. 153]

19.

I was raised with the amplified sense of nationalism that grows ever more rampant in exile, inextricably bound up with my father's palpable, entrenched longing for his family, land, food, traditions, and language – everything we did not have. But music we did. I remember spending hours fingering the worn cardboard sleeves of record albums with their unpronounceable words, staring at their images of people in incomprehensible clothing. How many times I carefully lowered the needle of our portable Victrola onto our battered vinyl recordings of Smetana's *Bartered Bride* and Dvořák's *Slavonic Dances*. Eventually, I played those dances too, as piano duets with my sister; their melodies still move me.

My father taught us folk songs from his childhood, but not his language; after his visit in 1971, he became ever more certain that the Czech language would die, consumed by the Russian that was compulsory in Czechoslovak schools. But I would always listen to him talking on the telephone to his fellow expatriates, speaking a language I knew by sound but could not understand: a quixotic, upside-down tongue in which "no" meant "yes." (*That* much I knew: *ano*, or *no* for short, is Czech for "yes." *No, no, no*, my father would patiently repeat as he paced the short length of the kitchen, smoking.) Perhaps I learned something else that way. Janáček observed that

> whenever someone spoke to me, I may have not grasped the words, but I grasped the rise and fall of the notes! At once I knew . . . how he or she felt . . . whether he or she was upset. As the person talked . . . I knew, I heard that, inside himself the person perhaps wept. Sounds, the intonation of human speech, indeed of every living being, have had for me the deepest truth. And you see – this was my need in life . . .
>
> [Janáček, 1989, p. 121, emphasis original]

Precisely because I did not understand, my mind is all the more etched, if not with the meanings, then with the *sounds* of the language that "calls for a Czech in the bosom of his land, rolling through the centuries with equal sorrow and harshness" (Janáček, 1989, p. 42). Although I could not understood my father's words, I knew the grief of a man desperate for his language, his country, his family, a family, for which we in the United States were no substitute.

I never listened to Janáček as a child; my father's tastes were too provincial for anything so different, so modern. But when in college I finally heard its exquisitely tuned emotion, faraway yet familiar intonations, and excitable, propulsive rhythms – and above all, the cadence and inflections of my father's voice – it felt so close, so immediately recognizable, that it seemed as though I had always known it. In a way, I had, and it called harshly, sorrowfully, for me.

20.

For what he somehow knew would be his last opera, the romantic pan-Slavist Janáček turned to Russia. As he did with *Jenůfa*, he wrote his own libretto for *From the House of the Dead*, from his beloved Dostoevsky. In the original, a group of prisoners discover an eagle with a broken wing; they feed and try to care for it, but it will not eat, and its wing does not heal. The prisoners decide to release him: "'Let him die, but let him die in freedom,' they said. 'To be sure, he is a free, fierce bird; he will never get used to the prison'" (Dostoevsky, 2004, p. 206). But in Janáček's

FIGURE 13.10 Closing scene, Metropolitan Opera production of Janáček's *From the House of the Dead*, New York, 2009.

operatic rendition, the prisoners nurse the eagle back to health, and it flies away at the opera's end, a marvelous gesture of transformative redemption and, perhaps, absolution (Fig. 13.10).

Jaroslav Vogel (1962) considers Janáček's late, great phase "intimately autobiographical" (p. 9). The changes the composer made to *House of the Dead* – let alone his choice of text – parallel his preoccupations with remorse and salvation as he reached the end of the life. Interviewed the year before he died, he confessed, "one day I would like to free myself even from the present. I would like to break the thread that binds me to the past, that restrains me" (Janáček, 1989, p. 126). But whereas Jenůfa, astoundingly, forgave the most grievous sin, Janáček had difficulty freeing himself from the cage of his crippling guilt. Perhaps setting his last opera in a prison reflected this; perhaps only in death could this eagle repair his broken wing.

From a different angle, the rehabilitated eagle – released to the cry, *Orel, car lesu!* ("Eagle, tsar of the forest!") – embodies the newly exultant Czech freedom: recall that the eagle is a symbol of the Czech lands, as well as of "Mother" Russia. Little did Janáček know how grimly ironic this allegory would become after the Czechoslovak state was again taken prisoner – this time, by Soviet Russia.

The overture of *House of the Dead* begins with a fraught, insistent, repetitive motif, the strings vibrating with anguish and strain. When repeated a while later, this theme is overlapped by a single trumpet playing a magisterial fanfare, which, although distant, evokes a memory of mysterious glory. This opening theme has always haunted me; when I looked at the score, I realized that it resembles the folk melody my father liked to tap out on the piano – black keys only – with fingers destined to never play an instrument. In Janáček's opera, the theme speaks of suffering and resilience, but I remember it as a sweetly sad, yearning tune, the only one my father could play; he would hum along, transported to another time and place. Unlike the other folk songs he taught us, this one had no words.

21.

Like my father and so many others, Sudek clung to the long-lost dream of a liberated Czech nation. People have asked: why didn't he just leave?[17] Such a question belies a lack of understanding of what it can mean to leave behind one's country, culture, and language. Hendrik, the protagonist of István Szabó's 1981 film, *Mephisto* (based on the eponymous 1936 novel by Klaus Mann), is an actor in Communist Hungary. In a brief but unforgettable scene, Hendrik visits Paris; the tempting possibility of defection is tacit. A camera pans around him from below as he exits the Metro steps and turns and looks around him, lost in the vortex of helpless confusion that faces every would-be expatriate in a foreign land. For Hendrik does not speak French, the language that has an untranslatable term for what he is feeling: *dépaysement*. He will do anything, it seems – even become an informant for the totalitarian regime – in order to stay in Hungary and work in the language he knows, for how can an actor possibly work in a foreign tongue?

Mann based Hendrik, a modern-day Faust, on Gustaf Gründgens, the actor who married Mann's sister. Gründgens' own careerist collaboration was well rewarded; excused from military duty, he was appointed director of the Third Reich state theater.[18] In 2006 it was revealed that Szabó had also bedded the enemy: he cooperated with the Communist secret police in exchange for membership in the Hungarian film academy. Well positioned to understand Gründgens' conflict, evidently he, too, had made a deal with the devil.

Although the nation in which Sudek and Janáček were raised was an oppressed one, it was their home. But the nation that my father called home was, at first, a free one; when its freedom was gone, home as he knew it was gone, too. To live, he had to leave and be free, like Dostoevsky's eagle, to die in freedom, just as so many others had to stay. He made a new home in New York where he was free, but his *dépaysement* remained. His *dépaysement*, his difference, his isolation were his prison now, and I inherited them, always feeling that he – and, by extension, *we* – belonged somewhere else, always feeling different from other children and their big, undisplaced, American families, families that were not (as far as I could see) living out a tragedy, and who, unlike me, seemed to know how to act and how to be – not knowing whether to be proud of that difference, or ashamed.

22.

In nineteenth century culture, much attention was directed to the identification of music with place. Barale (2009) writes that "The romantic-spiritualist notion of *Gemüth* . . . denoted a kind of spiritual entity or soul of a rhythmic nature which 'tuned' the psychic life of individuals, groups and even places – that is, the 'atmospheres' of a given environment" (fn, p. 49). Janáček (1989) extols the inexplicable rapport between music and the visual imagery of rural beauty: "even the tame look of a chick, the searching eye of a hawk . . . even the dreaming, pale blue of the forget-me-not, even the burning fire of the wild poppy evoke a chord within me" (p. 99). Indeed, he claimed that "to create an image through music is, in large part, one of the graphic arts. It becomes such an art when, as if by a miracle, the vision catches a glimpse of itself in a real being" (p. 118). Janáček achieves such a miracle in *Příhody lišky Bystroušky* (*The Cunning Little Vixen*), its sinuous rhythms, bounding themes and eerie piccolo replies summoning the primeval mystery of the forest. Its more expansive, exquisitely lyrical passages evoke the ecstasy of pastoral abundance: this is his memory, his vision, of Hukvaldy.

The connection between music and place – of which every exile and every family of every exile knows – also constitutes a critical part of the profound and mystical connection between Janáček and Sudek. Famous for his long exposure times (sometimes into the hours) that captured the movement of life through time, whenever Sudek opened the shutter by removing the lens cap, he would say, "And the music played . . ." Nowhere is this music more clear than in Sudek's last monograph, *Janáček-Hukvaldy*.

Like Janáček's music, Sudek's imagery conveys a quintessential sense of place. He treats every aspect of rural Hukvaldy with tender affection: the hayfields, the beehives, the springhouses with their little thatched roofs, the bright rushing streams. He gives the petite Baroque church, where young Leoš first heard and performed chamber music, a veiled, mystical treatment (Fig. 13.12). In Sudek's lens, even the imposing ruins of Hukvaldy Castle are approachable, habitable, even anthropomorphic; the tall iron gates at the foot of the hill, which remind villagers every day of the long-ago glory of the Great Moravian Empire, are gracious and welcoming. In the broad sweep of panoramic landscapes, Hukvaldy's luxuriant fields and undulating hills swoon with beauty. One can virtually hear the lilting birdsong and the thrum of humming insects, feel the trembling blackberries falling into the hand, the warm sun on the drying hay, and the cooling shade of the treelined paths that beckon and invite. It is as if Sudek visualizes the rhapsodic, tender *language* with which Janáček, a "son of the soil" (Kinnvall, 2004, p. 760), expresses his profound feelings for his country and his people:

It seems to me that the little rivers of Lachia are chased by the rhythm of its dances, as in old days; and as it was, so it is . . . Beautiful country, quiet people, and a dialect as soft as if you were cutting butter. (Janáček, 1982, p. 30)

FIGURE 13.11 The collapse of communism in Central Europe. Upper, the falling of the Berlin Wall, November 11, 1989. Lower, crowds mass in Václavské náměstí (Wenceslas Square), Prague, November 17, 1989.

23.

Janáček lived to celebrate the birth of the First Republic; Sudek lived to grieve its death. Sadly, he did not live to see the Berlin Wall fall, the Velvet Revolution that

FIGURE 13.12 Sudek, *Janáček-Hukvaldy*. Left, Kostel Sv. Maxmiliána (Church of St. Maximilian), 1759–1769, and behind it, the two-room *škola* (school) in which Janáček lived with his family. Right, a spring house in the Hukvaldy game preserve.

followed, and the birth of the Second Republic (13.11). But my father did. As if by a miracle or some other sort of divine magic, all barriers to travel vanished overnight; he got on the next plane to Prague and joined the excited crowds massing in the squares and boulevards, drinking it in – water after forty years in the desert. After forty years, this wanderer lived to see his promised land.

In a strange twist of fate, my father returned to his homeland just in time for his fiftieth year gymnasium reunion. Unannounced, he fell right into step with the other septuagenarians parading around the Baroque town square of Pelhřimov. There was much disbelief and celebration when he was finally recognized. Years later, my cousin Marta remembered how his classmates marveled at his language: he still spoke fluent Czech, but his diction and vocabulary were curiously antiquated, lacking any modern slang or idiom.

Language is a living thing; it breathes, it grows, and, sometimes, it dies. But my father's mother tongue remained more or less unchanged since the time he left his fatherland, as if kept under glass for four decades, retaining all the gentle formality and musical sweetness of old "high" Czech, filled with its characteristic diminutives and endearments. His language was a thing of the past, and it died with him. Yet some of it lives on in Janáček's music. Like Janáček, my father passed away a decade after the birth of a Czechoslovak state, their holy naïvety transformed into a viable reality.

24.

The mutilated trees of which Sudek was so fond, many of them in Hukvaldy, are natural metaphors for his mutilated right arm, which in turn embodies telescoping layers of trauma, including his other great loss, that of his father – a young boy's right hand man (Tutter, 2013).

When Sudek was a young man, Janáček was very much a public figure, his visibility enhanced by the popular *feilleutons* he wrote for the Czech daily, *Lidové noviny*. What did it mean for Sudek to hear Janáček's *Capriccio for Piano, Left Hand*, which premiered in Prague in the Jubilee year of 1928, the same year Sudek became famous for his first photographs of Svatý Vít? A music aficionado as serious as Sudek would have known that the person who commissioned and performed the *Capriccio*, the Czech pianist Otaker Hollman, had also lost his right arm in World War I. Sudek would have also been aware of the deaths of Janáček's children: the composer had publicly declared that *Jenůfa*, his most popular opera, was bound by "the black ribbon of the long illness, pain and cries of my daughter Olga and my little boy Vladimir" (Zemanová, 2002, p. 91).

Did Sudek – who lost his father when a two-year old boy – imagine Janáček as a spiritual surrogate father, one whose voice still spoke to him through his music? And did Sudek see himself as a spiritual surrogate son to Janáček – a man who lost *his* two-year old son, who wrote music for an amputee like him? In this family romance, Hukvaldy would have been more than Janáček's birthplace: it would have been Sudek's ancestral home, a source of constancy and consolation.

Janáček appears to have done something similar. Perhaps because his relationship with Kamila Stösslová was essentially impossible and largely epistolary, their correspondence was saturated with the fantasies that demonstrate his great imaginative capacity and that were transcribed and realized in the great music of his late period, fantasies in which he variously addressed his beloved Kamila as his mistress, his bride, his wife, and the mother of his children – and, at other times, his daughter.

25.

In 1982, just after graduating from college, I had the opportunity to visit Czecho-slovakia as a guest of the French government. Happy to stock up on sheet music at unheard-of prices, I visited a sheet music store in Prague. A clerk waited on me with a desultory, suspicious air as I satisfied my thirst for Bach and Brahms. But when I asked for Janáček, he came to life; elated, he eagerly showed me what he had.

My father worried that the appearance of a relative from "the West" would have repercussions for our family in Nová Cerekev; they did not enjoy the benefits of membership in the Communist Party. And, as a diplomatic guest, one or two Czech policemen followed me wherever I went in Prague, hanging back a few steps. One day I left the consulate apartments via a side exit in the small hours of the morning and boarded an extremely slow train to my father's village. My task was to find his elder sister, named, like Sudek's sister, Božena; fourteen years older than my father, it was she who had raised him, much as Rosalie had raised Janáček. My father was the youngest of twelve, and by then, Božena, his favorite, was the only one left.

Arriving at dawn, I found no street signs in the village, and the house numbers seemed random – 34, 78, 15, 4. I showed the only person I could find the piece of paper on which my father had written his sister's address, simply, "1, Nová Cerekev." He pointed in a direction, turned on his heel, and walked rapidly away. (Later I learned that the houses in the village were numbered in order of their age; Božena's house, #1, was the oldest.) I don't remember how I found the heavy wooden doors to the compound. With no forewarning, Božena knew who I was. She let me in and lit the fire.

Before long, a translator was found. The only local who spoke English distilled *slivovice* – plum brandy – in his cellar, and I was obliged to sample multiple vintages before beginning our tour of the village. I was a bit wobbly when we turned a corner and came upon the huge synagogue, an incongruous sight in such a tiny town. Noted for being the largest of its kind in Southern Bohemia, the synagogue of Nová Cerekev has since been lovingly reconstructed, but in 1982 it was empty, battered, and pockmarked with bullet holes. I asked about its desecrated state, and (I am embarrassed to say) why it was abandoned. My translator stopped and looked at me with an inebriated smile, and said, "Didn't you hear the good news? There are no more Jews!"

Before I returned to Prague, I felt compelled to photograph any element that might be identifiable with my father's village: the train station; the school; the synagogue; the square; the church, and the monuments in front of it; the lake; the hillside that shelters the village, and its forest where he loved to walk; and the graveyard, where, for the first time, I saw my surname on a headstone and had to turn away.

26.

My stay in Nová Cerekev was brief, that time: only two days, and I had to go, or else, it seemed, my heart would burst – not from sadness, as one might think, but from a hyperconcentration of pure, undifferentiated feeling, painfully intense, stronger and less coherent than physical pain. I was only twenty then and had no words for it. I do now.

When writing my first essay on Sudek, I reflected that nostalgia "is a yearning, a compulsion, to piece together the physical remnants of [a] formerly shared world, to remember and repair it, to refuse to ever fully relinquish it" (Tutter, 2013, p. 156). Now, I see that by photographing my father's village, I was not just documenting it: I was attempting to collect the fragments of a shattered past and make them whole and continuous with the present.

And yet even as I write these words, I realize that I have never been able to spend more than a few days at a time, and less than a handful in total, in Nová Cerekev – because of guilt, perhaps, or, and I think likely more so, out of an unconscious solidarity, or *Mit-Leiden*, with the cumulative burden of sorrow carried by my father, who for so many years could not go home. When I travel to my father's home, his yearning, his unbearable pain, comes too.

27.

In 1688, a physician named Johannes Hofer coined the term *nostalgia* from the Greek roots – *nostos* ("homecoming" or "returning home") and *algia* ("pain") – to describe a peculiar sickness that incapacitated Swiss soldiers away from home, typically triggered by "rustic mother's soups" and "the folk melodies of Alpine valleys" – especially the call to the cows, the *Ranz-des-vaches* (German, *Kuhreihen*; Boym, 2002, p. 4).[19] In his 1768 *Dictionary of Music*, Jean-Jacques Rousseau describes the *Ranz-des-vaches* as

> that Tune so cherished by the Swiss that they have forbidden it from being played in their Troops on pain of death since it would cause those who heard it to dissolve in tears, desert or die, so much would it arouse in them the ardent desire to see their country again. . . . These effects, which do not take place on foreigners, come solely from habit, from memories . . . recalling for them their country their old pleasures, their youth, and all their ways of living, arouse in them *a bitter pain for having lost all that*.
>
> [quoted in Illbruck, 2012, p. 88, emphasis added]

Milan Kundera (2003) notes that the

> Czechs have the Greek-derived *nostalgie* as well as their own noun, *stesk*, and their own verb [*stýská se*] which forms the root of the most moving Czech expression of love: *stýská se mi po tobe* ('I yearn for you,' 'I'm nostalgic for you'; 'I cannot bear the pain of your absence').
>
> [p. 3]

Like the similarly untranslatable Portuguese word *saudade*, *stesk* embeds within love the bitter pain of longing. This feeling is implicit in the Czech National Anthem, taken from *Fidlovačka*, a popular Czech revivalist opera. *Kde domov muj (Where is my homeland?)* speaks to the love of and longing for the pastoral splendor that represents home, and its history of loss, summoned its very name.

Kde Domov Můj, kde můj,	*Where is my homeland, where is my homeland,*
Voda hučí po lučinách,	*Water's rustling o'er the meadows,*
Bory šumí po skalinách,	*Pinewoods murmuring o'er the mountains,*
V sadě skví se jara květ,	*In the orchards with spring blossoms,*

Zemsky ráj to na pohled,	*Earth's paradise for the eyes,*
A to je ta krásná země,	*And that is that beautiful country,*
Zemé česká domov můj,	*The Czech land, home of mine,*
Zemé česká domov můj.	*The Czech land, home of mine.*[20]

28.

Three decades after my first visit, the Czech Republic is a very different place. Prague is no longer a shadowed, scaffolded city of melancholy beauty, but a scrubbed, bustling European metropolis clotted with tour groups and billboards. One can use a credit card in a taxi; there *are* taxis; no one stares at a visitor from 'the west.' I have mixed feelings about this. 'My' Prague was a ghost suspended in time, as if different clocks had stopped – in 1938, 1948, 1968; everywhere was felt an ineffable sadness, a suppressed pressure, the tense expectancy of a held breath. Actually, it felt a lot like home. Now Prague moves easily in the present tense; 'my' Prague, if ever there was one, and my father's Prague, as obsolete as his speech, have vanished. Only through Sudek can I draw back the curtain.

And so when in Lincoln Center I heard Janáček's extraordinary second quartet, *Intimate Letters*, virtually sobbing with longing for the woman he loved but could not have, it felt like an elegy for times past and for all that was lost in that great big space between leaving and returning – *the bitter pain for having lost all that*. My father's world – his family, language, and country – had changed and evolved without him, his entire past sealed off and disconnected from the present. Yet it was always pushing at the door, reopening the wound. There was no healing it, at least not for my father, not until 1989. And in a way that wound never completely closed.

29.

My father did not care for Dvořák's *Symphony No. 9* ("New World"), written in 1893 while the composer was living in New York – because, I am certain, it was not 'Czech' enough. But several years after my father's death, my dying mother chose for her own funeral service *Goin' Home*, a song based on its "Largo" theme.[21] I still cannot listen to this music.

My father returned from his 1971 visit to Czechoslovakia a defeated man, witness to a people held captive, his hope nearly extinguished. However, he managed a small but real victory: he smuggled home several tiny spruce seedlings in his socks. Two lived. Handsome and tall now, they stand, like parents, their feet in the earth, behind the row of spruce trees my father planted, one for each of his four children, by our farmhouse in the Catskills. These trees survived my parents, and the little house, and the big overshot barn, in whose lofty darkness I spent many a hot summer's day, sitting on fragrant bales of hay, reading, watching the dust turning in narrow ribbons of light.

FIGURE 13.13 Left, Sudek's photographs of Janáček's home in Hukvaldy and environs, from *Janáček-Hukvaldy*; right, the author's photographs of Nová Cerekev and environs, including the house in which Antonín Tutter was born (upper right), 1982.

30.

After I mistakenly searched for *Sudek* instead of *Janáček*, I ordered a copy of *Janáček-Hukvaldy*. Although I was familiar with Sudek's oeuvre, I had seen only a few of the Hukvaldy pictures: the chair, the castle ruins. Yet when the book arrived and I began to leaf through it, the pictures were precipitously familiar: the hillside that shelters the village, and the forest, where Janáček, and then Sudek, loved to walk; the house, the animals in their pens, the barnyard; the graveyard (Fig. 13.13). Here was the church, and the monuments in front of the church (Fig. 13.14). Again, I felt the spreading, by now familiar confusion: whose pictures were these?

FIGURE 13.14 Upper, Sudek's photographs of the statues of the martyrs Sts Florian (left) and John of Nepomuk (right), on facing pages in *Janáček-Hukvaldy*. Lower, the author's photographs of the Marian column (left) and the seventeenth century *boží muka* (wayside shrine, right) in Nová Cerekev, on facing pages in her 1982 photograph album.

After a while, I put down the book and found the photograph album from my trip to Nová Cerekev thirty years ago. I had not opened it in over a decade. Amateur attempts, and nowhere near the quality of Sudek's portraits of Hukvaldy, my pictures are nonetheless thematically the same (Figs. 13.13, 13.14). Here are the fields and the hillside forest that shelters the village, the house, the barnyard. Here is the church, and the monuments in front of the church. Here is the graveyard.

It was then that I sensed that just as I went to Nová Cerekev to find my father, Sudek went to Hukvaldy to find his. We sought out their 'songlines,' the paths they still take, their spirits alive and walking, music with pointing the way, as it always has.

You see, when I recognized my pictures of Nová Cerekev in Sudek's pictures of Hukvaldy, it was not the first time I had the seizing feeling that *I had been here before*. The first time was when I walked the forest of Nová Cerekev in 1982. My father's life project was the recreation of the landscape of his youth at our farm in New York, where he planted forty thousand trees over a period of forty years. Reflexively, unthinkingly, he transformed the land into a simulacrum of his home – its evergreen forests, meadows, paths, and lake – in Proust's words, *the deepest layer of his mental soil*. Looking to reclaim his past, I saw that I had in fact grown up with it: it was there all along (Figs. 13.15, 13.16). I knew my father's forest before I walked it, just as I knew Janáček's music before I heard it, as I knew Sudek's *Hukvaldy* before I saw it. For he recreated this piece of Bohemia, tree by tree – for himself, for his family, and for me.

FIGURE 13.15 Left, the pine forest in Nová Cerekev, photograph by the author, 1982; middle, Josef Sudek, *Březen (March)*, c. 1935; right, the forest that Antonín Tutter planted in New York State, 1965–2000.

FIGURE 13.16 Left, Josef Sudek in the Czech Middle Mountains; right, Antonín Tutter in his woods. Tutter shared with Janáček and Sudek the characteristically Czech feeling of communion with nature. He was never happier than when in the forest, taking care of his trees.

Notes

1 Athenaeus, *Deipnosophistai* 14:31.
2 Proust, 1992, pp. 259–260.
3 Rilke, 2010, Sonnets to Orpheus (1), trans. Robert Temple.
4 Janáček, 1989, p. 99.
5 Biographical information about Sudek is drawn from Bullaty, 1978; Fárová, 1990a, 1990b; and Kirschner, 1993; and about Janáček, from Tyrrell, 2006, 2007; Vogel, 1962; and Zemanová, 2002. The author's previous essay is currently the only psychoanalytic study of Sudek in English (Tutter, 2013). The only mentions of Janáček in the English language psychoanalytic literature are from Chipman, 2000, who compares his late creativity to that of Jean Sibelius, and Ginsburg and Ginsburg, 1992, who find Janáček of interest for his proximity to Sigmund Freud, born only two years after Janáček in the same village of Příbor, not five kilometers from Hukvaldy. Like Janáček, Freud also referred to Hukvaldy – more than once – as his "paradise" (Freud, 1872a, p. 9; 1872b, p. 16). See O'Donoghue's (2010) acute discussion on Freud's relationship to his hometown and environs.
6 The term "nationalism" is generally pejorative, carrying associations with German National Socialism. Adam Michnik's (1991) writes: "the aspirations to reclaim the national memory, to defend the cultural identity, to have an independent state do not qualify as Nationalism. Nationalism is not the struggle for one's own national rights but a disregard for someone else's rights to national and human dignity . . . Lenin was right

when he distinguished the nationalism of a conquered nation from the nationalism of the occupying nation" (pp. 758–759; Volkan, 1997 also makes this distinction.) In this essay, I use the term "Czech nationalism" in the former sense, which Michnik defines the latter *against*: a meaning closer to *národnost*, folk-allegiance. The pernicious species of nationalism that Michnik describes typically flourish when a country is liberated: witness, for example, the Czech expulsion of ethnic Germans from the Sudetenland after World War II, and the long-standing discrimination against the *Romy* ("gypsies") in the Czech and Slovak nations. See also Anderson, 1983 for a discussion of nationalism as an anthropological, rather than an ideological construct.

7 Like Béla Bartók, Janáček spent years recording Moravian folk music in the field. Many Moravians, including Janáček, resented the common automatic equation of "Bohemian" with "Czech." While the label "Czech" applies to all speakers of the Czech language, the Czech Republic (and the Czech portion of the former Czechoslovakia) is made up of three historically discrete kingdoms, Bohemia, Moravia, and Silesia, each with its own folk traditions and dialects of Czech.

8 These comments reflect Janáček's interest in Wilhelm Wundt's concept of *Völkerpsychologie*, which holds that psychological development depends on internal experience as well as the external influence of cultural and spiritual community. See Tyrrell, 2006.

9 As opposed to common belief, Janáček used speech melody less often as a template of musical melody, and more as a source of rhythm and prosody, especially when setting Czech lyrics and texts to music (see Tyrell, 2006 and Katz, 2009). Janáček presciently anticipated the subsequent importance of spoken language in music, from Cage to Stockhausen to Ligeti.

10 Language can also be enlisted as an instrument of subversion and resistance to political oppression (see Wierzbicka, 1990).

11 See Agnew, 2007, for an excellent discussion of the crucial role of nationalist symbolism in Czech nationalism.

12 Of interest, this is indeed the monastery where Gregor Mendel, monk and father of modern genetics, lived and bred his peas. In fact, for two years of Janáček's life, he reported directly to Mendel, whose stature at the time was completely obscure. See Tyrrell, 2006, pp. 56–57.

13 While the primacy of language as it relates to culture has been challenged in the contemporary critique, Lagerspetz (1998) offers that the right to one's language is an ethical, more than a cultural right.

14 Like Janáček, Lipps also was influenced by the psychologist Wilhelm Wundt; see fn. 7.

15 Apropos, Janáček was a famous eater, and food – the lack of it, the desire for it, the enjoyment of it – figured prominently in his letters to Kamila (Janáček, 1994), in which he variously uses food as bait, reward, and a means to provoke guilt.

16 Max Brod, a composer as well as a man of letters, translated Janáček's operas into German and was instrumental in bringing Janáček, along with Franz Kafka, to international attention.

17 Zdeněk Kirschner, personal communication, August 2013.

18 I thank my coeditor, Léon Wurmser, for this information about Klaus Mann's novel.

19 Léon Wurmser brought to my attention that a similar word exists in German: *heimweh*, best translated as "home-ache" or "home-woe."

20 The operal *Fidlovačka* was composed by Frano isek Skroup, with a libretto by Josef Kajetan Tyl.

21 Contrary to popular belief, Dvořák did not compose the "Largo" theme after Goin' Home; it was the other way around. William Arms Fisher wrote the lyrics for *Goin' Home* in 1922, adapting the "Largo" theme in the style of a Negro spiritual (Beckerman, 2003).

References

Agnew, H.L. (2007). Demonstrating the nation: Symbol, ritual, and political protest in Bohemia, 1867–1875. In: *The Street as Stage: Protest Marches and Public Rallies since the Nineteenth Century*, ed. M. Reiss. Oxford: Oxford University Press & the German Historical Institute of London, pp. 85–103.

Anderson, B. (1983). *Imagined Communities: Reflections on the Origin and Spread of Nationalism*. London: Verso.

Anzieu, D. (1979). The sound image of the self. *Int. Rev. Psycho-Anal.*, 6:23–36.

———. (1985/1989). *The Skin Ego*, trans. C. Turner. New Haven: Yale University Press.

Applebaum, A. (2012). *The Iron Curtain: The Crushing of Eastern Europe, 1944–1956*. New York: Doubleday.

Athenaeus, *Deipnosophistai*, trans. C.B. Gulick, Loeb Classical Library (7 volumes). London and Cambridge, MA: Harvard University Press, 1927–1941.

Barale, F. (2009). At the origins of psychoanalysis: Freud, Lipps and the issue of sound and music, trans. P. Slotkin. *Ital. Psychoanal. Ann.*, 3:37–54

Baranger, M., & W. Baranger, (2008). The analytic situation as a dynamic field. *Int. J. Psycho-Anal.*, 89:795–826.

Beckerman, M. (1986). In search of Czechness in music. *19th-Cent. Music*, 10: 61–73.

———. (2003), *New Worlds of Dvořák: Searching in America for the Composer's Inner Life*. New York: Norton.

Bick, E. (1968). The experience of the skin in early object-relations. *Int. J. Psycho-Anal.*, 49:484–486.

Boym, S. (2002). *The Future of Nostalgia*. New York: Basic Books.

Bullaty, S. (1978). *Sudek*. New York: Clarkson N. Potter.

Chipman, A. (2000). Janác?ek and Sibelius: The antithetical fates of creativity in late adulthood. *Psychoanal. Rev.*, 87:429–454.

Dostoevsky, F. (2004). *From The House of the Dead*, C. Garnett, trans. New York: Courier Dover. Originally published in Russian, 1861.

Fárová, A. (1990a). *Josef Sudek – Poet of Prague: Outward journey. Aperture*, 117:6–82.

———. (1990b). *Josef Sudek – Poet of Prague: A Deepening Vision. Aperture*, 118:83–92.

Freud, S. (1872a). Letter from Sigmund Freud to Eduard Silberstein, August 9, 1872. In: *The Letters of Sigmund Freud to Eduard Silberstein 1871–1881*, ed. W. Boelich, trans. A. Pomerans. Cambridge, MA: Harvard University Press, 1990, pp. 9–10.

———. (1872b). Letter from Sigmund Freud to Eduard Silberstein, September 4, 1872. In: *The Letters of Sigmund Freud to Eduard Silberstein 1871–1881*, ed. W. Boelich, trans. A. Pomerans. Cambridge, MA: Harvard University Press, 1990, pp. 14–19.

———. (1929). Civilization and its Discontents. Standard Edition, 21:57–146. London: Hogarth Press, 1961.

Ginsberg, L.A., & Ginsburg, S.A. (1992). Paradise in the life of Sigmund Freud: An understanding of its imagery and paradoxes. *Int. Rev. Psycho-Anal.*, 19:285–306.

Hollander, H. (1955). The music of Leoš Janáček – its origin in folklore. *Music. Quart.*, 41:171–176.

Illbruck, H. (2012). *Nostalgia: Origins and Ends of an Unenlightened Disease*. Evanston, IL: Northwestern University Press.

Janáček, L. (1982). *Leoš Janáček: Leaves From His Life*, ed. & trans. V. Tausky & M. Tausky. New York: Taplinger Publishing Company.

———. (1989). *Janáček's Uncollected Essays On Music*, ed. & trans. M. Zemanová. London: Marion Boyars.

_____. (1994). *Intimate Letters: Leoš Janáček to Kamila* Stösslová, ed. & trans. J. Tyrrell. Princeton, NJ: Princeton University Press.

Katz, D. (2009). *Janáček Beyond the Borders.* Eastman Studies in Music, ed. R.P. Locke. Rochester, NY: University of Rochester Press.

Kinnvall, C. (2004). Globalization and religious nationalism: Self, identity, and the search for ontological security. *Pol. Psychol.,* 25:741–767.

Kirschner, Z. (1993). *Sudek.* New York: Takarajuima & Prague: Museum of Decorative Arts.

Kristeva, J. (1982). *The Powers of Horror,* trans. L.S. Roudiez. New York: Columbia University Press.

Kundera, M. (2003). *Ignorance,* trans. L. Asher. New York: Harper Perennial.

Lagerspetz, E. (1998). On language rights. *Ethical Theory Moral Pract.,* 1:181–199.

Michnik, A. (1991). *Nationalism,* trans. E. Matynia. *Soc. Res.,* 58:757–763.

O'Donoghue, D. (2010). Moses in Moravia. *Amer. Imago,* 67: 157–182.

Proust, M. (1992). In Search of Lost Time, Volume I: Swann's Way, ed. D.J. Enright, trans. C.K. Scott-Moncrieff & T. Kilmartin. New York: Random House, Modern Library.

Rilke, R.M. (2010) *Sonnets to Orpheus,* trans. R.K.G. Temple, http://www.sonnetstoorpheus.com/, accessed March 21, 2014.

Said, E. (1994). *Representations of the Intellectual: The 1993 Reith Lectures.* New York: Vintage.

Sapir, E. (1949). The status of linguistics as a science. In: *Selected Writings of Edward Sapir in Language, Culture, and Personality,* ed. D. Mandelbaum. Berkeley, CA: University of California Press, pp. 160–166.

Šeda, J. (1971). Preface. In: *Janáček-Hukvaldy,* J. Sudek. Prague: Supraphon, 1971, unpaginated.

Stein, A. (2004). Music, mourning, and consolation. *J. Amer. Psychoanal. Assn.,* 52:783–811.

Sudek, J. (1971). *Janáček-Hukvaldy.* Prague: Supraphon.

Szabó, I., dir. (1981). *Mephisto.* Analysis Films.

Tausky, V. (1982). Recollections of Leoš Janáček. In: *Leoš Janáček: Leaves From His Life,* ed. & trans. V. Tausky & M. Tausky. New York: Taplinger Publishing Co., pp. 5–23.

Tucker, A. (1996). Shipwrecked: Patočka's philosophy of Czech history. *Hist. Theory,* 35:196–216.

Tutter, A. (2013). Angel with a missing wing: Loss, restitution, and the embodied self in the photography of Josef Sudek. *Amer. Imago,* 70:127–190.

Tyrrell, J. (2006). *Leoš Janáček: Years of A Life. Volume I. (1854–1914) The Lonely Blackbird.* London: Faber and Faber.

_____. (2007). *Leoš Janáček: Years of A Life. Volume II. (1914–1928) Tsar of the Forests.* London: Faber and Faber.

Urciuoli, B. (1995). Language and borders. *Ann. Rev. Anthropol.,* 24:525–546.

Vogel, J. (1962). *Leoš Janáček: A Biography,* trans. G. Thomsen-Muchová. London: Orbis Publishing, 1981.

Volkan, V. (1997). *Bloodlines: From Ethnic Pride to Ethnic Terrorism.* Boulder, CO: Westview.

Wein, M. (2009). Chosen peoples, holy tongues: Religion, language, nationalism and politics in Bohemia and Moravia in the seventeenth to twentieth centuries. *Past Present,* 202:37–81.

Weiss, M. (2001). The body of the nation: terrorism and the embodiment of nationalism in contemporary Israel. *Anthropol. Q.,* 75:37–62.

Wierzbicka, A. (1990). Antitotalitarian language in Poland: Some mechanisms of linguistic self-defense. *Lang. Soc.,* 19:1–59.

Woolard, K. & Schieffelin, B. (1994). Language ideology. *Ann. Rev. Anthropol.,* 23:55–82.

Zemanová, M. (2002). *Janáček: A Composer's Life.* Boston: Northeastern University Press.

14

DISCUSSION OF PART III

Image, Loss, Delay

Diane O'Donoghue

A strange phrase weaves through the narrative of Jacques Derrida's (2010) evocative meditations on a series of photographs of Athens taken by the French photographer Jean-François Bonhomme: "we owe ourselves to death" (*nous nous devons à la mort*). On first encountering this sentence, it seems simultaneously unsettling and incomprehensible. But as Derrida develops it – as a photographer would a picture – a representation emerges from what began as an unreadable surface. Framing it by the inevitability of death, Derrida discerns the possibility of temporal and visual resistance, where we are momentarily ransomed from mortality by a creative action that can live beyond us. It is here, in this site of delay, where objects can emerge into being. Derrida's *Athens, Still Remains* (*Demeure, Athènes*) finds copious evidence of demise in Bonhomme's photographs: buildings now in ruins, individuals preserved only as their headstones, a vaunted classical past preserved as mute residue amid bustling urban banality (Fig. 14.1). But in that strange phrase that haunts him – Derrida imagines it as a kind of unanticipated Delphic oracle – he also understands two aspects of the claim that these words exert: we cannot escape the final payment demanded by having been alive, but creative acts can incessantly defer a final extinguishing of meaning: art is both the still life as *memento mori* and reminder of what is alive, what *still remains*.

The two final essays in this volume, one by the psychoanalyst Adele Tutter and the other with Tutter in conversation with the sculptor Jane McAdam Freud, remind us that there is something missing in Derrida's essay: glimpses of the meaning these images had for Bonhomme himself. Were we given access to that aspect of the photographer's work, we might be afforded another way to understand Bonhomme's deep engagement with Athens and add another layer to Derrida's oracular refrain. Artists are often keen observers of their own mortality, as McAdam Freud notes when discussing how her work implicates her deceased father, Lucian Freud, and the awareness of the ultimate reality of her own death. So if one cannot escape the debt owed by one's life, how does the object, from the artist's perspective, cope with that reality? Losses and deaths can often open as well as close one's life story, along with threading through it, and we all risk becoming indentured in the servitude of traumatic events – familial, cultural, political. But, as we see in these chapters, amid what has gone before and what lies ahead, we need not fall into an abyss, something resembling the indecipherable surface of the undeveloped photograph. Rather, what emerges, after a delay, can be a remarkable image that serves as a bridge, exceeding the claims of either the legacy of trauma or the reality of death's extraction. Derrida recognizes this as a philosopher, but it is within the work of the artist, as discussed in Tutter and McAdam Freud's texts, that we see this at work in the creative process and, along with it, an additional understanding of an act of "transcendence."

Although philosophy and theology have often altered the direction associated with this word, the original Latin meaning of transcendence was "to climb across," rather than sweep upward. Commonly understood as a term for something apart from common, and in some cases mortal, limits, the original meaning of *transendere* was rather less grand: it meant to be able to bridge a gap. This usage is especially useful in both these essays, as it feels that in them there is an attempt to open a mediating space between past loss and the awareness of the fragility of the future. To climb across something suggests both movement and effort. In philosophical and religious transcendence, we can imagine the action as the end rather than the means and, even then, something that can be achieved without exertion. But the effort of the artists discussed here seems to provide a better definition of this, as they create a collusion of time and space that can give rise to aural and visual "objects." Their work does not emerge instantaneously, but develops, whether through a literal process, as in Tutter's discussion of Josef Sudek's photographs or through the delays that occur in the composing of music, with Leoš Janáček, and the "compositing" of sculpture, so evident in the multiple processes that are required to create some of McAdam Freud's pieces. These are moments of what can be a perilous creative passage, but, at least in the case of the artists discussed here, this *transcendence* does occur; the work eventually makes its appearance. To extend Derrida's mysterious phrase, might we also suggest that the space in life shadowed by loss and facing death, *owes a debt to being alive?* And that one of the most powerful traces of that debt is to create work that attests, not to some ethereal notion of aesthetics, but rather to a person's often hard-earned capacity to shape something that can live apart, and on, in often powerful and poignant ways?

Adele Tutter's essay weaves the legacies of loss endured in body and the body politic (in the case of the latter, that of the Czech-speaking lands) by two of its creative native sons, Janáček and Sudek. Alongside them, she also introduces her own father, Antonín Tutter, who shared a common homeland with the composer and photographer, and although not an artist in the conventional sense of the word, would eventually frame a rendition of his native landscape within the forests of upstate New York. He would transmit this sense of "displaced place" to his daughter; and who is to say that the sound made by those American pines did not have for him the same middle European cadence that we can more readily discern within Janáček's notes or Sudek's images? Evidence of potential transcendence – one that delays death and nourishes creative potential – was for all of these men deeply tied to the Czech soil, enduring, as they each did, the tumult of war and loss. This is particularly striking in Tutter's retelling of Sudek's yearly pilgrimage to Janáček's home in the Moravian town of Hukvaldy, whose medieval legacy was preserved in the striking remains of its vast castle, with foundations dated to the thirteenth century. Sudek would travel to the composer's modest cottage to photograph virtually identical images of its contents over more than twenty years.

This village has an interesting place in the history of psychoanalysis, too. From letters written by the adolescent Sigmund Freud, we learn that it was here, in the place he called *Hochwald* (Czech: Hukvaldy), that he found "a paradise without equal" (Freud, 1990, p. 9), where he would go to indulge in afternoons of youthful revelry.[1] Freud and Janáček were born in close proximity in both time – the latter being the elder by less than two years – and place. Freud's birthplace of Freiberg (Czech: Příbor) is six kilometers from Hukvaldy. Janáček's mother, Amalia Gruliclová, was also a native of Freud's town, and she and her husband lived there for a number of years before the elder Janáček was appointed teacher and choirmaster in Hukvaldy in 1848, six years before his famous son was born (Hollander, 1963, pp. 19–20.) Although there is no evidence that Freud knew the composer or his family, both certainly shared an attachment to the region. For Freud, it would be nurtured from afar, as the family left Moravia in his third year when his father hoped to establish residency in Leipzig; denied that, the family went on to Vienna, the hometown of Freud's mother, also named Amalia. Sigmund would return in the summer of 1872, at sixteen, and walk between his birthplace and that of Janáček with a pleasure and ease that he would never feel in Vienna, of which he would later say: "I never felt really comfortable in the town." (Freud, 1899, p. 311). The closest he would come to a *Heimat* – a homeland – was in these Moravian woodlands with their dramatic ruins, and one might speculate on the ways in which his imaginings of a psychical terrain bear traces of his first landscape.

Freud turned on a number of occasions to photography as a source for accessing the language of representation, memory, and image, as Mary Bergstein's (2010) work convincingly argues. What would Freud have found in Sudek's *Janáček-Hukvaldy* folios that might have resonated with, perhaps we might say, the long shutter speed of psyche? Such a delay would allow Sudek to create his haunting images of Janáček's objects – Derrida noted the same technique in Bonhomme's photographs – where the temporal specificity of the era of the image and that of its subject, such as the example of the composer's chair, becomes very indistinct. It is fascinating to consider that Freud introduced an important theory of memories and their development with examples from his experiences in earliest childhood and then adolescence in Freiberg. In "Screen Memories" of 1899, he not only introduces the most detailed glimpse into his Moravian past, but also how he remembered it: images rich in color, texture, sound.

Sigmund Freud and memory join in a different register through Adele Tutter's interview with his great-granddaughter. That Jane McAdam Freud, like her father, chose to be an artist sets her less apart from the paterfamilias than one might imagine. It is important to recognize that what Sigmund enunciated as the "unconscious" was a mechanism marked by its capacities for image-making (dreams, of course, being the hallmark of this) and the building of structures. McAdam Freud's grandfather, Ernst, was an architect, a profession for which he credited his father's interest in fostering. Ernst's son, Lucian, would become a world-renowned painter of the human figure, in all its visual and psychological complexities. With this lineage, it is impressive that an artist of the next Freud generation is able to create work that can acknowledge this past and yet not be lost within it. McAdam Freud's interview with Tutter begins with a discussion of a sepulchral-like sculpture that displays the word "THISHERE." Semantic ambiguities surround the alternative ways to read this – his/her, he/she, is/he. But in any rendition there is the sense of a cenotaph to an attachment and its loss. Derrida touches upon a similar affective response in his discussion of Bonhomme's photography of headstones in ancient cemeteries, some with carved names that make them feel quite akin to THISHERE. The departure of a paternal figure for McAdam Freud – she speaks both of the separation of her parents, with the resulting absence of her father, and her concurrent loss of belief in "Father Christmas" – informed the work when she created it in 2008. Revisiting it in this interview, after the death of her father in 2011, she reflects on this and on the inevitability of loss that cannot help but remind one of one's own death. She shares that a bust of her father, on which she was working at the time of his death, "helps me to keep him alive." This work thus allows for the finality of Lucian Freud's death to be delayed, postponed by an object that crosses over, bridges the gap from the time of his life to that after.

From a residency at the Freud Museum in London in 2005 and 2006, McAdam Freud created work inspired by her great-grandfather's vast collection, primarily of early objects from sites in the classical Mediterranean, Egypt, and middle Asia. This collaboration between the living and the dead has resonances in Sudek's "pilgrimages" each year to make work at Janáček's late residence, and amid his objects, in Hukvaldy. Arguably, of course, one could speak of the Freud relationships as more deeply familial, spanning three generations, and thus potentially far more intense. That said, Sudek does share with McAdam Freud a deep attachment to objects that touched, in every sense of the word, someone who, in both cases, the artist never met, and yet to whom they felt a profound connection. When McAdam Freud created work around her great-grandfather's collection, its presence for her extended through the ensuing years and generations. Although some of her work gestures to Sigmund's objects, there are others where a fainter echo of their presence may still be discerned, although the pieces themselves would not overtly suggest that. One looks at her double-sided sculptural plaques, where both Lucian and his grandfather can be carried forward. The paired images, looking in opposite directions, suggest father and daughter, and indeed some of the images appear based on their profiles. But as someone as familiar as the artist is with her great-grandfather's collection, there is also perhaps a nod here to his attachment to the Roman god of transitions,

Janus, who is depicted facing forward and backward, and whose name comes to refer to the first month of a new year, itself forming a threshold between past and future.

It is ironic that the notion of transcendence has been able to separate the "work of art" from both its maker and the historical and political moment they share. Aesthetics is a construction of both beauty and timelessness, and its ultimate residence, like all Platonic forms, is to be found in the heavens. The bi-directionality of Janus's gaze challenges this: it is decidedly horizontal and rather low to the horizon line at that. The view is filled with much that is not beautiful, in both what has now passed and what will follow it. "Art" may reside in immortality, but artists do not. Their work is often created out of the exquisite pain of many dimensions of loss, as we have seen in the individuals discussed in this volume. How does one extract a Czech identity from Sudek, Janáček, and Antonín Tutter or the Freud familial one from McAdam Freud and then tally what remains? It would seem very diminished indeed. Rather, their work has kept the power of connection and loss as places where "transcendence" occurs, and its alternative, disappearance – to death, time, and the erasure of aesthetic criteria – has been resisted. So the specter of mortality, Derrida's debt that all must pay, is not bested here by eternal life, but rather by delayed existence: one that keeps putting objects into the world, which allows for what is contained in a human life to remain visible, even after the creator of those objects no longer is. To understand the profound value of this is also a debt we owe – to ourselves.

FIGURE 14.1 Photographs of Athens by Jean-François Bonhomme, from Jacques Derrida, Demeure, Athènes.

Note

1 Freud's memories of his time in Hukvaldy are preserved in a series of letters he sent during his visit in 1872 to his school friend, Eduard Silberstein (Freud, 1990).

References

Bergstein, M. (2010). *Mirrors of Memory: Freud, Photography, and the History of Art*. Ithaca and London: Cornell University Press.

Derrida, J. (2010). *Athens, Still Remains: The Photographs of Jean-François Bonhomme*, trans. P.-A. Brault and M. Naas. New York: Fordham University Press, 2010.

Freud, S. (1899). Screen memories. Standard Edition, 3:300–322. London: Hogarth Press, 1962.

———. (1990). *The Letters of Sigmund Freud to Eduard Silberstein, 1871–1881*, ed. W. Boehlich, trans. A.J. Pomerans. Cambridge, Mass: Belknap Press of Harvard University Press.

Hollander, H. (1963). *Leoš Janáček: His Life and Work*, trans. P. Hamburger. London: John Calder.

EPILOGUE

"'Tis nameless woe"

Léon Wurmser

Grief's substance and shadow

As I discussed in Chapter 10, the "meal of healing" of the Shiv'a ritual traditionally consists of lentils and eggs. In fact, the egg assumed such a central role that in Spain, it was called *aveluz* (*aveluth*, Hebrew for mourning; Wieseltier, 1998, p. 320); during the Spanish Inquisition, its use was viewed as evidence for secret "Judaizing" and cause for persecution. We also saw how these foods were chosen as specific symbols because they had no opening, "no mouth," and thus beautifully symbolized the wordlessness and namelessness of overwhelming grief and sadness.

A few quotes from Shakespeare's tragedy *Richard II*, which contains particularly striking references to sadness, psychic pain, and mourning, illustrate grief beyond words, though not beyond images. The assassination of this rather wayward, incompetent, feckless monarch brought about the ascension to the throne of the dynasty of the House of Lancaster, specifically of Henry Bolingbroke, who became King Henry IV. Yet it is as if the bloodguilt for the murder and usurpation of Richard II, no matter how seemingly justified, led to one hundred years of civil war, the War of the Roses. In the prophecy of the Bishop of Carlisle: "The woe's to come. The children yet unborn/ Shall feel this day as sharp to them as thorn" (IV: I). As presented by Shakespeare, this fatal deed haunted the row of kings until Richard III, that horrific, monstrous descendant and end of the dynastic line. He served as its ghastly endpoint: the hated deformed child avenging his resentment and nameless shame ("unacknowledged shame," Lansky, 2015), a harbinger of many future horrors as a prototype of the ruthless, amoral tyrant – for the abused, shamed, and, perhaps, deformed children who would become the gigantic murderers of history – Hitler, Stalin, Saddam Hussein (and perhaps Goebbels and Mao Tse Tung).

Yet the beginning of the sequence in Richard II is distinguished by repeated expressions of woe, of sorrow, of grief. There is, almost at the beginning, the lament of the Duchess of York (the aunt of both the King and his usurper), directly followed by the Queen's woeful foreboding. The duchess compares her sorrow to a tennis ball bouncing off a wall:

> Grief boundeth where it falls
> Not with the empty hollowness, but weight,
> I take my leave before I have begun,
> For sorrow ends not when it seemeth done.

[Shakespeare, 1952, I: II]

Then the Queen speaks of premonitions of sorrow: "Yet again, methinks, / Some unborn sorrow, ripe in fortune's womb, / Is coming toward me, and my inward soul / With nothing trembles." The courtier Bushy tries to soothe her:

> Each substance of a grief has twenty shadows,
> Which shows like grief itself, but is not so;
> For sorrow's eye, glazed with blinding tears,
> Divides one thing entire to many objects. . .
> 'tis with false sorrow's eye,
> Which for things true weeps things imaginary.

The Queen retorts:

> It may be so, but yet my inward soul
> Persuades me, it is otherwise . . .
> But what it is, that is not yet known—what
> I cannot name. *'Tis nameless woe, I wot.*

[II: II, emphasis added]

But grief has layers, and it has inside and outside meanings: both "substance" and "shadow." Betrayed and deposed, his identity shattered, the King asks for a mirror "that it may show me what a face I have, / Since it is bankrupt of his majesty." Staring at it, he exclaims:

> Hath sorrow struck
> So many blows upon this face of mine
> And made no deeper wounds? O flattering glass
> A brittle glory shineth in this face –
> As brittle as the glory is the face.
> [He dashes the glass against the ground.]
> For there it is, cracked in a hundred shivers.
> Mark, silent King, the moral of this sport,
> How soon my sorrow hath destroyed my face

His foe, Henry Bolingbroke, counters: "The shadow of your sorrow hath destroyed/ The shadow of your face." Richard II replies, in ironical disbelief:

> Say that again,
> The shadow of my sorrow! Ha! Let's see,
> 'Tis very true, my grief lies all within.
> And these external manners of laments
> Are merely shadows to the unseen grief
> That swells with silence in the tortured soul.
> There lies the substance, and I thank thee, King,
> For thy great bounty, that not only givest
> Me cause to wail, but teachest me the way
> How to lament the cause.

[IV: I]

Our book is an attempt to approach the *substance* under the *shadow*: to give to "nameless woe" and "unseen grief" word, imagery, memory, and a deeper understanding.

Often with our patients, regardless of diagnosis, we encounter a profound nothingness and emptiness, an inner abyss, a feeling state reaching into the deepest inwardness of the soul. Some speak of a "black hole" within them. The contradiction posed by the profound inner emptiness, that of the devouring "black hole," and the need to adapt to external demands leads to massive despair and the sense of broken reality. Many want to recognize in this contradiction a psychotic core and its encapsulation. But I have rather often seen it occurring not only in the severe neuroses, especially in severe neurotic depressions, but also in states of profound grief, during which one's very existential foundations are shaken. We may alternatively explain it as a manifestation of severe traumatization. Anxieties and other emotions connected with severe trauma, usually repeated and chronic, fail to find adequate expression, any words, even any images – "'tis nameless woe." As a child expressed in therapy: "There were black hells I had no words for." Earl Hopper (1991) uses a poignant simile: "an infinitely powerful cauldron of pain that annihilates all that enters it" (p. 609). It is the onrushing torrent of feelings of panic, of guilt, and of shame that evoke that experience of Psalm 42.8: "Abyss calls the abyss, to the roar of Your cataracts (*tehóm el tehóm qore leqól tzinnorécha*). All Your breakers and billows have swept over me" (the Hebrew Bible, *Tanakh*). If we take these verses as a metaphor for the traumatic experience, then what are the disasters to which they refer? In the biblical text, it is grief, scorn, and despair, and having been forgotten and abandoned by divinity that oppresses the soul.[1]

Especially, shame and guilt can be such profound affects; both call forth the abyss of despair; both submerge the sufferer in absolute abjectness. And mourning is perhaps always accompanied by profound feelings of guilt and, at least I believe so, also by shame. Certainly in the papers collected in this volume, we find their double shadow haunting the background.

But we may add more to this study of "nameless woe." In regard to early trauma – and loss, mourning, and grief are trauma par excellence – Joachim Küchenhoff (1990) writes,

> in contrast to later trauma, it does not remain external to the psychical appa-
> ratus, but becomes part of it. In other words, the *traumatic experience becomes a*
> *transcendental part of the categories of experience, a subjective* a priori *of all possible*
> *experience.* In this regard, the early trauma poses an entirely different psycho-
> dynamic problem. Its assimilation is so total that the trauma becomes the
> image of self and world whereas later trauma remains a foreign body for
> experience which could still infect all other forms of experience. It is the
> early trauma that is therefore used for the formation of identity.
>
> [my translation, p. 18]

We therefore should speak not of "early trauma," but rather of "traumatic identity" or "traumatic identity formation," Küchenhoff says, which is manifest in a
basic sense of unpredictability.

> Due to a trauma in the first months of life, the development of basic trust may
> be interrupted; no memory image of a good breast arises that could form the
> background for any possible experience; the trauma becomes incorporated
> like a bad and unpredictable breast, leading to the basic conviction that life
> unfolds within a basic unpredictability. [p. 18]

> (...) "Personification in the traumatic object" can defend against early trauma, a
> bondage to an evil object as fundamental to life and perpetuated in the archaic
> superego (with the alternating solutions of submission to it or triumph over it);
> so can "the rejection of the relationship to the traumatic object," "attacks on
> linking," and the establishment of "the phantasma of the empty space."
>
> [pp. 24–26]

We also see, in the parlance of André Green, and again as a defense, that "the
disobjectalizing function [leads] to an *absence of representation* rather than to depression"
(Green, 1993, as translated by Reed & Baudry, 2005, p. 127), resulting in what he
terms "the pathological negative" (p. 130) or "the void" (p. 132; see also Jarass and
Wurmser, 2007): *abyss calls the abyss.*

The healing power of transcendent tradition

How do we as therapists respond?

A brief answer is: we must find a path back to broader, sheltering contexts and connections, in the web of relationships and of relatedness, with our contemporaries,

the intimate Other (the You, *das Du*); but we must also find a path back through long stretches of time.

Just now I have read a very wise comment by David Brooks (2014) in the *New York Times*, who writes,

> Most of our core beliefs originated with some great figure from the distant past. These ideas, creeds or faiths were then nurtured by generations of other people, who are also now mostly dead. They created a transcendent tradition which we embrace and hope in turn to pass along to generations as yet unborn. No sensible person would ever be happy betraying the approval of the admiring dead just to win some passing approval in the here and now.
>
> [p. A23]

What I shall next say speaks to several strands of such transcendent traditions that are particularly relevant for today's psychoanalyst, but which are also of great value to every person who tries to grapple with overwhelming grief, that "nameless woe," even if they do not necessarily connect those traditions with the same "great figures from the distant past."

There are three such dimensions in dealing with mourning, all found to various degrees in every contribution to this book. Although they may appear to some too general or too philosophical, I find them useful; all three are anchored in my identity and very long experience as a psychoanalyst who has faced many forms of mourning and grief, not only in my patients, but very much in myself, as I describe in my own contribution to this volume. They are: (1) the fundamental nature of inner conflict, (2) the fundamental importance of intimacy and the Intimate Other, and (3) the fundamental wisdom of the psychoanalytic ethic – to always dignify rather than shame, and to always revere and explore the realm of inner life and what is yet unknown.

Conflict and complementarity

The first strand is the use of the fundamental nature of inner conflict as a means of self-understanding and empathy for others, be it one dealing with "normal" grief, be it "pathological mourning," be it overwhelming trauma like the Holocaust, or simply emotional pain of any kind.

We encounter beautiful words in the Book of Job, in Elihu's answer of reproof and rebuke to Job's accusations of God:

> For God speaks time and again, though man does not perceive it, in a dream, in a night vision (*bachalom chezion layla*), when deep sleep falls upon men, while they slumber on their beds. Then he opens men's understanding, and by disciplining them he leaves His signature to turn men away from an action, to suppress pride in men. He spares him from the Pit, his

person, from perishing by the sword. He is reproved by pains on his bed, and strong conflict ("we*riv*," an alternative reading for "we*rov*") tears his inner being apart.[2]

[33.15]

Here the dream reveals and warns about inner dangers: God speaks to man through his dream conscience and dream knowledge and tries in this way to save his soul. In essence, Job said: "I have no guilt that would justify the punishment I suffer," and Elihu replied (I paraphrase): "How can you dare to say such a thing? Surely you must be guilty, and your dream will show you how." Elihu, Job's apparent friend, appears here as a humiliating accuser; although applying a good, theoretically psychoanalytic interpretation of the superego function of dreams, he comes across as an utterly unempathic, judgmental therapist.

But the most important thing is the alternative reading: *"the soul is torn apart by conflict."* This image of being *inwardly* torn apart fits well with the ethical conflicts that were vastly sharpened by the emphasis on "inner man," related (but not restricted) to the advent of radical monotheism (Assmann, 2003; 2006; also Wurmser, 2012) and, more generally, with the new consciousness connected with Jaspers' "axial time" ("*Achsenzeit*," 800–200 BC; Jaspers, 1949), evident, for example, in Greek tragedy and shortly thereafter in Plato.

A famous phrase by the pre-Socratic Heraclitus points in a similar direction: *Polemos pater panton* (fr 53; if I do not simply translate *polemos* as "war" or "fight," but in a broader sense as "conflict"): "conflict is the father of all, the king of all, and some he reveals as gods, and some as men; some he makes slaves, and some he makes free." The consciousness of inner conflict has accompanied Western thought and creativity throughout its history and with it its guiding metaphors for self-understanding, especially when faced with the inevitable traumata of human existence.

Ancient Greek tragedy revolves around the pivot of the tragic choice – the necessary decision between opposing commitments to enormously important values, ideals, and loyalties. Many symbols or metaphors in Greek tragedy reflect the consciousness of inner conflict – for example, the *Symplegades*, "blue clashing rocks" (*symplekein*, to clash, to fight, almost synonymous to "conflict," *confligere*) in Euripides's *Medea*. There is also the repeated use of the term *diphrontis*, "of two minds," in Aischylos's *Libation Bearers* and in Euripides's *Hippolytos*, which appears to refer with particular poignancy to what I have referred to as the shame-guilt dilemma (Wurmser, 1981; 1989).

Speaking in the *Phaidros* of "the soul being like the combined force of the winged pair of horses and the charioteer," Plato describes how "the bad horse pulls the chariot down" and then adds, "and then pain (*ponos*) and extreme conflict (*agon eschatos*) are inflicted upon the soul" (246/247).

Before our modern age, however, such inner conflict has, to my knowledge, nowhere been more keenly expressed and reflected upon than in Augustine's

Confessions, even in its unconscious dimensions and in the very concept (metaphor) of conflict at its center: "So stood two wills of mine in conflict with each other, one old, the other new, one carnal, the other spiritual, and in their discord they laid waste my soul." *(Ita duae voluntates meae, una vetus, alia nova, illa carnalis, illa spiritalis,* configebant *inter se, atque discordando dissipabant animam meam)"* (8.5). Here is even the very root of "conflict," namely, the verb *configere*: "clashing together, crashing, fighting."

> This was the controversy I felt in my heart, about nothing but myself, against myself. *(Ista controversia in corde meo non nisi de me ipso adversus me ipsum).* [8.11] ... it was myself who willed it, and myself who nilled it; it was I myself. I neither willed entirely, nor yet nilled entirely. Therefore was I at strife with myself, and distracted by mine own self *(Ideo mecum contendebam et dissipar a me ipso).*
>
> [8.10]

At the same time, this is an inner compulsion, opposed to free choice: "This discord happened against my will" *(et ipsa dissipatio me invito quidem fiebat)"* (8.10).

And crucially Augustine immediately adds that there are many such inner conflicts: "For if there be so many contrary natures in man, as there be wills resisting one another; there shall not now be two natures alone, but many" *(Nam si tot sunt contrariae naturae, quot voluntates sibi resistunt, non iam duae, sed plures erunt)* (8.10). A multiplicity of inner conflicts tear apart the will and hence the consciousness of the cohesive self.

He even comments upon the complementarity between these opposite parts of his self: "Hence it is that there be two wills, for that one of them is not entire: and the one is supplied with that, wherein the other lacks *(Et ideo sunt duae voluntes, quia una earum tota non est, et hoc adest alteri, quod deest alteri)"* (8.9).

Indeed, this thought is taken up by Richard II, the tragedy that frames this Epilogue: "Thus play I in one person many people, / And none contented" (V:V).

It was Goethe who took up the concept of "inner conflict" as an explanatory metaphor when, in 1815, he described how Shakespeare foregrounds "the inner conflict" between "*Sollen*" and "*Wollen*" – between what man ought to do and what he wants to do. This inner conflict converges with an external one: "a wanting that goes beyond what the individual is able to, is modern" (Goethe, 1961, p. 186).

The philosophical knowledge about inner conflict becomes dominant in Nietzsche. In *The Dawn* (1886), he addresses "the essential *fight of motivations* – for us something *entirely invisible and unconscious*" (II, 129, p. 113, my emphasis).[3] In *The Gay Science* (1887), he describes the man who is told to control himself: "he always stands there with a defensive gesture, armed against himself, with a sharp and suspicious eye, the eternal guardian of his castle which he has made himself into" (IV, 305, p. 204).[4]

There is a *defiance against oneself* manifested in many forms of askesis [harsh self-discipline]. Certain people have such a great need to exert their violence and domination that, lacking other objects or because they have otherwise always failed in it, they finally turn to tyrannize certain parts of their own being, as it were segments or steps of their own selves.[5]

[emphasis added; I, 137, p. 123]

There is hardly any moment in psychoanalytic work or self-analysis, as I also showed in my contribution to this volume, where we are not aware of different voices of the personality that contradict each other, of parts that struggle with each other: "Into a thousand parts divide one man" (Prologue, *Henry V*). Such inner splits are the hallmark of the mind when studied with the psychoanalytic method, the a priori starting point for our systematic efforts to understand our inner lives and our dialogue with others. As Freud (1916/1917) notes:

We seek not merely to describe and to classify phenomena, but to under-stand them as signs of an interplay of forces in the mind, as a manifestation of purposeful intentions working concurrently or in mutual opposition. We are concerned with a *dynamic view* of mental phenomena. In our view the phenomena that are perceived must yield in importance to trends which are only hypothetical. [p. 67] (. . .) It is important to begin in good time to reckon with the fact that mental life is the arena and battle-ground for mutually opposing purposes or, to put it non-dynamically, that it consists of contradic-tions and pairs of contraries. Proof of the existence of a particular purpose is no argument against the existence of an opposite one; there is room for both. It is only a question of the attitude of these contraries to each other, and of what effects are produced by the one and by the other.

[pp. 76–77]

The central concern for psychoanalysts is the consistent, systematic exploration of inner conflict, especially of unconscious inner conflict. No matter how we try to define our work, it always comes down to the fact that, at its best, the focus, the center of our interest during our analytic work lies in inner conflict. Everything else moves to the periphery, not because it is irrelevant, but because our inner ori-entation regards it as part of the surrounding field and not the beacon that guides us. Thus psychoanalysis is grounded in a philosophy – in fact, a "transcendent tradi-tion" – that sees its center in *conflict and paradox, in polarity and complementarity*, and that seeks on many levels the dichotomies of knowing, acting, and feeling.

Dialogue and the intimate other

The second dimension in transcending mourning is the cardinal and essential nature of dialogue and intimate relationship. I referred to it in my contribution to this volume with the tale of the Circle Drawer, about the legendary Talmudic figure

Choni and the Aramaic saying: "*O chevruta o mituta*" ("either togetherness [community, friendship, belonging] or death").

In this context of this second dimension, I find Buber's addition to Freud of great help. His distinction between two principal dimensions of human existence, under the headings of the relations "*I-You*," and "*I-It*," refers to something most essential to human nature, and which permeates all our work and our understanding of mankind: "The world of experience belongs to the basic word *I-It*. The basic word *I-You* creates the world of relatedness" (p. 18; this and all translations of Buber are mine).

In "*Zwiesprache*" ("Dialogue," Buber, 1930, p. 169), Buber, in a sharp break with the German philosophical tradition, particularly Hegel, quotes the philosopher Ludwig Feuerbach: "The true dialectic is not the monologue of the solitary thinker with himself, but it is a dialogue between *I* and *You*." Buber declares:

> Relationship is reciprocity . . . When I am facing a human being as my *You*, meaning the basic word *I-You*, he is not a thing among things and does not consist of things . . . everything else lives in *his* light . . . Experience is distance from *You*. [p. 20] . . . the development of the ability to experience and to use [things] mostly occurs by diminishing the power to relate – the power with whose help alone man can live a life in the spirit" (in other words, "in the world of the mind").
>
> [p. 48]

But the dialectic is inescapable:
> This is however the sublime melancholy of our fate, that every *You* in our world has to turn into an *It* . . . Every *You* in the world is destined in its essence to become thing or again and again to enter into the thingness . . . The *It* is the eternal chrysalis, the *You* is the eternal butterfly. Only these are not always states that are clearly separating out, but they are often in profound doubleness, indistinguishably intertwined.
>
> [p. 29]

Very importantly, Buber talks about the *"drive to make everything into a* You, *the drive for all-relatedness"* (p. 38). Anticipating present-day views of early infant development, he declares:

> It is not so that the child would first perceive an object and then put himself into relation to it; rather, the striving for relationship comes first; it is the open hand which the other (*das Gegenüber*) nestles against. The relationship to this other, a wordless prototype for saying *You*, is the second. But the constitution of an object is a late product that has emerged from the dividing out of the primal aliveness, from the separation of the conjoined partners – like the arising of the I (*Ichwerdung*). *In the beginning there is the relationship*: as category of the essence, as readiness, as receiving form, as model of the soul; the a priori of relatedness, *the inborn You* (emphases original). The lived relationships are

realizations of the inborn *You* in the encounter. That this other can be conceived of as the encountering one (free translation of *"als Gegenüber"*) and taken into the exclusivity is founded in the relationship.

[p. 39]

Decisively, *"man becomes I [in this relatedness to] the You"* ("Der Mensch wird am Du zum Ich," p. 40). "the separate *It* of institutions is a Golem and the cut-off *I* of feelings is a soul bird that flutters around. Neither does know man" (p. 54).

For us who work especially with patients who are severely and early traumatized and thus always live under the shadow of a deep sadness, this dialectic is decisive: the real relationship on the *I-You* level and the eminence of empathy is indispensable; but the precise comprehension in terms of conflict, defense, and unconsciousness is just as necessary, a form of *I-It* relation. In short, we need both Freud and Buber.

And finally,

A few reflections on wisdom

Wisdom is more than philosophy or psychoanalysis.

First, I take a parable from the *Zohar* (1864, 2:176a-b), which its translator, Daniel C. Matt, introduces with the remark: "although usually essence is the goal of mystical search, here essence is inadequate unless it stimulates you to explore ever deeper layers, to question your assumptions about tradition, God, and self."

There was a man who lived in the mountains. He knew nothing about those who lived in the city. He sowed wheat and ate the kernels raw. One day he entered the city. They offered him good bread. The man asked, "What's this for?"

They replied, "It's bread, to eat!"

He ate, and it tasted very good. He asked, "What's it made of?"

They answered: "Wheat."

Later they offered him thick loaves kneaded with oil. He tasted them and asked: 'And what are these made of?"

They answered: "Wheat."

Later they offered him royal pastry kneaded with honey and oil. He asked, 'And what are these made of?'

They answered: "Wheat."

He said: "Surely I am the master of all of these, since I eat the essence of all these: wheat!"

Because of this view, he knew nothing of the delights of the world, which were lost on him. So it is with one who grasps the principle but is unaware of all those delectable delights deriving, diverging from the principle.

Matt notes that the wheat and its products (kernels, bread, cake, and pastry) may symbolize four levels of meaning in Torah: simple, homiletical, allegorical, and mystical.

What is concrete, what is singular, what is immediately experienced, has just as much dignity as what is general and abstract. The *I-You* precedes the *I-It* – especially also in the practice of psychoanalysis when dealing with great trauma.

Second, I present a few thoughts of life wisdom from the fourth chapter of the *Pirqei Avot*, "Sayings of the Fathers," an early part of the Talmud, from about the second century CE.

> Ben Zoma says: Who is wise? One who learns from all people; as it is said: "From all those who have taught me I obtained understanding for your testimonies are my pursuits"(Psalm 119.99). Who is mighty? One who conquers his passions, as it is said: "One who is slow to anger is better than the mighty, and one who rules over his spirit is better than one who conquers a city" (Proverbs, 16.32). Who is rich? One who rejoices in his portion, as it is said: "When you eat of the labor of your hands you shall be happy and it shall be well with you" (Psalm 128.2). ". . . you shall be happy' – in this world; 'and it shall be well with you" – in the world to come. Who is honored? One who honors the created beings (*"habriyot"*: mankind, but also the animals), as it is said: "for those who honor Me I will honor, and those who despise Me shall be held in contempt" (1 Samuel 2:30).
>
> [Bulka, 1993, pp. 141–143]

Third, "[Ben Azzai] used to say: 'do not despise any person, and do not consider anything impossible, for there is no person who does not have an hour and no thing that does not have its place'" (Bulka, 1993, p. 145).

We may see this as a kind of ethics of the psychoanalytic attitude and its aim: the dignity of every person and the importance of every detail in mind and life; the avoidance of shaming and the profound reverence about the unknown; the constant curiosity about what is still to be learned; and the restlessness of the mind, the realm of the inner life and its expression in dialogue – all this seems to me to be contained in these sayings.

"*Rastlosigkeit und Würde – das ist das Siegel des Geistes*" ("Restlessness and dignity – this is the seal of the mind [or spirit]"), says Thomas Mann (in *Joseph und seine Mann*, 1933, p. 50).

And finally, again some words from Heraclitus (fr 22b45), uniting and encompassing all these dimensions: "The boundaries of a soul you can never find, no matter whether you walk on all the paths; such deep meaning has she."

Notes

1 In contrast, the great German mystic Meister Eckhart (c.1260–1327) uses the same passage, *abissus abissum invocate*, to ask that the depth of the mystical word be mirrored by the depth of its interpretation (Ruh, 1989, p. 51).

2 I follow the English translation by the Jewish Publication Society, except for the last sentence, where it is translated, "and the trembling in his bones is constant."
3 Translations from the German are mine: eigentliche *'Kampf der Motive'*: – etwas für uns völlig *Unsichtbares und Unbewußtes.*
4 *er [der Mensch, dem es anbefohlen wird, sich zu beherrschen] steht beständig mit abwehrender Gebärde da, bewaffnet gegen sich selbst, scharfen und mißtrauischen Auges, der ewige Wächter seiner Burg, zu der er sich gemacht hat.*
5 *Es gibt einen Trotz gegen sich selbst, zu dessen Äußerungen manche Formen der Askese gehören. Gewisse Menschen haben nämlich ein so hohes Bedürfnis, ihre Gewalt und Herrschsucht auszuüben, daß sie, in Ermangelung anderer Objekte oder weil es ihnen sonst immer mißlungen ist, endlich darauf verfallen, gewisse Teile ihres eigenen Wesens, gleichsam Ausschnitte oder Stufen ihrer selbst, zu tyrannisisieren.*

References

Assmann, J. (2003). *Die mosaische Unterscheidung oder der Preis des Monotheismus*. München: Carl Hanser Verlag.

————. (2006). *Monotheismus und die Sprache der Gewalt*. Wien: Picus Verlag.

Augustine. *Confessiones*. Loeb Classical Library, Cambridge: Harvard University Press, 1968.

Brooks, D. (2014). Other people's views. *The New York Times*, Feb. 7, 2014, p. A23.

Buber, M. (1930). *Dialogisches Leben*. Zürich: Gregor Müller Verlag, 1947.

Bulka, R.P. (1993). *Pirqei Avot (Chapters of the Fathers)*. Nortvale: Jason Aronson.

Diels, Hermann. *Die Fragmente der Vorsokratiker*. ed. Walther Kranz. Berlin, 1951.

Freud, S. (1916/1917). *Introductory lectures on psychoanalysis*. Standard Edition, 15/16:15–463. London: Hogarth Press, 1963.

Goethe, J.W. (1961). *Gesamtausgabe (Complete Edition)*. Munich: Deutscher Taschenbuch Verlag.

Green, A. (1993). *Le travail du negative*. Paris: Edition de minuit.

Heraclitus. *Fragmente. Tò Biblion*. Insel Bücherei, No. 49, ed. G. Burckhardt. Wiesbaden: Insel Verlag.

Hopper, E. (1991). Encapsulation as a defense against fear of annihilation. *Internat. J. Psycho-anal.*, 72:607–624.

Jarass, H. & Wurmser, L. (2007). "The burned hedgehog skin": Father's envy and resentment against women perpetuated in the daughter's superego. In: L. Wurmser & H. Jarass: *Jealousy and Envy: New Views About Two Powerful Feelings*. Psychoanalytic Inquiry Book Series, London: Routledge.

Jaspers, K. (1949). *Vom Ursprung und Ziel der Geschichte*. Zürich: Artemis Verlag.

Küchenhoff, J. (1990). Die Repräsentation des frühen Traumas in der Übertragung. *Forum der Psychoanalyse*, 6:15–31.

Lansky, M.E. (2015). "O, coward conscience, how dost thou afflict me": Ruthlessness and the struggle against conscience in *Richard III*. In: *Psychoanalysis and Tragedy – Awe, Hubris, and Shame and Their Clinical Significance*, ed. L. Wurmser. *Psychoanalytic Inquiry*, 35:117-135.

Mann, T. (1933). *Joseph und seine Brüder*. Frankfurt am Main: Fischer, 1966.

Nietzsche, F. (1887). *Die Fröhliche Wissenschaft (The Gay Science)*. Stuttgart: Kröner.

————. (1886). *Morgenröte (The Dawn)*. Stuttgart: Kröner.

Plato. *Phaidros*. In: Plato, *Platonis Opera (5 volumes)*, ed. J. Burnet, Oxford Classical Texts. Oxford: Clarendon Press, 1967; English trans., *Great Books of the Western World*, Vol. 7, ed. R.M. Hutchins, trans. B. Jowell, D. Matt & J. Harward. Chicago: Encyclopaedia Britannica.

Reed, G.S. & Baudry, F.D. (2005). Conflict, structure, and absence: André Green on borderline and narcissistic pathology. *Psychoanal. Quart.*, 74:121–156.

Ruh, K. (1989). *Meister Eckhart. Theologe, Prediger, Mystiker.* Munich: C.H. Beck.

Shakespeare, W. (1952). *Complete Works*, ed. G.B. Harrison. New York: Harcourt, Brace & World.

Tanakh: A New Translation of the Holy Scriptures According to the Traditional Hebrew Text. Philadelphia, New York & Jerusalem: Jewish Publication Society, 1985.

Wieseltier, L. (1998). *Kaddish.* New York: Random/Vintage.

Wurmser, L. (1981). *The Mask of Shame.* Baltimore, Johns Hopkins University Press.

_____. (1989). *Die zerbrochene Wirklichkeit. Psychoanalyse als das Studium von Konflikt und Komplementarität.* Heidelberg: Springer.

_____. (2012). "Archaic heritage," the self-contradiction in monotheism, and the Jewish ethos of being a *Mensch (Menschlichkeit)*—Thoughts of a psychoanalyst about a triple centenary. *American Imago*, 69: 401–429.

Zohar: Aramaic edition in 5 volumes, Livorno: Israel Koschta, 1864. Pritzker Edition, Vol. 1–8, trans. D.C. Matt. Stanford: Stanford University Press, 2004–2013.

INDEX

Note: page numbers in italics indicates figures